Genders and Sexualities in History

Series Editors: **John H. Arnold, Joanna Bourke and Sean Brady**

Palgrave Macmillan's series, *Genders and Sexualities in History,* aims to accommodate and foster new approaches to historical research in the fields of genders and sexualities. The series promotes world-class scholarship that concentrates upon the interconnected themes of genders, sexualities, religions/religiosity, civil society, class formations, politics and war.

Historical studies of gender and sexuality have often been treated as disconnected fields, while in recent years historical analyses in these two areas have synthesised, creating new departures in historiography. By linking genders and sexualities with questions of religion, civil society, politics and the contexts of war and conflict, this series will reflect recent developments in scholarship, moving away from the previously dominant and narrow histories of science, scientific thought and legal processes. The result brings together scholarship from contemporary, modern, early modern, medieval, classical and non-Western history to provide a diachronic forum for scholarship that incorporates new approaches to genders and sexualities in history.

Queer 1950s: Rethinking Sexuality in the Postwar Years challenges popular and scholarly perceptions of the 1950s as a decade of overwhelmingly conformist attitudes towards gender and sexuality. In this groundbreaking collection, the authors provide meticulously researched, incisive, international and interdisciplinary new scholarship that questions the ubiquity of the postwar nuclear family and concomitant cultural clichés in the historical analysis of the decade. The collection repositions our understanding of the significance of the 1950s, which has tended to serve either as the end point for studies of the war years, or as the oppressive starting point for analysis of sexual liberation in the 1960s and beyond. *Queer 1950s* recasts the analysis of sexual lives and politics in the decade, through a range of disciplinary, national and transnational perspectives. It brings together historians and literary and cultural critics, who, in common with all volumes in the *Genders and Sexualities in History series,* presents a multifaceted and meticulously researched study of the past.

Titles include:

John H. Arnold and Sean Brady (*editors*)
WHAT IS MASCULINITY?
Historical Dynamics from Antiquity to the Contemporary World

Heike Bauer and Matt Cook (*editors*)
QUEER 1950s
Rethinking Sexuality in the Postwar Years

Cordelia Beattie and Kirsten A Fenton (*editors*)
INTERSECTIONS OF GENDER, RELIGION AND ETHNICITY IN THE MIDDLE AGES

Chiara Beccalossi
FEMALE SEXUAL INVERSION
Same-Sex Desires in Italian and British Sexology, c. 1870–1920

Peter Cryle and Alison Moore
FRIGIDITY
An Intellectual History

Jennifer V. Evans
LIFE AMONG THE RUINS
Cityscape and Sexuality in Cold War Berlin

Kate Fisher and Sarah Toulalan (*editors*)
BODIES, SEX AND DESIRE FROM THE RENAISSANCE TO THE PRESENT

Christopher E. Forth and Elinor Accampo (*editors*)
CONFRONTING MODERNITY IN FIN-DE-SIÈCLE FRANCE
Bodies, Minds and Gender

Dagmar Herzog (*editor*)
BRUTALITY AND DESIRE
War and Sexuality in Europe's Twentieth Century

Andrea Mansker
SEX, HONOR AND CITIZENSHIP IN EARLY THIRD REPUBLIC FRANCE

Jessica Meyer
MEN OF WAR
Masculinity and the First World War in Britain

Jennifer D. Thibodeaux (*editor*)
NEGOTIATING CLERICAL IDENTITIES
Priests, Monks and Masculinity in the Middle Ages

Hester Vaizey
SURVIVING HITLER'S WAR
Family Life in Germany, 1939–48

Forthcoming titles:

Matt Cook
QUEER DOMESTICITIES
Homosexuality and Home Life in Twentieth-Century London

Rebecca Fraser
GENDER AND IDENTITY IN ANTEBELLUM AMERICA FROM NORTHERN WOMAN TO PLANTATION MISTRESS

Julia Laite
PROSTITUTION AND REPRESSION IN THE METROPOLIS
Criminalization and the Shaping of Commercial Sex in London, 1885–1960

Melissa Hollander
SEX IN TWO CITIES
The Negotiation of Sexual Relationships in Early Modern England and Scotland

---

Genders and Sexualities in History Series
Series Standing Order 978–0–230–55185–5 Hardback 978–0–230–55186–2 Paperback
(*outside North America only*)

You can receive future titles in this series as they are published by placing a standing order. Please contact your bookseller or, in case of difficulty, write to us at the address below with your name and address, the title of the series and one of the ISBNs quoted above.

Customer Services Department, Macmillan Distribution Ltd, Houndmills, Basingstoke, Hampshire RG21 6XS, England

---

Queer 1950s

Rethinking Sexuality in the Postwar Years

Edited by

Heike Bauer
Senior Lecturer in English Literature and Gender Studies,
Birkbeck College, University of London

and

Matt Cook
Senior Lecturer in History and Gender Studies,
Birkbeck College, University of London

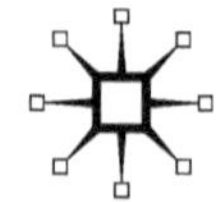

Softcover reprint of the hardcover 1st edition 2012 978-0-230-30069-9

First published 2012 by
PALGRAVE MACMILLAN

Palgrave Macmillan in the UK is an imprint of Macmillan Publishers Limited, registered in England, company number 785998, of Houndmills, Basingstoke, Hampshire RG21 6XS.

Palgrave Macmillan in the US is a division of St Martin's Press LLC, 175 Fifth Avenue, New York, NY 10010.

Palgrave Macmillan is the global academic imprint of the above companies and has companies and representatives throughout the world.

Palgrave® and Macmillan® are registered trademarks in the United States, the United Kingdom, Europe and other countries

ISBN 978-1-349-33648-7 ISBN 978-1-137-26471-8 (eBook)
DOI 10.1057/9781137264718

This book is printed on paper suitable for recycling and made from fully managed and sustained forest sources. Logging, pulping and manufacturing processes are expected to conform to the environmental regulations of the country of origin.

A catalogue record for this book is available from the British Library.

A catalog record for this book is available from the Library of Congress.

10 9 8 7 6 5 4 3 2 1
21 20 19 18 17 16 15 14 13 12

Transferred to Digital Printing in 2013

To the memory of Joseph and Gwladys Cook
and Karl Bauer

Contents

Figures

Acknowledgements

This book emerges out of the Queer 50s conference we organised at Birkbeck, University of London, in May 2009. The event brought together activists, artists and academics to think through the first full postwar decade. We are grateful to all the participants and especially to our colleagues from BiGS (Birkbeck Interdisciplinary Gender and Sexuality) for their enthusiastic support. We would also like to thank Sean Brady and Joanna Bourke, the series editors, for their endorsement of the book project, and Michael Strang, Ruth Ireland, Clare Mence and Vidhya Jayaprakash at Palgrave Macmillan. Huge thanks finally to our partners – Diane Watt and Ben Tooke – for their love, care and enthusiasm.

Contributors

Andrew Asibong is Senior Lecturer in French and Co-Director of Birkbeck Research in Aesthetics of Kinship and Community (BRAKC) at Birkbeck, University of London. His research focuses on aesthetics of the fantastic and the ways in which these can potentially reconfigure subjectivity and modes of belonging. He is the author of *François Ozon* (2008) and co-editor of *Marie NDiaye: L'Etrangeté à l'œuvre* (2009).

Heike Bauer is Senior Lecturer in English and Humanities at Birkbeck, University of London. Her publications include a monograph, *English Literary Sexology: Translations of Inversion 1860–1930* (2009) and a three-volume anthology of texts titled *Women and Cross-Dressing 1800–1930* (2006). She has also published on sexology, nineteenth-century literary culture, race and the histories of female and male same-sex sexuality. She is currently working on a book about Magnus Hirschfeld, hatred and the queer developments of modern sex research and is leading a related collaborative project on sexology and translation.

Justin Bengry is a SSHRC Postdoctoral Fellow in History at McGill University, Canada. His research on the relationship between homosexuality and consumer capitalism in twentieth-century Britain has appeared in *History Workshop Journal* and *Socialist History*. He is working on a book titled *The Pink Pound: Queer Profits in Twentieth-Century Britain*.

Chris Brickell co-ordinates the Gender Studies Programme at Otago University, Dunedin, New Zealand. He has published widely on the history and sociology of sexuality, including *Mates & Lovers: A History of Gay New Zealand* (2008). He is working on a cultural history of adolescence in New Zealand.

Matt Cook is Senior Lecturer in History and Gender Studies at Birkbeck, University of London, and co-director of the Raphael Samuel History Centre. His publications include two books, *London and the Culture of Homosexuality, 1885–1914* (2003) and *A Gay History of Britain: Love and Sex Between Men since the Middle Ages* (2007), as well as numerous articles and chapters in the history of sexuality and the history of London in the nineteenth and twentieth centuries. He is working on a book and a series of articles exploring queer families and domesticity in the twentieth century and co-editing a book on queer Europe since the Second World War.

Jennifer V. Evans is Associate Professor of History at Carleton University in Ottawa Canada, where she teaches a variety of courses in 20th century German history with a primary interest in the history of sexuality. Her book, *Life Among the Ruins: Cityscape and Sexuality in Cold War Berlin* (Palgrave, 2011) explores the rebirth of the city's various subcultures in the aftermath of World War II. She has also written about same-sex sexuality in Nazi and post-1945 Germany, juvenile delinquency, and queer memorial cultures. In addition to editing a book on queer urban history, she is currently researching the role and potential of social media in countering online hate alongside a project examining the function of 1970s and 1980s queer erotic photography as a claim to sexual freedom in the pre- Aids era.

Amanda Littauer is Assistant Professor of History and Women's Studies at Northern Illinois University. She earned a PhD in History, with a designated emphasis in Women, Gender, and Sexuality, from University of California, Berkeley in 2006. She has published in the *Journal of the History of Sexuality* and is completing a book titled *Sex Anarchy: Women, Girls, and American Sexual Culture in the Mid-twentieth Century.*

Kaye Mitchell is Lecturer in Contemporary Literature at the University of Manchester, where she is Director of the MA Contemporary Literature and Culture. She is the author of two books, *A.L. Kennedy* (2007) and *Intention and Text* (2008), and numerous articles and chapters on contemporary literature, literary theory, gender and sexuality.

Alison Oram is Professor in Social and Cultural History at Leeds Metropolitan University, UK. Her research interests centre on the history of sexuality and gender in twentieth-century Britain, and on the representation of gender, sexuality and family in public history. Her recent books are *'Her Husband Was a Woman!' Women's Gender-Crossing and Modern British Popular Culture* (2007) and *The Lesbian History Source Book: Love and Sex between Women in Britain 1780–1970*, co-authored with A. Turnbull (2001).

Antu Soreinen is Postdoctoral Research Fellow at the Academy of Finland. She has published a book on lesbian fornication trials in Finland, journal articles on queer history, edited a special issue *Queering the Home* of the SQS (1/2011) and co-edited a book *Siveellisyydestä seksuaalisuuteen* [From Decency to Sexuality] with Tuija Pulkkinen (2011).

Elizabeth Stephens is Research Fellow at the Centre for the History of European Discourses, University of Queensland. Her books include *Queer Writing: Homoeroticism in Jean Genet's Fiction* (2009) and *Anatomy as Spectacle: Public Exhibitions of the Body from the Nineteenth-Century to the Present* (2011). She has published more than a dozen articles and chapters in edited collections on masculinity, queer theory and non-normative bodies.

Introduction: Queer 1950s: Rethinking Sexuality in the Postwar Years

Heike Bauer and Matt Cook

This collection has two main aims. Firstly, it seeks to excavate and rethink some of the specific cultural, political and experiential contingencies that shaped sexual lives and thought during the 1950s. Secondly, it aims to expand the boundaries of modern sexuality debates and their transnational dimensions. It does this by presenting alongside each other chapters which scrutinise familiar and less familiar material, and which are orientated around but also depart from the well-established Anglo-American axis of analysis in gender and sexuality studies. Our investigation speaks to recent work in queer theory and historiography on the potential for queer modes of life, which, as Judith Halberstam argues, emerge through 'subcultural practices, alternative modes of alliance, forms of transgender embodiment, and those forms of representation dedicated to capturing...willfully eccentric modes of being'.[1] Where Halberstam especially scrutinised the temporal shapes of queer lives, this collection explores what it may mean to think of the 1950s as a queer time, both for our understanding of the history of that decade and for queer studies more broadly.

We understand queer as a critical method, politics and orientation and as a concept associated with desire, intimacy and belonging. We also associate it with the troubling of norms and conventions and the seeking out of blind spots in existing narratives about the present and the past. In the 1950s, the term 'queer' was used in related ways to describe the unusual and the odd and was often a derogatory term – one which makes some of the men and women who lived through the decade uncomfortable with its more recent reclamation. *Queer 1950s* utilises and marks such shifting meanings and perceptions by shuttling between recent theory and accounts on the one hand and conceptualisations, writings and archival holding from the period on the other. In this way, we explore the diverse and sometimes unexpectedly resonant ways in which queer lives were imagined, theorised and lived in a decade associated with a (perhaps rather queer) *in-betweeness* – sandwiched as it was between the war years and the social transformations of the 1960s.

Critically queer 1950s

Histories of sexuality, literature and social change have often located the 1950s as the beginning or end of analysis, the place to stop an examination of the war years, or to start on the 1960s and the social, sexual and cultural changes that are seen to mark that later decade. Until recently, long histories of modern sexuality have tended to give significance to the 1950s mostly in terms of repressive norms, against which the gay and women's liberation movements reacted in the decade that followed.[2] The axiomatic example of this problematic remains the insistent rhetoric of the nuclear home and family, which pervaded European and especially Anglo-American debate and policy in the drive for postwar reconstruction. However, as a renewed scholarly focus on the postwar period is beginning to show, this rhetoric belied the daily grind, poverty and pragmatic impossibility of living up to circulating ideals. Dagmar Herzog, Julian Jackson, Frank Mort and Susan Stryker, amongst others, illustrate vividly that people's everyday lives rarely accorded to the patterns of sexual and gendered behaviour apparently prescribed in popular literature, legislation, trials and the newspaper press.[3] They make clear that the 1950s should not be defined only by overtly repressive and conformist attitudes towards gender and sexuality, as queer life sometimes flourished despite persecution. Yet these critics also acknowledge that it is often the ideals and ideologies of the 1950s, rather than their fault lines, underlying uncertainties and confusions, which have taken the firmest hold in popular imaginings of the decade.

From Hollywood glamour through to the nuclear family and the beginning of the nuclear age, many images of the 1950s have become cliché, a notion which implies a certain stasis, as it describes what Ruth Amossy calls 'stylistic features frozen by usage'.[4] The chapters in this collection, however, show that movement, relocation and migration were defining features of the 1950s as were the concomitant unsettling and reorienting of lives in new spaces and contexts. Nevertheless, each of the contributors and those of our subjects who lived through the

1950s have had to negotiate those ideals and clichés in their memories, accounts and analyses. From our twenty-first-century vantage point and with such clichéd conceptions of the decade, it is hard to grasp fully the ways in which the rupture, tragedy and dislocation of the war years played out in the 1950s in national and international politics and economics and in individual lives and communities. But the profundity of the personal and national tragedies accompanying the war made it equally hard at the time to comprehend its impact let alone to contextualise or historicise it. Carolyn Dean has illustrated vividly how what she calls a 'fragility of empathy after the Holocaust' characterised public discourses about the war years, especially in countries such as France and Germany, where the memory of collusion with, and support for, the Nazi regime has sometimes been impossibly hard to work through.[5] Indeed, it is no coincidence that in many texts of the period we find a sense of separation from the immediate past and an insistent focus on the future. While for many who had lived through the war it was too soon and possibly too dangerous to remember and process this trauma, those experiences surely inflected and modulated lives and relationships – not least because in different ways and in different places the war exposed the shallowness and fragility of apparently entrenched norms.

Queer 1950s recuperates traumas and pleasures of the everyday and rethinks the boundaries of science and popular culture then, and of critical theory now. This kind of history and analysis builds on the pessimistic turn in queer studies, which has complicated queer scepticism about notions of identity and community.[6] A number of the chapters engage with the work of Heather Love, who has so influentially refocused debates – including centrally in terms of how to think about identity in the past without essentialising or overdetermining it. Love calls for new histories of identity that account for its various meanings and utilities at and across different moments in time.[7] Our contributors respond in various ways by seeking out the intersections between subjective, sexual and emotional lives and social, cultural and political events, dynamics and changes, such as postwar reconstruction, housing shortages, decolonisation, and the onset of the Cold War. The collection as a whole is itself also a contribution to these debates. Our title has obvious similarities with that of Patricia Juliana Smith's collection, *The Queer Sixties*. Smith focuses on art, literature and film to provide a 'new and different means of looking at the queer cultural and subcultural expression of that decade, which culminated in the closet doors swinging open, dramatically and irrevocably'.[8] While sharing

Smith's sentiment about the importance of looking queerly at the past, *Queer 1950s* is not driven by the same progressive impulse as *The Queer Sixties*. By losing the definite article, we indicate our commitment to the multiplicity of queer perspectives while our decision to use a full rendering of the date ('1950s' instead of 'Fifties') signals a decade which has a less prominent place than the sixties in the contemporary (queer) critical landscape.

Queer 1950s, then, is committed to careful contextualisation and to thinking conceptually across time and space. In a recent collection of essays on the *Lesbian Premodern*, the editors make a persuasive case for the productivity of the 'deliberate anachronisms' of the book's title, presenting it as an invitation to the reader 'to think across time, geographies, disciplines and methodologies' to produce 'a relational space where dialogue begins'.[9] The notion of a 'queer 50s' similarly seeks to initiate dialogue by bringing together terms that do not normally stand in close temporal proximity – for while the 'queerness' of others might have been in common parlance in insult and description during the fifties themselves, we are today more familiar with the different understandings of queer which emerged through critical theory in the 1990s and which initially found limited resonance with that earlier decade.[10] Our project, therefore, is partly recuperative in the sense of tracking queer histories and genealogies of which we still know relatively little. It is also, though, about seeking new points and modes of access to this past that will allow us to push the boundaries of critical practice.

Snapshots

Queer 1950s brings together historians, literary and cultural critics who draw on a range of particular, localised and transnational perspectives to scrutinise the complexity of sexual lives and politics in this decade and also to discern its reach backward and forward in time. The chapters provide snapshots – glimpses at queer life, art and thought in the mid-twentieth century. Some of the texts and figures discussed will be familiar – iconic or mythologised even – but the collection also reaches for other sources and representations which complicate entrenched understandings and modes of analysis. What becomes clear through this material is that while most of the individual figures discussed in this book did not conceive of themselves as radical queer activists and while an organised collective sexual politics was only just beginning, life and thought in the fifties was noticeably marked by a process of reshaping, reforming and flux. Some of the chapters explore the limits of sexual politics in the 1950s. Others question how and where resistance and change might happen, and so the very nature of radicalism during this period. Being queer did not at this time necessarily mean being part of a political or intellectual avant garde – and sometimes quite the contrary. In these and many other respects the decade holds up only the most fractured of mirrors to our contemporary sexual selves.

Brought together, the individual chapters speak to each other in multiple and sometimes surprising ways. The book has three parts which deal with aspects of 'Representing', 'Living' (in) and 'Thinking' (about) the 1950s. We deliberately use the continuous form as a linguistic indicator of the continuities and sense of being-in-process that marks debates then and now. The collection opens with chapters that explore the representations of queer life and desire in the 1950s and show how careful readings expose queer dynamics in lived experiences and cultural logics of the time. The chapters in part two examine ways of living the 1950s. Drawing especially on oral history and life testimony, they reflect on ways in which individuals orientated themselves in particular contexts then and in relation to that decade (and so also the period of their youth) since. The chapters in the final part explore ways of thinking about sex in the 1950s and how the decade has continued to be a significant reference point in conceptualisations of gender, sexuality and the body. Each contributor asserts the significance of the particularities of this time and of different places and ways of being. They share a commitment to grounding and contextualising their work precisely. This approach chimes with the work of queer literary critic Elizabeth Freeman, who observes that 'perhaps the queerest commitment' of her book *Time Binds: Queer Temporalities, Queer Histories* is 'close reading: the decision to unfold, slowly, a small number of imaginative texts rather than amass a weighty archive of or around texts, and to treat these texts and their formal work as theories of their own, interventions upon both critical theory and historiography'.[11] While Freeman speaks specifically about visual and verbal artistic projects, we share her concern with the particular as a way into understanding larger contexts as we bring together diverse critical voices and a range of approaches and sources, not to create a harmony but to let the dissonances speak and to let connections emerge. Across the chapters, we find, for example, that in very different contexts youth and immaturity are key affinities in lived experiences of queer cultures. Our imagined reader is one who might find through the perspectives offered such new access points into the intricacies of life, art, popular science and thought in the 1950s in ways that complicate existing assumptions about the decade.

The chapters interrogate specific sites of sexuality debate in the 1950s within and across national boundaries; transnationalism and transregionalism are as much threads in this book as any settled nationalism. We see people, ideas and cultures moving across the borders which the warring nations had just before been fighting to define and lock down. What emerges strongly, though, as we move between New Zealand, Finland, the USA, England, France and Germany, and their cities and countrysides, is a coalescing of white (same-sex) sexual identities and identifications within and amongst these countries. This, we suggest, is indicative of the process by which racialised subjects have been produced as insiders and outsiders to our postwar sexuality categorisations.[12] In such ways, the chapters – taken together and individually – extend our understanding of the meanings and relevance of identity at the time. Indeed, they often guide us away from those identity narratives through which we are accustomed to looking at past lives and direct us instead towards the ways in which individuals and groups of individuals drew on multiple resources, places and pasts to orientate themselves. Some of the chapters recuperate particular histories – of New Zealand's queer subculture in Chris Brickell's piece and of Finnish female religious communities in Antu Sorainen's. Others suggest new approaches to the 1950s – via a queered post-colonialism with Andrew Asibong, and with crip theory in Elizabeth Stephens' chapter. Asibong draws the bloody battle for Algerian independence into his examination of the queer dynamics of 1950s French cinema in a nuanced dissection of the impact of colonial oppression on the racialised postwar French cultural imagination. The Coney Island Freak Show, examined by Stephens, in turn focuses on a well known but under-analysed group to explore how people created a space in which lives could be lived differently yet which were also simultaneously embedded in and reliant on mainstream understandings, mores, and money. Heike Bauer rethinks the relationship between textual and sexual politics by looking at translations of ideas about male homosexuality between Europe and the U.S., and Jennifer Evans uses the figure and photography of Herbert Tobias to interrogate the importance of other boundary crossings (between metropolis and its peripheries, between mainstream and counterculture, between nations) in understanding sexual subjectivities and their representations.

The book thus draws out the transnational and transcultural dimensions of postwar sexuality, and their regulation, partly through comparison of different geopolitical national contexts. But transnationality also has a particular temporal dimension, as the chapters by Evans, Stephens and Bauer illustrate. If one image of the 1950s is as fiercely forward-looking, Bauer makes the case that instances of looking backward towards the pre-war period are equally important for our understanding of the fifties. Tracing Alfred Kinsey's references to Magnus Hirschfeld, the radical pre-war German sexologist, internationalist and homosexual rights activist, Bauer shows that Kinsey's rejection of his predecessor underpins the 'straight turn' of sex research in the postwar years. Stephens meanwhile conjures a Janus-faced 1950s – harking back to the Victorians and forward to the fifties motifs in the recent revival of the Freak Show. This and other chapters indicate that queerness might be (to use Halberstam's useful phrase) be 'an outcome of strange temporalities' – a melding of different time frames to produce new formations and understandings.[13]

Queer 1950s makes clear that both women and men seized, twisted and refigured dominant discourses to provide support and impetus to different ways of living and different understanding of the self. Amanda Littauer and Kaye Mitchell, for example, show that in North American pulp fiction and scientific writings there is an archive testifying to the proliferation of female same-sex discourses, including by women writing about themselves. Alison Oram, on the other hand, makes the case that in 1950s Britain, lesbianism lacked the domineering line of investigation and understanding that male homosexuality acquired in that decade. These essays especially re-examine emblematic indicators of the era, such as sexology, pulp fiction and the sensational newspaper press. The focus on these sources is important because the postwar era is marked by an explosion in these popular and expert genres, facilitating the broader and transnational spread of ideas about sex, desire and sexuality. And yet, while the impact of these texts is profound, it also becomes clear that they failed to dictate, sum up or fully capture the queer lives that were being lived and which we glimpse through the testimonies of individual men and women.[14]

The collection reveals different motors for shifts in representation, action, identity, and community formation. These include the economics underpinning newspaper coverage identified by Justin Bengry and the subjectivities orientated around religion dissected in Sorainen's piece. Where Bauer focuses on the exchange between male sexologists, Mitchell identifies a textual community associated with lesbian pulp sexology, whilst Brickell conjures the diverse queer spaces and networks of 1950s New Zealand. Littauer portrays the complex relationship between reading, acting out and shared experience for teenage girls in the U.S. Oram and Matt Cook, meanwhile, reinvestigate the relational potential of that mainstay of postwar culture – the home. They allow us to see how queer women and men made a claim on the domestic sphere in ways which allowed them to both fit in and stand out. Oram reveals how 'domesticated' married women, their sexuality apparently fixed heterosexually, often had close relationships with other women in ways which did not necessarily feel contradictory or hypocritical to them. Via the oral and fictionalised testimony of former teacher Rex Batten, Cook indicates the equivocal meanings of home – a site variously of danger, betrayal, reassurance and security, and a repository of memory. He shows how that sphere allows Rex to recapture a sense of himself and of that decade for himself and for other audiences now. In this way he folds his own experiences into stories and myths about the decade. The contributors thus interrogate sources for the potency of their claims to truth and to be representative. It is partly for this reason that we do not want to dismiss mythologies of the 1950s even as we question them. We rather want to suggest that in and of themselves, they had and continue to have real power.

* * *

Queer 1950s provides new insights, opens out questions for further analysis – about the relationship of race, gender and sexuality most especially – and signals the utility of queer approaches to the study of the past. The trick for us is to find what queer men and women did, how they did it and how they understood what they were doing, but also to think in fresh ways about the relationship between discourse, experience and politics. We hope that by the end of this volume – with its multiple crossing of spatial, linguistic, temporal, generic and disciplinary boundaries and frames – those doings, beings and understandings might be more imaginable. We hope, too, that the harsh judgments made of that decade – about the apparent attachment to the closet, to privacy, respectability, to not saying – might be understood as part of a more complex picture. It may not have been that these girls and boys, and women and men, were insufficiently liberated, but that their loves and lives were differently ordered and organised in ways that might have facilitated as well as inhibited daily pleasures. This is not to be nostalgic but rather to recoup for the 1950s a complex sense of its multiple and varied pleasures, traumas, possibilities, and structures; to give credence to the felt desire to tell stories about that period then and since; and to give the decade more texture than we tend to accord it.

Notes

1. Judith Halberstam, *In a Queer Time and Place: Transgender Bodies, Subcultural Lives* (New York: New York University Press, 2005), 1.
2. See, for example, John D'Emilio and Estelle B. Freedman, *Intimate Matters: A History of Sexuality in America* (New York: Harper & Row, 1988) and Patrick Higgins, *Heterosexual Dictatorship: Male Homosexuality in Postwar Britain* (London: Fourth Estate, 1996); Janice M. Irvine, *Disorders of Desire: Sexuality and Gender in Modern American Sexology* (Philadelphia: Temple University Press, 2005).
3. Carolyn Steedman's *Landscape for a Good Woman: A Story of Two Lives* (London: Virago, 1986) was groundbreaking in terms of this nuanced approach to the past. Since then, and especially in the last ten years, cultural, literary, social and sexuality histories of the 1950s have become increasingly sensitive to the multiple intersections between sexual, subjective and social worlds. See, for example, John Howard, *Men Like That: A Southern Queer History* (Chicago: University of Chicago Press, 1999); Elizabeth Lapovsky Kennedy and Madeline D. Davis, *Boots of Leather, Slippers of Gold: The History of a Lesbian Community* (New York: Penguin Books, 1993); Chris Brickell, *Mates and Lovers: A History of Gay New Zealand* (Auckland, NZ: Godwit for Random House New Zealand, 2008); David Kynaston, *Family Britain, 1951–1957* (New York: Walker & Co, 2009); Matt Houlbrook, *Queer London: Perils and Pleasures in the Sexual Metropolis, 1918–1957* (Chicago: University of Chicago Press, 2005); Dagmar Herzog, *Sexuality and German Fascism* (Berghahn, 2005), and her *Sex After Fascism: Memory and Morality in Twentieth-Century Germany* (Princeton: Princeton University Press, 2007); Richard Hornsey, *The Spiv and the Architect: Unruly Life in Postwar London* (Minneapolis: University of Minnesota Press, 2010); Judith Halberstam, *Female Masculinity* (Durham: Duke University Press, 1998); Julian Jackson, *Living in Arcadia: Homosexuality, Politics, and Morality in France from the Liberation to AIDS* (Chicago: University of Chicago Press, 2009); Susan Stryker, *Queer Pulp: Perverted Passions from the Golden Age of the Paperback* (San Francisco: Chronicle Books, 2001); Mort, Frank, *Capital Affairs: London and the Making of the Permissive Society* (New Haven: Yale University Press, 2010); Alan Sinfield, *Literature and Culture in Postwar Britain* (Berkley: University of California Press, 1997); Alistair Davies and Alan Sinfield, *British Culture of the Postwar: An Introduction to Literature and Society 1945–1999* (London: Routledge, 2000); Lesley Hall, *Sex, Gender and Social Change in Britain Since 1880* (Basingstoke: Palgrave Macmillan, 2000); James Gilbert, *Men in the Middle: Searching for Masculinity in the 1950s* (Chicago: University of Chicago Press, 2005).
4. Ruth Amossy, 'The Cliché in the Reading Process', *SubStance*, 11.2 (1982), 34.
5. Carolyn Dean, *The Fragility of Empathy after the Holocaust* (Ithaca: Cornell University Press, 2004). See also Herzog, *Sex After Fascism*.
6. Annamarie Jagose, *Queer Theory: An Introduction* (New York: New York University Press, 1996), and William B. Turner, *A Genealogy of Queer Theory* (Philadelphia: Temple University Press, 2000), amongst others, have charted the emergence of queer theory and its impact on gay, lesbian and feminist studies. For an account of the impact of the queer and cultural is 'turn' on

social research, see Sasha Roseneil and Stephen Frosh, *Social Research After the Cultural Turn* (London: Palgrave Macmillan, 2011).
7. Heather Love, *Feeling Backward: Loss and the Politics of Queer History* (Cambridge, Mass.: Harvard University Press, 2007).
8. Patricia Juliana Smith, 'Introduction' to *The Queer Sixties*, ed., Smith (New York: Routledge, 1999), xii.
9. Noreen Giffney, Michelle Sauer and Diane Watt (eds), *The Lesbian Premodern* (Basingstoke: Palgrave Macmillan, 2011), 7.
10. See note 2.
11. Elizabeth Freeman, *Time Binds: Queer Temporalities, Queer Histories* (Durham and London: Duke University Press, 2010), xvii.
12. On this, see Charles. I. Nero, 'Why Are Gay Ghettoes White?' and other essays in E. Patrick Johnson and Mae G. Henderson, eds, *Black Queer Studies* (Durham: Duke University Press, 2005); and the debates provoked by Jasbir Puar's work on 'homonationalism' *Terrorist Assemblages: Homonationalism in Queer Times* (Durham: Duke University Press, 2007).
13. Halberstam, *In a Queer Time and Place*, 1.
14. For some of the problems (and possibilities) associated with the use of 'the evidence of experience' see Joan W. Scott, 'The Evidence of Experience', *Critical Inquiry*, 17.4 (1991), 773–797.

Part I
Representing

1

The Long 1950s as Radical In-Between: The Photography of Herbert Tobias

Jennifer V. Evans

For years, Elaine Tyler May's 1988 *Homeward Bound* set the tone for the way we understood the 1950s. Using the metaphor of containment to explain gender roles and sexuality in the post-WWII era, she argued that the Cold War West linked sexual deviance to political deviation, necessitating the containment of communism via the promotion of marriage and matrimony, isolating queers from public life in a series of lavender scares. In this telling, the 1950s were a period of intense sexual conservatism where 'fears of sexual chaos made non-marital sexual behaviour in all its forms...a national obsession'.[1] On both sides of the Iron Curtain, non-normative, non-marital sex threatened more than moral decline; if left unchecked, it could imperil reproductive citizenship and undercut the strength of the nation.[2] This yearning for heteronormative ideals was a response to postwar scarcity, piecemeal living conditions, and increasing antagonism on the Cold War stage.[3] But as Dagmar Herzog has argued for the West German case, sexuality was not just a marker of stabilisation. In the postwar decades, sexual relations 'became premier sites for memory-management' as successive governments attempted to come to terms with the lingering impact (and in some cases continued appeal) of Nazism. In her compelling account of the sexual politics of 1960s social movements, student radicals and members of the New Left perceived their own healthful embrace of sexual impulses in contradistinction to the perceived sexual conservatism of the 1950s, which was not only a misnomer but also a misremembering of sexual attitudes and practices from the first half of the twentieth century. In other words, Herzog suggests that the 1950s paints a more complicated picture beyond the three r's of regression, regulation and repression.

As Rebecca Jennings and Matt Houlbrook have shown in their respective analyses of postwar London, regulation often existed side by side with sexual liberalism through what John D'Emilio and Estelle Freeman referred to over ten years ago as 'contradictory patterns of expression and constraint'. At times, the erotic was quite explicitly celebrated, especially if kept within a heterosexual framework or imagined within the contours of respectability and committed monogamous relationships.[4] If the containment thesis tends to emphasise national security, welfare policies, citizenship and the state, especially in regulating men's behaviour, the literature on incitements to desire extends the focus to erotic publications, sex advice literature and popular and bar culture, tracing in provocative detail the contours of a variety of same-sex desiring subcultures in the urban milieu. But let's not forget Herzog's claim that 1950s sexuality also represented a site of contestation in the period itself, and in terms of how subsequent generations memorialised their own sexual lives. Indeed, the 1950s have been doubly, perhaps even triply, memorialised, first and foremost by the post-Stonewall gay liberation movement, and then by successive generations of social historians spurred on by Foucault's injunction to view sexuality as the 'impersonal operation of discourses, institutions, and social practice', at once deeply political and central to the operation of the modern liberal state.[5] 1950s homophile organisations may have taken up the mantra of sexual liberalism, but as recent work by David Churchill, Julian Jackson and Domenico Rizzo has shown, in adopting an accomodationist stance they cast same-sex desire as a personal matter deserving of protection as a form of individual self-expression and civil rights, provided it was conducted with a degree of sexual sobriety far from the taint of the street.[6] As George Chauncey argued in *Why Marriage?* the search for respectability meant that certain homophile groups sought 'to restrain the public behavior of those homosexuals who did not share their assimilationist intentions'.[7] While this self-loathing was itself loathed by early gay and lesbian activists who sought out defiant expressions of oppositionality in history, both groups found affinity in the denigration of the gutter. As Rosa von Praunheim and New Left activist-sexologist Martin Dannecker pronounced in their provocative film *It's Not the Homosexual Who is Perverse but the Conditions Under Which He Lives* – which galvanised the West and East German gay liberation movements – true acceptance could only be secured by taking lust, love, and desire 'out of the urinal and in to the streets'. By this, they meant first and foremost the need to organise and make public the issue of gay rights. This message of openness turned on the image of the eternally abject, the blackmailing hustler, cruising in the shadows and street-level sex. In attempting to construct a positive genealogy of gay identity, these early queer critics found themselves unable to account for the rent boys and aging queens whose image fit untidily into the new found optics of empowerment and pride. It was only in the mid-1970s, with the consolidation of the porn industry and an increased number of sociological studies of gay life, that the queer cultural imaginary expanded to embrace a wider array of subjectivities.

With the formation of organised gay rights movements and activist scholarship slowly taking root inside and outside the hallowed halls of academe, it seemed that the quest to revivify those 'hidden from history' was finally underway.[8] And while the gains made were significant, in casting the 1950s as 'the period before', we threaten to reproduce the notion that little good came out of it. In our emphasis on the political arc of rights and normalisation, we have succeeded in foregrounding gay identity by backgrounding subjectivity, including the wants and desires of those whose lives fail to fit into this teleological paradigm. Too busy mapping the impact of milieu, habitus and environment, generations of the well intentioned have privileged analyses of regulation and control over sexuality's role in the cultivation of contradictory selves based on highly subjective (and often changing) wants and needs.

Drawing inspiration from Heather Love, who argues that we need to look backward in a way that considers the losses as well as the gains, I wish to suggest a way of reassessing the long 1950s as a period of postwar transition, disavowal, anxiety, scrutiny and control, certainly, but also one marked by lust, desire, beauty and love.[9] I wish to think about these middle years between the war and the riots, between the horrors of the Holocaust and that iconic skirmish outside New York's Stonewall Inn as more of a radical in-between instead of a lost decade. Just as it is fair to say the 1950s did not singularly usher in widely-sweeping changes in official and popular morality, so too is it important not to overstate the late 1960s as that quintessential moment of radical change. The 1950s are best understood, I wish to suggest, by looking at the lives of those whose position within society was more ambivalent, reproached, rejected and sometimes downright loathed. To do this, I will focus on the visual archive of German photographer Herbert Tobias and the ways in which his work helped construct a pre-Stonewall aesthetics of desire that went well beyond the discourse of self-hatred, despair and denial that all too often marks analyses of the period. Tobias's work is useful in the way in which it challenges the earlier homoerotic canon, introducing new social and aesthetic ways of viewing and understanding the shameless queer subject. I will argue that insofar as Tobias's photography helped create a visual vernacular of the erotics of the street, it went a long way in resisting contemporary discourses of abjection. His photos were more than mere depictions of a day in the life, however. They served as visual templates of memory and longing, at once registering and working through the anxieties of the period by aestheticising a range of abject masculinities – those of the rent boys, pick-ups and casual encounters that made their way through his home studio in West Berlin. Tobias's aesthetic was not completely new, drawing as it did on the Weimar fascination with friendship and brotherhood in staging alternative visions of male desire. While there is a rich tradition of homoerotic photography pre-dating Stonewall, much of what little historiography exists suggests that it was in fact the 1970s that bore witness to a collective affirmation of identity and belonging – what George Stambolian has called 'a modern echo of the civic and cultural pride' of gay liberation.[10] Far from simply 'the time before' liberation, I will demonstrate with attention to Tobias's work ways in which the 1950s provided a vocabulary of homoeroticism charged with passion and desire that transcended the repressive inheritance of post-Nazi Germany and the identity politics of the homophile movement, creating a knowledge of the body on display that was forward thinking and liberatory.

Envisioning desire in homoerotic photography

Herbert Tobias contributed to a grand tradition of homoerotic visual appreciation of the young male form. Already in the eighteenth century, Johann Winckelmann revelled in the aesthetic eroticisation of Greek art, especially the way in which paintings and sculpture idealised the strength and universal beauty of the young male form.[11] Prussian photographer Wilhelm von Gloeden consciously evoked this style in over 3,000 images of Sicilian boys posed lounging in Arcadian scenes donning wreaths and amphoras.[12] Aside from the cultural pretention of wealthy aesthetes who consumed his images, von Gloeden's homoerotic vision of physicality was similarly taken up by the European middle class given the perceived links between male nudity, ascetism, morality, self-discipline and proximity to nature – all traits increasingly embraced across the political spectrum by nationalist movements of the nineteenth century, including Zionism and relatively apolitical movements like the *Wandervögel*.[13] In these contexts, intergenerational sex, like the boundary between homoeroticism and homosexuality, was often crossed in the spirit of male bonding. Although outright homosexuality was certainly policed more energetically once the Nazis seized power, homoeroticism flourished in the filmic style of Leni Riefenstahl, whose veneration of the male form combined noxious patriotism with echoes of this earlier tradition.

But as Thomas Waugh has demonstrated, photography served as a privileged medium for gay eroticism and flourished especially in the 1920s and 1930s for what he also terms the 'Glamour Generation' – those members of a transatlantic web of gay intelligentsia and high bohemia that had made inroads into the fashion industry between the wars.[14] These decades gave rise to a self consciously open gay aesthetic in photography, despite the fact that the early artistic and social movements were likewise defined by nascent homophobia. A raft of openly identified cosmopolitans circulated in Europe's capitals, conjoining the fashion and fine arts industry to high and low culture. Still, these were largely small enclaves of the like minded, yet they were able to tap into the anti-establishment sentiment within the various body culture movements, from free love to FKK (*Freie Körper Kultur* or Free Body Culture). The photography of Herbert List and George Platt Lynes enjoyed a particular resonance among these various anti-bourgeois artistic circles, many of which shared the call (if not acceptance) of 1930s Surrealists, who delighted in liberating bourgeois society from traditional taboos and repressed forms of sexuality. List and Lynes, like Tobias in the 1950s, made their living primarily in the fashion industry of the 1930s or shooting portraits of such luminaries as Christopher Isherwood, Carmen Moranda and Orsen Wells. Shots of starlets in dream-like settings with props, mirrors, veils, busts and statues stood in direct opposition to the photojournalism of the day, which dominated the liberal German press and the populist *Life* magazine. Drawing on the revolutionary tactics of surrealist art while honing their skills in an industry of illusion and spectacle, List and Lynes laid a foundation for a more metaphysical staging of irony and reverie that Tobias would draw on explicitly in his own oeuvre. World War II and total war would bring back the classical fixation with ruins and antiquity as List, who had fled Nazi Germany for Greece before returning under duress and serving in the map-designing office, used stylised images of broken male statuary to symbolise the end of beauty, innocence lost and German guilt.

Beyond simply serving as a canvas upon which memories of total war and destruction took shape, the male forms immortalised by List and Lynes and later Tobias represented an aesthetic corollary to sexology's categorisation, providing a visual archive of a variety of masculine archetypes beyond the staged exoticism of the Italian or Greek boy or the physical power of body-building lads. The different gradations of homoerotically-charged masculinity epitomised in the bodies of dancers, actors, sunbathers and aesthetes communicated a multivalent masculinity within same-sex spheres. Although List was able to earn a decent living as a photojournalist with the celebrated Magnum agency, and Lynes enjoyed commercial success with his portrait photography of Hollywood stars, both men circulated their most explicitly homoerotic images among a close coterie of friends out of fear of jeopardising their livelihoods. Lynes did publish a series of photos in *Der Kreis*, the Swiss homophile magazine, but used a pseudonym to ensure anonymity. Gaining newfound notoriety shortly before his death in 1955, Lynes was approached by American sex researcher Alfred Kinsey, who asked permission to publish 200 photographs of his male nudes, since, as he put it, 'there wasn't any record of the homosexual aesthetic in any form that was as interesting as this because it...was perfectly open.'[15] But this perceived openness was nothing more than an artistic variation of bodybuilding physique culture, which came to dominate the visualisation of 1950s homoeroticism. Rooted in the erotics of the street and not in the classical tradition or body building aesthetic, Tobias's photography provided a new and unique take on the visibility of abject desire.

From the studio to the street

Tobias came to his craft while still a young man, after serving in the Wehrmacht and deserting behind the lines in late 1945. Upon his release from a Prisoner of War Camp, he enrolled in a theatre course and began a life of creativity. After touring with a small theatre troupe, he met his first real love, Dick – an American civilian working for the occupation government. Theirs was a passionate relationship, but one which, like so many in the postwar period, garnered the attention of neighbours, and they were denounced to the police. Evading capture, which would result in Dick's return to the US, they fled to Paris, where Tobias began shooting photos with the camera Dick had given him as a present. While working in the darkroom of a photography studio, his talent was discovered and his work passed on to contacts at *Vogue Paris*. Before he could enjoy his newfound fame, in 1953 he himself was forced to flee the city after an incident in a teahouse with an undercover police officer brought a charge of indecency. He returned to West

Germany, which he referred to as the 'successor state to Hitler's Reich' given the continuation of the 1935 law against homosexuality that remained in the criminal code until 1969. Labelled a sexual offender, he moved first to Frankfurt where his November 1953 cover shot in the *Frankfurter Illustrierte* won a 3,000 DM competition, ensuring him some measure of acclaim and success as one of the most sought after fashion photographers of the postwar generation.

It was the divided city of Berlin that would capture both his imagination and desire. In relocating to the former capital in 1954, he sought out the 'remnants of what remained from the legendary 1920s'.[16] Informed by this quest to 'research and document this lost past', Tobias took to the city streets, photographing children at play amidst what appear to be the still smouldering ruins ten years after capitulation. Although he chronicled the bleakness of life in stark black and white hues, West Berlin's foremost art critic recognised Tobias's talent at capturing the complexity of life in vivid texture.[17] As art historian Will Grohmann commented in the magazine *New Times*, 'Tobias uses the camera like a painter his palette.'[18]

During his time in Berlin in the 1950s, he was well supported with numerous contracts from various fashion magazines. He had prestigious advertising gigs with Berlin's public radio, and even held contracts for record art from Deutsche Grammophon. Although he began taking photographs of his male lovers in Paris, it makes sense that it would be the city of Berlin that would help forge his artistic and aesthetic sensibilities, given the way the ruins disrupted the cohesiveness, tidiness and easy separation of high and low, past and present. As people suffered through temporary housing, stood in queues waiting for transportation or rations, or were pressed into police vehicles after an untimely raid on an underground bar, the city's scarred landscape forced a confrontation with the nakedness of existence with the past rubbing up against the present. Realising that there was beauty and transcendence in destruction, Tobias opted for a personal mediation on the place of the sublime within the sordid. This approach to photography was certainly in keeping with existential philosophy, and he had mixed and mingled with Genet and Cocteau in Paris, but it was also supremely political, both for the ways in which his photos served as a guide into his own existential interiority and the way they laid claim to freedom of desire and choice, whether melancholic, euphoric, poetic or carnal. This emphasis on erotic individualism over shame may have begun in Paris, at his lover's behest, but it blossomed in Berlin, where he discovered that 'either one lives a situation or photographs it'. Often, he asserted, 'I have done both.'[19] Still, the irrepressible nature of his art was not forged in a vacuum, and his experiences in the repressive climate of Christian democracy and the Konrad Adenauer state meant every effort to remain true to his vision came at a cost, both personal and political. Looking back on these unstable years in a piece of writing that took its name from the preamble of the West German constitution 'The Dignity of Man is Inalienable,' Tobias went so far as to lament that this decade was especially difficult for him since 'it was hard to retain any sense of loyalty to a state that allowed such wrongs to continue to transpire.'[20] This profound sense of disillusionment helps explain Tobias's itinerant lifestyle as he migrated first to Hamburg, then to New York and back again, in search of the support of an international queer community.

To be fair, West Germany was not the only postwar regime to have done injustice to Tobias. His homosexuality had made him *persona non grata* at *Vogue*, despite the fact that it was common knowledge in the industry that, according to Tobias himself, 'any fashion photographer worth his salt was likely gay'.[21] But the fact that the Adenauer regime had persecuted at least as many men for same-sex infractions over the course of the 1950s as had the Nazis before and during the war should not be forgotten.[22] Worse still, case files from the Nazi period were entered as evidence in postwar trials, drawing a direct line of continuity between the two regimes. Although the methods for collecting evidence were less traumatic, certainly, the effects of a charge remained crippling for the accused. After a series of trials in Frankfurt in 1950–1951, six young men made headlines for resorting to suicide rather than being called to testify. With no legal protection, men lost their livelihoods, and despite creative attempts to circumvent the vice squad through the installation of controlled entry systems to underground bars, until decriminalisation in 1969 queer life in West Berlin was marred by the spectre of prosecution. Besides reinforcing a siege mentality, illegality and censorship made organising an opposition exceedingly difficult, and explains why homophile organisations and pro-decriminalisation advocates agitated for change via models of respectability and legal reform. Outright expressions of love for love's sake were soft peddled in favour of respectability and the right to personality as framed by the tenets of the constitution on human dignity.[23]

Efforts to repeal Paragraph 175 came from a variety of places, from progressive-minded jurists to philosophers like Theodor Adorno. But the message of toleration often turned on a particular image of gay respectability, and the image of the citizen worthy of membership was one who practiced restraint and sexual sobriety. Part of that sobriety extended to recriminations about cruising and male prostitution in particular; indeed, it was not until the mid-1970s that sociologists at the University of Hamburg humanised the plight of the rent boy as part of the urban gay scene. One prominent West German jurist, the stridently outspoken Botho Laserstein, who defended gay clients caught in the police dragnet and wrote advice manuals to help men navigate through the legal process, warned against the dangers of the trade and the malevolence of the hustler.[24] Drawing on contemporary sexological literature from Frankfurt's Institute for Sexual Studies, Laserstein argued that since it was greed and not sexual orientation that induced rent boys to prey on innocent men, as long as consensual sex between men was criminalised, new clients for the boys would be generated, putting honest and otherwise law-abiding men in harm's way.[25] According to Laserstein, rent boys were the 'worst kind of criminal there is'.[26]

Staging the homoerotic self

Situated against this backdrop of respectability and disavowal – for as one can imagine, the tearoom trade, cruising, and rent boys continued to hold firm as features of gay life in the 1950s – Tobias's photographs (although highly staged) appear as a stridently political affront to the official morality of the Federal Republic, to the dictates of contemporary sexological thinking, and to the unfortunate hypocrisy of the reform movement. Not only does Tobias make his own self a subject and object of the photographic gaze, but he brings into focus elements of the unacknowledged everyday in all their manifestations. As Andreas Sternweiler has said elsewhere, his photos constructed a 'poetics of living homosexuality' that went far beyond camp, classicism, pure show or theatre.[27] In flying in the face of conformity on three levels, the photos from the 1950s suggest a radical in-between, jostled between echoes of Weimar libertinism and the unbridled self-assertion of Stonewall-era activism.

This is most visible in Herbert's choice of composition and staging. Gone is the academic imagery of List or Lynes. Nor are there visions of grand balls or exotic bars in the soon-to-be commodified West German gay scene. Although stylised, each subject is positioned to simultaneously evoke and embody a mix of quotidian everydayness organised around the spectacle of sensual pleasure. Most importantly, the masculinities encapsulated in these photos communicate a subjectivity of self-assuredness that might be cerebral as well as physical, a synthesis of brains and brawn quite unlike Genet's prisoners in the 1950s film *Un Chant d'Amour* or the beefcake masculinity that dominated the mail order trade. We see this especially in an image of Dick taken in 1951, labelled simply 'Without Title'.

When compared to the photo spreads in *Der Kreis* (the Circle), the legendary Swiss magazine and symbol of the international homophile movement, Tobias's photos were anything but high-brow and classical. Despite being embraced by the art world, Tobias was ever the outsider who went out of his way to develop his artistic vision independent of current trends. He even refused inclusion in the 1955 Family of Man show at the Museum of Modern Art in New York, the exhibition that brought international fame and exposure to contemporaries Doisneau, Brassai, Dorothy Lang, Robert Capa and Ansel Adams. Within the gay scene, his aesthetic diverged significantly from that which graced the pages of the friendship magazines and homophile papers. Despite the inclusion of near-nude inserts and fetishised images of manual labourers, a 1958 reader survey in *Der Kreis* exposed the readership's more traditional taste with the overwhelming majority opinion was that the magazine should showcase more classical nudes.[28] German publications like *Die Gefährten* (The Companion), *Der Weg* (The Path) and the *Amicus Brief* (or Amicus Letter) mixed 1920s eroticism with commercial success. The *Amicus Brief* newspaper even had contacts-desired pages in the back – but these soon fell into obscurity following the promulgation of West Germany's 1953 law for the protection of minors, which was explicitly designed to prevent a return to sexually permissive anarchy of Weimar-era kiosk and newspaper stands. This crackdown on gay print culture made an impact in forging real limits to what images could be showcased within the public sphere. It is not insignificant that the protective legislation corresponded directly to the worst years of anti-gay persecution, contextualising homophile reaction against more self-conscious displays of sexuality.[29] Viewed in this light, Tobias's photos were doubly subversive, providing images of intimacy and desire unfathomable in contemporary print culture.

It is not insignificant that it would be in his Parisian photos that Tobias concerned himself with themes of tenderness, longing and intimacy, since it was there, in his hotel room in the Rue Gregoire de Tour, that he explored the full range of his feelings for Dick. In these photos, and those of the friends and lovers who stopped by, he embeds his subjective experience of desire in the fabric of subculture, taking them out of the sanctuary of the hotel room into the public, to the parks, street corners, toilets and gardens of the Jardin du Luxemburg, known nodes within cruising culture and the Parisien gay scene. In a photo labelled simply '140', the subject's half-smile and well-placed hand on a companion's knee are certainly not images of shame and derision, but claims to self-expression within a still repressive climate. A photo of two men walking down the street with shopping bags in hand (it turns out, two friends of Tobias) takes an even more interesting gendered claim to desire by showcasing queer intimacy through the lens of domesticity and cohabitation. It does not matter whether it was fleeting or temporary; it is its everyday ordinariness that lends affirmation and meaning, especially considering that domestic realm offered no sanctuary to the preying eyes of the state. Of course, Tobias was very much aware of the fact that these gestures of intimacy were enacted in a world still hostile to queer sociability. We see this in evidence in a photo labelled simply 'Ohne Title' (Without Title) where the faces of two men staring out of their apartment door are literally enveloped by branches, symbols of the tentacles of the contemporary moral canon.

This moral universe is not simply accessible via the dichotomy homo-versus-straight. Implicit in Tobias's photography is a self-conscious engagement with the vicissitudes of same-sex sexuality within the various 1950s gay subcultures, those constructed within the literary realm as well as in the everyday. We see this especially in the way in which his photos tackle the problem of shame and of self-loathing, two issues hotly debated in queer theory today.[30] As Regina Kunzel has noted, queer history almost exclusively focuses on historical moments of opposition to oppression, while more recently suffering and shame have come under the microscope for the way they helped forge affective responses to the conditions of social exclusion. Kunzel argues that historians have failed to pay suitable attention to those 'sideways' moments where subjects negotiate their existence between and beyond the dichotomy of shame-versus-pride. Tobias takes up this challenge visually in sitting as subject in *Day-Dream after Querelle de Brest*, a photograph named after the fourth novel by Jean Genet, which itself would be made into a film in 1982 by Rainer Werner Fassbinder, the last of the West German gay icon's films before his own overdose. The madcap story of a sailor who encounters a motley crew of whores, thieves and grifters in northwest France, before falling into a murder cover-up, after having more than his fair share of sexual encounters, is a graphic meditation on sex, violence and desire. In Tobias's self-portrait, we are made witness to what appears at first glance to be the subject's suffering, in a cellar squat or dank hovel, mirroring one of characters in the novel whose elaborate rape fantasy includes his desire to be dominated by his underlings in the hull of his ship. Without knowledge of the novel's theme of murder and carnality, we might assume the photo is a commentary on the stultifying repression of the day. But the novel from which it gained inspiration – written in 1947 and published in 1953, and coincidently illustrated with sketches by Jean Cocteau, purported to have been not just one of Herbert's admirers but lovers – is both a crime story and meditation on masculinity, seduction, and self-delusion which turns on assumptions surrounding the putative active-equals-masculine, passive-equals-feminine subject positions within same-sex sexuality. In the midst of the story of libidinous desires, Genet presents an argument of moral transgression, pride in abjection, and the celebration of betrayal – in this case, a cover-up of a murder housed within a discussion of repressed desire. In his staging of the rape fantasy, meanwhile, Tobias reclaims vulnerability (and passivity) as an emblem of masculinity, while rendering violence beautiful – perhaps the ultimate transgression after all.

This celebration of the abject would continue into his Berlin phase, where, leaving Dick behind, Tobias further integrated the abject into his portrait of subculture. From the safety of his apartment, a testament, perhaps, to the intensification of surveillance in West Berlin or an effort to further lay claim to the domestic as political, he styled and photographed his pick-ups, boys, friends and acquaintances in a series of positions drawing on echoes of earlier emblems of gay sociability. Unlike the Paris photos, however, these images have one thing in common: the composition of the photos, the narrative scenarios presented or hinted at, and the resistant stare or gaze suggest that these were anything but the 'sad young men' Richard Dyer has described emerged on screen in 1950s film.[31] In these photos of couples, the boy next door, working-class men in their gear, or tattooed trade, we confront a gaze of innocence, trust, playfulness, longing and allure. These are not simply objects of desire but subjects who push back against the lens. In this sense, Tobias implicates the viewer in the construction of an embodied masculine sensuality, one that virtually penetrates the lens. With all the accoutrements of the various subcultures, tattoos, costumes, accessories, hairstyles, gestures and, in some cases, foliage/nature, these figures participate in their self-narration. This represents the first time that a subcultural community participated in the representation of its own desire.[32] More importantly, it did so through an erotics of intentionality, where the private and domestic laid claim to the public as sites of intimacy, fantasy and desire, a kind of working-through of the supposedly shamed self. It is more than that, too. It is a quiet, but persistent, assertion of the right to desire in both domestic and public space, and in this sense it was deeply political.

Conclusion

Looking backward as Heather Love suggests, the 1950s were much more than a period of sadness, disavowal and self-loathing. At the very least, it was a decade of suspended existence, a 'sideways moment' or radical in-between. Imbuing his subjects with an embodied shamelessness, albeit a still selective one based primarily on lithe and boyish masculinity, rehabilitating the hustler but not the faerie or the aged queen, Tobias created a unique and alternative education of desire to that espoused by police, jurists, progressive-minded sexologists and artists in the queer canon. Unlike the strategic silences of the homophile movement, however, Tobias's photography exalted in the forbidden by simultaneously drawing on past aesthetic language and harking forward to the post-Stonewall claims to individual sexual autonomy.

In conclusion, let me make four quick points to better understand Tobias's place within the 1950s. Firstly, Tobias's work raises the issue of how we might all negotiate in our work what Sara Ahmed calls 'the affective economy' – the circulation of emotions such as desire, joy, lust, as well as shame in the years before decriminalisation. In Tobias's photography, we see the artist attempting to transcend loneliness in an alternative performance of self-formation. But this is not out-and-out pride – more a transitional expression of self-narration that might provide pause for a reconsideration of how we conceptualise the time before Stonewall. Secondly, part of Tobias's allure, certainly, is the way in which his work is not simply a staging of reality but an active exercise in self-fashioning, one that drew inspiration, strength and permanence from everyday elements of contemporary gay life. This raises a rather significant question: How might we gauge and measure the effect of these significant yet smaller, subtler, claims to queer sociability within politics at large, among the macro-level debates on decriminalisation and emerging psychosocial definitions of 'the homosexual', and especially amidst the night raids, and police clampdowns that also marked the Queer 1950s? We often assume a causal connection between cultural visibility and political change, but more often than not, there is actually some measure of disconnect between the two. What is the place of aesthetic questions within the slow and meandering march to legality? And, more importantly, given Tobias's own cosmopolitanism, what is the transnational element to this discussion? To what extent did international communication networks, modernist aesthetics and the international art market help bring what Michael Warner has called the queer counterpublic to being?[33]

Thirdly, along this vein, how might we further develop the link between the representational and the 'real', as it were, in order to trace the feedback loop from the discursive to the material and back again? One way is to place greater emphasis on the body as a spatialised site of regulation, memory, and resistance. For Tobias, the body and its desires are understood spatially, forging notions of conjugality, of domesticity, as well as constituting a cartography of the city's gay scenes. In drawing on past and contemporary visual imaginaries, perhaps an art of arousal even, he depicts the body as having a history in a demographic sense and in an iconographic one as well. In historicising the place of the abject and the honourable, we might be better able to articulate moments of resistance to the status quo, but also (and this brings me to my fourth and final point) to move beyond the simple dichotomies of assimilation and opposition, regulation and reaction, shame and pride, state control and individual autonomy that lie at the heart of our linear sense of the postwar decades. One step in that direction is the recognition that the 1950s were a period in flux, marked seductively by twilight moments amidst baleful persecution. Tobias's work is suggestive of a third path beyond mere containment and self-loathing, to bring back into view some of the ideas from the outset of this chapter. His photography opens up new and imaginative spaces at once recognisable and familiar while new and enticing.

Notes

1. Elaine Tyler May, *Homeward Bound: American Families in the Cold War Era* (New York: Basic Books, 1988), 93–94.
2. Jennifer V. Evans, 'Decriminalization, Seduction, and Unnatural Desire in East Germany', *Feminist Studies*, 36.3 (October 2010), 553–577.
3. Hanna Schissler, '"Normalization" as Project: Some Thoughts on Gender Relations in West Germany during the 1950s', in Hanna Schissler, ed., *The Miracle Years: A Cultural History of West Germany, 1949–1968* (Princeton: Princeton University Press, 2001), 366.
4. D'Emilio and Estelle, *Intimate Matters*; 2nd expanded edition, University of Chicago Press, 1997).
5. David M. Halperin, *What Do Gay Men Want? An Essay on Sex, Risk, and Subjectivity* (Ann Arbor: University of Michigan Press, 2007), 3.

6. David S. Churchill, 'Transnationalism and Homophile Political Culture in the Postwar Decades', *GLQ: A Journal of Lesbian and Gay Studies*, 15.1 (2009), 31–66, Julian Jackson, 'Arcadie: Sense and Issues of the "Homophile" in France, 1954–82', *Revue d'Histoire Moderne & Contemporaine*, 53.4 (2006), 150–174, Domenico Rizzo, 'The Ideal Friend: The Homophile Canon and "Market" of Relations in the 1950s', *Revue d'Histoire Moderne & Contemporaine*, 53.4 (2006), 53–73.
7. George Chauncey, *Why Marriage? The History Shaping Today's Debate over Gay Equality* (New York: Basic Books, 2004). For a larger discussion of homophile movements and their changing orientation, see Churchill, Transnationalism and Homophile Political Culture.
8. Martin Duberman, Martha Vicinis, and George Chauncey, *Hidden from History: Reclaiming the Gay and Lesbian Past* (New York: Plume, 1990); see also Jeffrey Weeks, *Sexuality and Its Discontents. Meanings, Myths, and Modern Sexualities* (London: Routledge, 1990).
9. Love, *Feeling Backward.*
10. George Stambolian in Allen Ellenzweig, *The Homoerotic Photograph: Male Images from Dureiu/Delacroix to Mapplethorpe* (New York: Columbia University Press, 1992), xviii.
11. Johann Joachim Winckelmann, *History of the Art of Antiquity* (Los Angeles: Getty Publications, 2006), discussed further in Eric O. Clarke, *Virtuous Vice. Homoeroticism and the Public Sphere* (Durham: Duke University Press, 2000), 137.
12. Hans-Joachim Schickedanz, ed., *Wilhelm von Gloeden: Akte in Arkadien* (Dortmund: Harenberg, 1987). Jason Goldman, 'Nostalgia and the Photography of Wilhelm von Gloeden', *GLQ: A Journal of Lesbian and Gay Studies*, 12.2 (2006), 237–258.
13. Daniel Boyarin, *Unheroic Conduct: The Rise of Heterosexuality and the Invention of the Jewish Man* (Berkeley: University of California Press, 1997); Yaron Peleg, 'Heroic Conduct: Homoeroticism and the Creation of Modern, Jewish Masculinities', *Jewish Social Studies*, 13.1 (2007), 33.
14. Thomas Waugh, *Hard to Imagine. Gay Male Eroticism in Photography and Film from Their Beginnings to Stonewall* (New York: Columbia University Press, 1997), 106.
15. Glenway Werscott quoted in Ellenzweig, *The Homoerotic Photograph*, 104.
16. Herbert Tobias, 'Leben zu Protokoll ... "fast ein Augenblick von Glück."' Ein Gespräch zwischen Herbert Tobias und Hans Peter Reichelt in *Him Applaus*, 1977 (Heft 11), 11.
17. Pali Meller Marcovicz, 'Fremder, der du vorübergehst ... Ein Freundeswort zu Herbert Tobias' in *Herbert Tobias Photographien* (Berlin: Fröhlich and Kaufmann, 1985), 15.
18. Will Grohmann, 'Ausstellungskalendar' in *Die Neue Zeit* (15 November 1954).
19. Herbert Tobias, *Die anderen Fotos* in Konvolut unveröffentlichter Schriften, ohne Jahr, 24 Seiten (Typoskript, Kopie. Verblieb des Originals unbekannt), 1. Berlinische Galerie, Landesmuseum für Moderne Kunst, Fotographie und Architektur, Fotografische Sammlung.
20. Herbert Tobias, 'Die Würde des Menschen ist unantastbar' in Konvolut unveröffentlichter Schriften, ohne Jahr, 24 Seiten (Typoskript, Kopie. Verblieb

des Originals unbekannt), 23. Berlinische Galerie, Landesmuseum für Moderne Kunst, Fotographie und Architektur, Fotografische Sammlung.

21. Tobias, *Him Applaus*, 39.
22. Robert Moeller, 'Private Acts, Public Anxieties, and the Fight to Decriminalize Male Homesexuality in the Federal Republic of Germany', *Feminist Studies*, 36.3 (October 2010), 528–552.
23. Andreas Pretzel and Volker Weiss, *Ohnmacht und Aufbegehren: Homosexuelle Männer in der frühen Bundesrepublik* (Hamburg: Männerschwarm, 2010).
24. See *Der unaufhaltsame Selbstmord des Botho Laserstein: ein deutscher Lebenslauf*, ed. Herbert Hoven (Frankfurt am Main: Luchterhand-Literaturverlag, 1991).
25. Botho Laserstein, *Strichjunge Karl: Ein kriminalistischer Tatsachenbericht*, (Hamburg: Schmidt, 1954) 54. Of course, the fear of solicitation and blackmail was intense during the Nazi period. In Hamburg, for example, members of the Hitler Youth served as decoys, pretending as Stefan Micheler argues 'to offer sexual services in order to entrap men'. See Stefan Micheler, 'Homophobic Propaganda and the Denunciation of Same-Sex-Desiring Men under National Socialism', *Journal of the History of Sexuality*, 11 (2002), 125.
26. Botho Laserstein, *Strichjunge Karl*, 37.
27. Andreas Sternweiler, 'Poesie of a Gay Everyday', *Herbert Tobias, 1924–1982: Blicke und Begehren* Hrsg. von Ulrich Domröse (Hamburg: Haus der Photographie Deichtorhallen Hamburg, 2008), 42.
28. Waugh, *Hard to Imagine*, 406; see also Hubert Kennedy, *The Ideal Gay Man: The Story of Der Kreis* (New York: Routledge, 1999).
29. Elizabeth D. Heineman, 'The Economic Miracle in the Bedroom: Big Business and Sexual Consumption in Reconstruction West Germany', *Journal of Modern History* (December 2006), 846–877.
30. David M. Halperin and Valerie Traub, *Gay Shame*, Pap/DVD (Chicago: University Of Chicago Press, 2010); Regina Kunzel, 'Queer Studies in Queer Times: Conference Review of "Rethinking Sex," University of Pennsylvania, 4–6 March 2009', *GLQ: A Journal of Lesbian and Gay Studies*, 17.1 (1 January 2011), 155–165.
31. Richard Dyer, *Heavenly Bodies: Film Stars and Society* (New York: Routledge, 2003).
32. Waugh, *Hard to Imagine*, 158.
33. Michael Warner, *Publics and Counterpublics* (New York: Zone Books, 2005).

2

Nouveau Désordre: Diabolical Queerness in 1950s French Cinema

Andrew Asibong

1950s France was not the safest cultural terrain on which to build queer cinematic images.[1] The gay men of the 1930s French cinema glory days had beaten a sharp retreat back into the celluloid closet.[2] The Nazi Occupation introduced anti-gay legislation in France for the first time since the 1791 reforms (and this regression was to remain in place until François Mitterand's 1981 victory). Yet after the war, gay people were associated with collaboration and decadence and seen as agents of corruption that the shiny, new, post-Résistance French nation needed to scrub away from its guilt-sodden consciousness as quickly as possible. These were the years of 'fast cars and clean bodies', not transgression, experimentalism, or anything remotely 'queer'.[3] Even the major visible counter-cultural movement in France at the beginning of the decade, Existentialism, was overwhelmingly heterosexual in its Sartre-Beauvoir-Camus-branded café manifestations. If it undoubtedly had its queerer undercurrents and associated players (such as the bisexual writer Violette Leduc, author of the censored adolescent lesbian novel *Ravages* (1955) and the melancholic autobiography *La Bâtarde* (1964)), these elements remained muted, unthreatening, in the background.[4] Existentialism would be supplanted by cinema's *Nouvelle Vague* (or New Wave) towards the end of the decade as France's hippest left-field export. This movement, too, was characterised by an ostentatious heterosexuality: its occasional flashes of queerness (one thinks of the discreet homo-eroticism of Claude Chabrol's 1958 film *Le Beau Serge/Handsome Serge*; the vaguely gender-bending aesthetics of Jean-Luc Godard's 1959 film *A bout de souffle/Breathless*; the homosocial bonding of François Truffaut's 1962 film *Jules et Jim*) are generally drowned out by the interminable postures, conversations and cigarettes of the iconographic male-female Gallic couple.[5]

There are, of course, notable exceptions to this portrait of a deeply unqueer French 1950s. Perhaps the most arresting is Jean Genet's notorious, now semi-legendary 1950 short film, *Un chant d'amour/A Song of Love*, in which various naked and semi-naked male prisoners (and one warder) writhe, exchange cigarette smoke through holes in the walls, full-frontally masturbate, wave flowers, fall in love and fantasise. Genet's beautiful black-and-white images have had an enormous impact on international culture, avant-garde and mainstream, high and low, gay, straight and everything in between. From the artwork of The Smiths to the videos of P.J. Harvey, from the acclaimed HBO television show *Oz* (1997–2003) to mainstream gay pornography, from the filmmaker Todd Haynes to the Breton pop duo Mansfield TYA, the implications of the film's ultra-modern iconicity seem far more significant for the twenty-first century's celebrations of an internationally 'cool' queerness than for any representably queer French sensibility of the 1950s.[6] Genet's outrageous and unapologetically homosexual over-exposure carves out an extreme and deliberately unintegrated gay male (sub-)cultural space for itself. Long unavailable in France and frequently banned in the US and UK (as recently as 1989, it was withdrawn from an arts cinema in Hull)[7], its explicit, stripped-down gayness has only recently been allowed to show itself in public. *Un chant d'amour* is by no means an irrelevant document for scholars of the 'queer 50s', and yet it is, in many ways, so radically at ease within its own homosexual desire as to appear singularly 'ahead of its time' and, thus, strangely, perhaps more 'at home' in a post-Stonewall cultural landscape. Like Genet's novel *Notre-Dame-des-Fleurs/Our Lady of the Flowers* (1943), in which the drag queen Divine cavorts, masturbates, and engages in multiple instances of gay group sex with her friends Mignon-les-Petits-Pieds, Seck Gorgui and Notre-Dame-des-Fleurs in 1930s Montmartre, the activities and identities depicted obviously represent activities and identities which did have a real subcultural existence for a limited number of men, but which were almost entirely separated from the mainstream, and consequently censored in all sorts of ways.[8]

At the opposite end of the scale in the decency stakes is Marcel Carné's 1954 film *L'Air de Paris*, in which a young boxer (Roland Lesaffre) and his macho trainer (Jean Gabin) play out a sort of Platonic romance. In a recent critical article, Richard Dyer probes this film for evidence of its inherent homo-ness, seemingly frustrated by his discovery of it everywhere and nowhere at the same time, and concluding with the observation that the film's improbably magical final shot suggests that 'there is no place for Victor and André, for homophilia, in Paris or anywhere else'.[9] *L'Air de Paris*, queer but stiflingly coy, gags itself from start to finish, and consequently is able to enjoy the mainstream appeal clearly unavailable (and undesirable) to Genet. The end result, though, is a film in which all we can do (and, ultimately, all Dyer can do) is desperately read for fleeting signs, as underexposed and evanescent as the tight vests and erect penises of *Un chant d'amour* are overexposed, overwhelming and consequently censored.

Neither *Un chant d'amour* nor *L'Air de Paris* experiments with the queerness of interpenetration between straight and gay dimensions of 1950s France. Both remain so resolutely in their chosen realms – either unapologetically subcultural transgression or repressed, buttoned-up acceptability – that their usefulness for a theorisation of queer 1950s French film and culture is perhaps limited. Equally limited and limiting are the somewhat more frequent, generally melodramatic representations of lesbian desire on the French screens of the 1950s, the vast majority of which tend to frame the women in question in vaguely pathologising terms ('mad girls' or 'bad girls', as Lucille Cairns's study puts it), generally without the disruptive aesthetic complexity that might be posited as essential to queer film (as compared to film containing potential queers).[10]

It might seem odd to turn to either Jean Cocteau (1889–1963) or Henri-Georges Clouzot (1907–1977) for a theorisation of subversive French 1950s cinematic queerness. At the dawn of the 1950s, Clouzot was middle-aged and Cocteau was old, and neither was associated with anything remotely cutting-edge. Though gay, and despite his early championing of then-convict Genet, Cocteau was firmly established at the heart of a wealthy and powerful Parisian high-culture set. His 1940s films, such as *Les Parents terribles/The Terribles Parents* (1948) and *La Belle et la bête/Beauty and the Beast* (1946), had been great popular successes, camp eccentricities to be sure, but an essential part of the mainstream French film fabric. The Existentialists, self-proclaimed guardians of all that was edgy, found Cocteau outmoded and fussy – a relic of pre-war, pseudo-transgressive, faux-aristocratic posturing.[11] As for Henri-Georges Clouzot, certainly *not* gay as far as we know (he was married to the actress Vera Clouzot), his cinema has long been considered the archetypal 'cinéma de papa': precisely the sort of stuffy, traditional fare derided by Godard, Truffaut and the late-1950s rebels of the New Wave. His macho high-action romp *Le Salaire de la peur/The Wages of Fear* (1953) was a big commercial success, but hardly indicative of anything socially disruptive. Moreover, both Cocteau and Clouzot emerged from the Occupation with reputations more than slightly sullied by what was perceived as a far-too-agreeable manner with the Nazi authorities, neither one having been even vaguely active in the Resistance, and both having carried on applying for funding, grants, and general state protection and support throughout the darkest days.[12]

Cocteau and Clouzot certainly do not come from any of the places we might start looking for queer 1950s images with impact, then. However, as I suggested above, who in 1950s France *did* come from such a place? Sartre and his friends were, at the beginning of the decade, no 'queerer' than Jean-Luc Godard, François Truffaut and the other *Cahiers du cinéma* New Wavers were at the end of it. Marcel Carné, with *L'Air de Paris*, was playing his cards too close to his chest for them to be visible, while Jean Genet, as we have seen with *Un chant d'amour*, was so far out on his own underground limb that queer subversion of the cinematic mainstream was an impossibility. In a way, it makes sense that Cocteau and Clouzot can ultimately be credited with providing 1950s French cinema with its most clearly visible, most widely disseminated queer images: both directors were caught in the quintessentially queer position of simultaneous public acceptance and lingering, unspeakable shame.

Cocteau's *Orphée*, released in Paris in September 1950, and Clouzot's *Les Diaboliques*, released in Paris in January 1954, have attained the status of world-renowned popular classics as well as critically-acclaimed gems, but in what follows I want to try to speak of them together (as they rarely, if ever, are) as fundamentally unstable, hybrid, fantastical – and deeply queer – 1950s films. *Orphée* stars Cocteau's former lover Jean Marais as the eponymous Left Bank poet. Orphée has reached a position of public celebrity, thanks to his successful poems, and lives with his devoted – if slightly dull – wife Eurydice (Maria Déa), but this is amid the general contempt of the hip new generation of Parisian artists and activists (embodied in Juliette Gréco's Aglaonice), who see Orphée as a tedious old has-been. When Orphée is kidnapped by a mysterious Princess (Maria Casares), who later reveals herself as an avatar of Death, he finds himself pulling away from both his domestic set-up with Eurydice and the mundane judgments of the 'boho' set, only to move more and more deeply into the unthinkable (since undead) world of transgression, fantasy and destruction offered by the Princess and her all-male community (two named, white, speaking assistants, Cégeste (Edouard Dermithe) and Heurtebise (François Perier), two nameless, silent, Chinese servants, and a whole horde of leather-clad demon bikers). The film veers amongst domestic comedy (Orphée and Eurydice rowing about magazines and mirrors and knitted woollen bootees), detective inspector shenanigans, social satire at the expense of the

Existentialist café-brigade, and the utterly demented proto-science-fiction that unfolds in the underworld.

Clouzot's *Les Diaboliques* is apparently easier to pin down. Set in a stale private boys' school run by a cruel and sadistic headmaster Michel (Paul Meurisse), the film follows the unlikely decision of Michel's timid, God-fearing, weak-hearted wife Cristina (Vera Clouzot) and his butch blonde bombshell mistress Nicole (Simone Signoret) to team up and kill him. Luring Michel to Nicole's house in the provinces, the two women drown him in the bathtub and dump his body in the school swimming pool. But when the pool is drained, Michel's body has disappeared. It seems to have come back to life, turning up in group photos, punishing errant pupils, and eventually rising from a new bathtub to scare Cristina literally to death. It turns out that Michel was not dead at all but had plotted the whole thing with Nicole as a way of getting rid of Cristina. The wicked pair of lovers are arrested at the end of the film by a slightly spectral retired detective, though, and Cristina's ghost now seems to be the returning phantom, wandering the hallways of the disintegrating school to chat with the most rebellious of the frustrated pupils.

Such as I have described them, it is probably not difficult to see why both films have become classics. If *Orphée* has always appealed to lovers of dreamy, opium-fuelled, overblown 1950s-ness, *Les Diaboliques* is rightly considered to be one of the darkest and most terrifying films of its era. But the films' supreme interest lies, perhaps, in their acute awareness of the interaction between the legally and conventionally cruel 'everyday' in which their narratives are at first realistically anchored, and a queerly out-of-control dimension of exception which keeps threatening to submerge this first world of sanctioned, knowable sadism. The films slide and oscillate wildly between these two realms, between the spaces of straight, realist, readable cruelty, and unmoored, fantastical, impenetrable horror, pulling protagonists and spectators alike between old and new orders.

What of their specifically sexual queerness? Surely queer status cannot be claimed for these films merely on the basis of their foundation on shifting, unstable signifiers of ontology? In fact, both films do contain a very specifically sexualised queerness, playing with their protagonists' sexual identities in a manner quite unlike that of the majority of films being made during that era, and inspirational of a whole slew of more recent queer cinema, both French and otherwise. Despite the alleged central romance between Orphée and the princess, most of the iconic images of *Orphée* are indisputably gay: the famous shot of Jean Marais collapsing longingly against the unyielding mirror and his own reflection (this would be used as the cover for the Smiths' 1983 single 'This Charming Man'); the various unspoken gazes and interactions between Orphée and, first, Cégeste (played by Edouard Dermithe, Cocteau's lover at the time), then Heurtebise; and, of course, the silent, identikit, leather-clad motorcyclists who flank the princess wherever she goes, carrying off her various targets to the nether regions of the underworld. These motorcycle men would give rise to the all-masculine worlds of Kenneth Anger in *Scorpio Rising* (1964), Marlon Brando in László Benedek's *The Wild One* (1953), and, in the wake of these influential American films, a whole generation of gay biker iconography.[13] Their cinematic influence can even be felt as late as the gay 1970s: the world of the princess and her motorbike men resembles nothing so much as the parallel (and definitely queer) netherworld of Mortville to which the quintessential buttoned-up, middle-class housewife Mink Stole escapes halfway through John Waters's 1977 lesbian camp-trash masterpiece *Desperate Living*.

As for *Les Diaboliques*, the entire film is soaked in an atmosphere of barely concealed lesbianism. While the 1952 Boileau-Narcejac novel upon which the film is based, *Celle qui n'était plus*, reserves a gay female relationship as its 'shock ending' (the wife and mistress are revealed to have been in league all along, and it is the husband who is the final dupe), the film takes lesbianism as its point of departure, revelling in a bizarre and 'unnatural' bond between the two women from the outset (pupils and colleagues alike remark on the two women's inexplicable intimacy), using that connection as the emotional meat of the entire film before reverting to an unconvincing and insubstantial heterosexual 'shock ending', in which the wife, not the husband, is proved 'really' dead. There is little need to expend too much energy trying to set about trying to prove the sexual closeness of Cristina and Nicole in the film: it exists as a given. The women share a bed wherever they are located, display a sometimes heartbreaking closeness (making the final betrayal of Cristina by Nicole all the more sickening), bicker like lovers, have no reason other than intimate emotional involvement to be carrying out the plot in the first place (all the married couple's money, we are reminded many times, comes from Cristina), and eventually separate (before Cristina's death) with all the pathos of a regular couple. No, the women at the centre of *Les Diaboliques* are quite obviously not just good friends but instead form the prototype for many a criminal (yet oddly sympathetic) female couple striking back (if here only apparently) against bestial male oppression. (One thinks of Ridley Scott's 1991 film *Thelma and Louise*, Andy and Lana Wachowski's 1996 film *Bound*, and

Alexandre Aja's 2003 film *Haute Tension/Switchblade Romance*, even if the latter work slides disappointingly in its final minutes towards an almost hysterical homophobia.)

French film specialists have recently begun to explore the queer dimensions of *Orphée* and *Les Diaboliques* beyond the remit of mere imagery and iconography, though. In his recent monograph on Cocteau, James S. Williams expresses the desire to 'resist the temptation merely to search for hidden or repressed gay images or symbols in Cocteau's work'[14] and instead sets about instigating a fascinating unpacking of a whole queer aesthetic across the whole of the Coctelian *œuvre*. Williams locates this aesthetic at the level of Cocteau's obsession with all that pertains to 'rearness' or 'behindness'. Persuasively demonstrating how key relational moments and interactions occur between male characters precisely when one is standing or sitting behind the other, forcing the 'front' interlocutor to turn his head to look at one at his back or on his tail, Williams argues for a fundamentally 'anal drive' governing all the films, with *Orphée* and its 1960 sequel *Le Testament d'Orphée* operating as prime examples.[15] This, Williams insists, is the true queer aesthetic at work within Cocteau, a male-male back-to-frontness to be found not through plot or characterisation, but through *mise en scène* alone, and strengthened by Cocteau's relentless utilisation of reverse-motion photography, in which objects and men (and men-as-objects) are forever being projected backwards, falling supine in space and time, only to spring up again, improbably erect, when the film is turned back in the opposite direction.

Equally ingenious is Susan Hayward's recent revisiting of *Les Diaboliques*, in which she calls for the recognition of Clouzot's classic as a queer text not necessarily because of any putative relations occurring between Nicole and Cristina (Hayward even suggests that the relationship might not be drawn explicitly enough as lesbian, claiming that Clouzot has to some extent 'heterosexualized' the original literary source),[16] nor especially because of Nicole/Signoret's troubling, anti-Monroe blonde butchness (although Hayward is struck by the significance of Nicole/Signoret's unpainted nails and carpet-slippers),[17] but above all because of the way in which the film, essentially a kind of French film noir, upsets the conventional allocation of hero/*femme fatale* roles. Finding that Nicole/Signoret shifts too disconcertingly between archetypal *femme* and masculinised thug to function as a watertight repository of paranoid heterosexual fantasy, Hayward argues that the film's true *femme* is the shifty, unlocatable, disappearing figure of Michel. The film thus redistributes normative film noir gender roles, leaving the tiny, bird-like Cristina to occupy the role of anxious, 'castrated' hero.[18]

As well as confidently and cleverly insisting upon the two films' queerness at these subtle levels, recent study of *Orphée* and *Les Diaboliques* also calls attention to their latent political content, highlighting moments in *Orphée*, for example, that appear uncomfortably to recall France's recent immersion in a twilight world of interrogation and torture,[19] or those in *Les Diaboliques* that seem to make baleful references to the burgeoning practice of bathtubs and water torture across the Mediterranean in French Algeria.[20] If I am seeking to bring anything new to the queer or historical table in my own presentation of *Orphée* and *Les Diaboliques*, it would be to suggest that we would do well to consider the films together in order to explore how it is not merely a case of their tendency to indulge in thrilling moments of troubling queerness or their flirtation with a certain kind of political allusiveness that should be at stake for the modern critic, but rather the manner in which the two things – queerness *and* an attention to traumatic French recent histories – are in fact welded together via the films' indulgence in the excessive aesthetics of the overblown fantastic.

Both films use the hyperexpressionism of horror to point to an overwhelming and uncontainable trauma at the heart of so-called 'normal' domestic and socio-political relations of the everyday. As in the cinema of George A. Romero (both with his *Living Dead* series and with *sui generis* pieces such as *Season of the Witch* (1973) and *Martin* (1977)), David Cronenberg (from his early 'body horror' films of the 1970s to later works such as *M. Butterfly* (1993) and *Crash* (1996)), or the HBO television series *True Blood* (2008–present), a straight, hegemonic order that poses as knowable, reasonable, 'real', is incessantly tainted and penetrated by a seeping surplus of socially demanding being that is at once both queer and fantastical. This surplus threatens to submerge both films before being apparently despatched in the final frames by a return to 'business as usual' that is as banal as it is unconvincing. If, as Hayward and Williams persuasively suggest, nods to the Occupation and colonial horrors do pop up from time to time in these films, apparently alongside all the randomly queer goings-on, it is because they are – in just the same way as the queer identities and practices they flank – insidious, irrepressible elements of these films' unconscious, elements that will return no matter what.

Orphée presents the spectator with an everyday world of realism and order that is governed at every stage by surveillance and sadism. Orphée is excluded, judged, ridiculed and metaphorically torn to pieces by a postwar society that poses as transgressive but is, in fact, constructed upon norms every bit as conservative as the ones it claims to have sprung up against. If his wife, Eurydice, offers at least an escape from the assessments and vilifications of the self-styled bohemian Aglaonice and the hateful *Café des Poètes,* she is nevertheless linked to them by some unspecified past association. The oppressiveness of the world Eurydice offers Orphée is symbolised throughout the film by her stifling involvement with domestic interiors, boiling kettles, and glossy magazine spreads.

Every bit as satirically irreverent with regard to the state of everyday 1950s France, *Les Diaboliques* shows us a world in which sadism is sanctioned and nourished by the institutions of marriage and school, interwoven in literally nauseating knot (one thinks of Cristina's near-vomiting at the school dinner table) by the husband-and-wife-led private institution in which the sordid action takes place. Everywhere Cristina and Nicole go – and long before they commit their apparent murder – they are spied and eavesdropped on by neighbours, colleagues and pupils, all of whom whisper the same insistently repeated refrain: 'Ce n'est pas normal!' ('It's not normal!'). But what both films instigate via their very different lurches towards something unnameable – the princess and her underworld in *Orphée,* the murder plot and subsequent hauntings, both orchestrated and possibly authentic in *Les Diaboliques* – is a refusal of these everyday, 'straight' forms of sadism, and a flight (on which the spectator, too, is uncompromisingly dragged) into a queerer, more intense form of torture, expressed in a mode of non-realist hysteria. In *Orphée,* the princess's world is simultaneously queer and oneiric. Her sex appeal, as with nearly all the heroines in Cocteau's films, is usually (and somewhat unsatisfactorily) described by critics as 'phallic', but perhaps more important is the fact that it is inextricably bound up with the fetishistic apparel and paraphernalia of the gimp-like men and automata who flank her. If Orphée is uncontrollably drawn to the world of the princess's death-driven sexuality, it is not because he wants to set up a suburban home with her in a comfy second marriage that will mirror his present arrangement with Eurydice. No, the sexuality, the modes of relation offered to Orphée by the princess and her community will literally immolate him, squeeze him to something like death, act on him in frenzied, ritualistic movements that resemble nothing so much as a Bataillean orgy of disintegration. When, in the film's final sequence, he is held down and stretched by Heurtebise and Cégeste, while the princess rants her incomprehensible instructions, the spectator is left in no doubt that the struggle taking place within this film is that between a sexuality and a mode of existence in the world that at once refuses all appellation and all knowability.

In the same way, the adventure towards which Cristina and Nicole pull the spectator from the start of *Les Diaboliques* is not merely one of heavily-coded lesbianism. It is a descent into a world of ghosts, unruly bodies[21] and magic, every bit as disorderly and anarchic as the cinematic phantasmagoria initiated by later filmic lesbians, such as the eponymous heroines of Jacques Rivette's *Céline et Julie vont en bateau/Céline and Julie Go Boating* (1974), Millie Lammoreaux and Pinky Rose in Robert Altman's *3 Women* (1977) or David Lynch's Betty and Rita of *Mulholland Drive* (2005). And even if the film appears to overrule the validity of that world, negating simultaneously its queerness and its fantastical nature in one fell swoop in the nasty revelation not only that Nicole has been on the demon headmaster Michel's side all along, but that the entire ghost story has been a hoax, the very last suggestion – that the dead Cristina now haunts the school despite everything – represents an irrepressible return, a permanent presence of fantastical queerness, in the form of a melancholic lesbian ghost.

I am not suggesting that either *Orphée* or *Les Diaboliques* are, in fact, manifestoes for queer surrealist revolution. Both highly ambivalent with regard to their often weak, unsympathetic, sometimes even closet-fascistic protagonists, they offer nothing so much as sheer thrilling provocation. Nor am I arguing that the conflation of queerness and the excessive genre of the fantastic as I have presented it is, in itself, helpful or liberating. But what is inescapable is that the films, made just five years apart, sling a sort of magical catapult at that purportedly 'reasonable' and 'realistic' way of life that is normative and institutionalised postwar French heterosexuality. Intriguingly, both films find the same powerfully disparaging way to describe the framework of straightness, that hegemonic matrix that appears ultimately to prevail: it is presented as nothing more than a cesspit of liquid abjection. *Les Diaboliques* shows us constant images of Michel – punitive guardian of the institutional, heterosexual order – immersed in and emerging from different containers of dirty water (river, pool, bath). The film's opening images are of a filthy pool of water, images of liquid putrefaction which lead us seamlessly to the interiors of the unhappy school ruled over by the corrupt headmaster. As for the angel Heurtebise in *Orphée,* himself about to be led with the princess to something worse than Death, there is only one conclusion he is able to draw from the return of Orphée and Eurydice to their bourgeois 1950s domestic interiors: 'Il fallait les remettre dans leur eau sale' [We had to put them back into their mire]. Straightness may ineluctably return to centre stage, these queer 1950s films seem to be saying, but it can no longer pretend to be either solid or clean.

Notes

1. As Richard Dyer reminds us: 'The post-war period was markedly homophobic. The anti-gay legislation introduced under Vichy in 1942 was maintained, and the Paris police began cracking down on homosexuality from 1949 on; anti-gay laws were to be strengthened under Charles de Gaulle.' Richard Dyer, 'No Place for Homosexuality: Marcel Carné's *L'Air de Paris* (1954)', in Susan Hayward and Ginette Vincendeau's (eds) *French Film: Texts and Contexts* (London/New York: Routledge, 2000), 128.
2. Dyer lists a remarkable number of classic French films in which gay men were featured during the 1930s – *Le Sang d'un poète* (1932), *Paris-Béguin* (1931), *Zéro de conduite* (1933), *La Kermesse héroïque* (1935), *Hôtel du Nord* (1938), *La Règle du jeu* (1939) – before noting that lesbian representation was relatively plentiful in both the 1930s *and* the 1950s, for example, *Club de femmes* (1936), *Les Collégiennes* (1956), *La Garçonne* (1957). Dyer, 'No Place', 128.
3. See Kristin Ross, *Fast Cars, Clean Bodies: Decolonization and the Reordering of French Culture* (Cambridge: MIT Press, 1996).
4. Leduc's narrative of lesbian worship for Beauvoir, *L'Affamée/Starved* (Paris: Gallimard, 1948), cast Leduc herself in the position of self-effacing gay underling, slavishly attendant upon the (only apparently heterosexual) Beauvoir's every whim.
5. Consider, for example, Godard's *Le Mépris* (1963) and *Masculin/Féminin* (1966), or Eric Rohmer's *Ma nuit chez Maud* (1969).
6. Contemporary pop culture seems extremely comfortable appropriating images which, at the time Genet made *Un chant d'amour*, were anything but 'pop' but rather emerged from a context of crime and extreme stigmatisation. Today, it seems almost *de rigueur* for the ambassadors of 'MTV cool' to combine the iconography of homosexual prison activity with the normalising programmes of mass advertising. (Consider the 2010 Lady Gaga promotional video 'Telephone' for a disquieting case in point.)
7. See Jane Giles, *The Cinema of Jean Genet: Un Chant d'Amour* (London: BFI, 1991), 31.
8. *Notre-Dame-des-Fleurs,* circulated anonymously for much of the 1940s, was considered by many who read it to be mere pornography, and was published in truncated form by Gallimard in 1951. For a useful analysis of 'actual' homosexual life in 1950s France, as opposed to literary/cinematic fantasies of it, see Julian Jackson's *Living in Arcadia: Homosexuality, Politics and Morality in France from the Liberation to AIDS* (Chicago: University of Chicago Press, 2009).
9. Dyer, 'No Place', 138.
10. See Lucille Cairns's study of lesbianism on the French screen, *Sapphism on Screen: Lesbian Desire in French and Francophone Cinema* (Edinburgh: Edinburgh University Press, 2006).
11. As James S. Williams puts it: 'he was considered after the war to be *passé* in an age of political engagement'. James S.Williams *Jean Cocteau* (London: Reaktion, 2008), 114.
12. See Williams, *Cocteau,* 176–186, and Christopher Lloyd, *Henri-Georges Clouzot* (Manchester: Manchester University Press, 2007), 29–63.

13. Among the most celebrated and instantly recognisable of these eroticised gay motorcyclist images are surely the drawings of the cult artist and illustrator Tom of Finland.
14. Williams, *Cocteau*, 158.
15. Williams, *Cocteau*, 157–186.
16. Susan Hayward, *Les Diaboliques* (London/New York: I.B. Tauris, 2005), 35, 52.
17. Hayward, *Les Diaboliques,* 46.
18. Hayward, *Les Diaboliques,* 50–51.
19. Williams, *Cocteau*, 124–130.
20. Hayward, *Les Diaboliques,* 55–57.
21. Hayward, *Les Diaboliques,* 59–61.

3
Love 'Off the Rails' or 'Over the Teacups'? Lesbian Desire and Female Sexualities in the 1950s British Popular Press

Alison Oram

In 1954, an article headlined 'Love Off The Rails' appeared in the mass market Sunday newspaper, The *People*.[1] Framed as giving advice to worried parents, it examined the implications of the recent New Zealand murder case, in which two teenage girls, Juliet Hulme and Pauline Parker, involved in what other press reports described as an 'unhealthy relationship' and a 'wild infatuation...for each other', were convicted of murdering Parker's mother because they feared she might separate them.[2] The author deployed a range of psychiatric theories of the family and parenting to instruct fearful readers on how to prevent their own daughters 'develop[ing] unnatural love affairs with members of the same sex'.[3] The sensational headline is of the type often linked to 1950s scare-mongering about out-of-control teenagers or the threat of homosexuality. Yet, the discussion moves on to a quieter, more privately-situated vision of same-sex love in asserting that many wives had 'a homosexual background', which meant that 'their real love life is spent over the teacups with their girl friends'.[4] This domestic image of housewives chatting at home suggested that lesbianism might also be found in the heart of the apparently normative family and contrasts strongly with the violent disorder evoked by 'love off the rails'. This chapter explores the territory surrounding and connecting these representations of female homosexuality, in a period when mass media ideas about lesbianism were becoming more clearly formulated.

Historians of sexuality have argued that homosexuality took shape as a distinct modern identity in 1950s public consciousness in Britain.

Jeffrey Weeks sees this happening in relation to both male and female homosexuality: the homosexual person was now delineated as 'a particular type of being with his or her distinct desires, ways of being and identity', though he also acknowledges that this process 'was partial and uneven in its impact'.[5] For male homosexuality, this transition into a public identity had taken place by the end of the 1950s, as result of high-profile prosecutions sensationally depicted in the press.[6] There was less media attention paid to lesbianism, and postwar public knowledge and perceptions of same-sex love between women deserves further research.[7] This chapter will discuss the varied set of ideas through which lesbian desire and sexuality became identifiable and personified in 1950s news reporting. At the same time, I also wish to complicate the notion that female homosexuality was emerging as a discrete – boundaried – form of public identity, by looking at the relationship of lesbianism to married heterosexuality. When lesbianism appears in conjunction with marriage and the family, it reveals considerable uncertainty about the nature of women's sexual desires and the shape that modern marriages should take.

Revisionist historians are dismantling the idea that the long 1950s (from the 1930s to the early 1960s) were the 'golden age of marriage'.[8] Marriage, heterosexuality and family life comprised the hegemonic model of mature sexuality, household formation and national stability, but individual adherence to such a perfect structure proved to be short-lived. Lesley Hall suggests that the fifties might be seen more as a period of sexual instability than one of unthinking orthodoxy.[9] Ideal marriage now included larger goals: it was to be a companionable partnership between wife and husband. In tension with its status as a social institution, marriage was increasingly seen as a *relationship* of continuing love and mutual sexual pleasure as women's sexual desires were acknowledged from the mid-twentieth century.

It is difficult to exaggerate the social importance of marriage to women's identity and life course in this period. It remained the most obvious and pragmatic route to adult status and security, in a period in which women's average wages remained around 55 per cent of men's, and their employment opportunities were only gradually widening.[10] It was also key to women's gendered self-identity, offering the fulfilment of motherhood and family life, as well as a re-valued sexual pleasure – it was the privileged affective and romantic partnership.[11] Whether marriage could successfully function as the bedrock of national social stability in a time when divorce rates were perceived to be high, and young people were casually jumping into marriage at ever younger ages, was a matter of anxious debate.[12] Lesbianism was figured as the 'other' to heterosexual normality in the fifties' popular press, but it also served to raise troubling questions about female friendship, women's sexual agency, and the place of sex and love within marriage.

Reaching into almost every home and creating a shared public language in its news reporting of sexual transgression, the popular press is an important source of evidence for analysing the changing forms of sexual knowledge circulating in mass culture and available to its mainly working-class and lower middle-class readers. Newspaper stories are highly sensitive to what is topical and what will be acceptable to readers and hence are useful barometers of social change. Yet, they are not straightforward reflections of popular views and knowledge, nor an accurate record of events. While the press increasingly provided sexual information, it did so with the commercial aim of entertaining its readers while remaining sufficiently respectable. Sexual content, whether in relation to crime, divorce or other human interest reports, was delivered in a limited format; suspended between the registers of titillation and moral condemnation, with much material censored, omitted or described in euphemistic language.

This analysis of how lesbianism was reported is based mainly on my survey of the two best-selling British Sunday newspapers, the *News of the World* and the *People*, which had a huge reach in mid-twentieth century Britain. In 1950, the *News of the World* had 17.6 million readers (over half the adults in Britain), and the *People* 13 million readers.[13] The *News of the World* had a reputation for reporting a whole range of crime stories and human interest news, treading a thin line between salaciousness and 'decency'. The *People* was less sensational and seen as more respectable, though it frequently trumpeted about morality and at times set itself the task of educating readers on these new sexual topics.[14] Some sections of the postwar press were keen to provide more enlightening information on sexual matters, while the saturated market for newspapers in the 1950s, pressurised further by competition with television, encouraged some papers, including the *News of the World*, to become more detailed and explicit in their coverage of sex crime and scandal. Mass-market newspapers took an obsessive interest in male homosexuality from the early 1950s, reaching a peak with the 1954 Wildeblood trial, and reporting it in generally hostile and sensationalist terms. This contributed, along with the 1957 Wolfenden Report which it had prompted, to the idea of the male homosexual as a particular type of person.[15]

Female homosexuality, in contrast, was not a preoccupation of the 1950s press, but it was more directly and less ambiguously reported than it had been before the war.[16] The formulations that were used to refer to sex between women typically included 'perverted passion', 'improper association' or 'abnormal friendship'.[17] The term 'homosexuality' was rarely used of women, and 'lesbianism' appeared for the first time only in 1959, in the *News of the World*.

Unlike male homosexuality, lesbianism was neither a criminal offence nor the subject of a moral panic, and the idea of homosexuality among women emerges mainly within two press genres, crime stories and divorce court reporting. As well as the stock narrative forms common to these genres, such as titillating suggestiveness or moral outrage about law-breaking and violence, some of these reports deploy humour, a form of presentation which also reveals contemporary unease about female sexual desire and the institution of marriage.

Lesbianism in crime stories

Lesbianism did gradually gain a public image in this period, albeit an inchoate one. In the crime reports, love between women was generally positioned as existing outside the family; indeed, it was often a threat to the normal processes of courtship and marriage. Lesbian identities were knitted around four themes of deviance. The first was criminality itself, including crimes of violence. Psychological excess could be another marker. Psychiatric discourses were increasingly in play in the postwar years, often used in a rather vague form. The woman who desires other women might be neurotic and display uncontrolled emotion. The third element, gender deviance expressed as masculinity, is frequently assumed to feature strongly in 1950s media stereotypes of lesbianism. In these press reports, the lesbian may have a masculine appearance, or even cross-dress, but not necessarily. Finally, female homosexuality was associated with moral transgression, as the language used to describe it (cited above) demonstrates. Some reporting of lesbianism was inflected with a commentary of right and wrong and shamefulness. Many of these themes were already established in the older professional literature of sexology and psychology, but they were new in popular culture and debate in the fifties. Sometimes, the lesbian figure in the press was over-determined by these discourses; at other times, she escaped most of them. This was not yet a solid or consistent public identity.

The crime stories were often intertwined with discourses of psychiatry. The woman who had sex with other women was represented as a socially marginal individual with an unbalanced personality; the adolescent who had taken the wrong path, or the adult woman who could not control her emotions. Excessive sexual jealousy prompted criminal violence in a case involving an army husband in 1949, when Margaret Snelgrove tried to hit Captain Hill with a metal bar outside his home in Richmond, Yorkshire. She also had a sheath knife strapped to her wrist. Her probation officer said that she 'was an unhappy woman who had formed a strong attachment for Capt. Hill's wife'. The magistrates remanded her to 'a home' for 21 days to be examined by a psychiatrist.[18] Psychiatric explanations of criminal behaviour had developed between the wars in relation to specific groups such as juvenile offenders and male homosexuals, but now reached across all types of crime and offender as new responsibilities were given to the courts.[19] Typically, as in the Snelgrove case, an imprecise, non-technical language was used by the police, probation officers or social workers as they commented on the mental health of the women involved in assaults or suicide attempts.

As descriptions of lesbian desire became more explicit in crime reports in the 1940s and 50s, this strengthened the links between a pathologised lesbianism, criminality and female deviance, a theme which was common across all kinds of popular media, including pulp fiction, social problem novels and film.[20] The danger of homosexual contagion in all-female environments (such as prisons) was one aspect which occasionally surfaces in the popular press. After four convictions for theft and fraud during the Second World War, Ellen Young was sent to Holloway Prison. There 'she was brought into contact with a form of perversion through an older woman', an event which was used by her defence to account for her subsequent masquerading as a man and her brief marriage to a more sexually innocent girlfriend.[21]

Despite the appearance of psychiatric explanations, female homosexuality as gender deviance – that is, as expressed through masculine appearance – was only an intermittent theme in the popular press stories. Into the early 1950s, wearing slacks was often seen as an almost accidental hangover from the war years of women's work in factories and in the uniformed military services. With growing affluence, it became increasingly reprehensible in a period when gender differentiation could flourish, and women could make a choice for greater femininity. Muriel Johnson, who worked as a pastry cook, served in the ATS and intermittently dressed like a man, was arrested and charged in 1951 after becoming engaged to two young women who had complained to the police. She had 'become a menace' because of 'her associations with other women who took her to be a man'.[22] In this kind of case, the mannish woman not only sexually deceives a younger woman but also disrupts the normal path towards marriage, demonstrating the significance of courtship as a key transitional (and potentially dangerous) moment of feminine self-hood.

In some criminal cases, the youthful lesbian expresses shame and remorse or decides to pursue a heterosexual life, emphasising the moral deviance of love between women. Joyce Irons, who had passed as a man (at least to some of her friends), got engaged to another woman in the mid-1950s, who broke off the relationship after they quarrelled and the other woman found a boyfriend. Irons paid a boy of 13 to throw acid in her ex-fiancee's face and was jailed for three years. Speaking to the *News of the World*, Irons said she wore slacks for practical reasons, and back-pedalled rapidly to conventional womanhood. 'In every other way I was a perfectly normal girl. I had been kissed by men and did not find it unpleasant.' Bitterly regretting her incitement to violence, she said that she had since met a man and hoped to 'settle down as an ordinary housewife' with him after her prison term. Irons was pictured in before and after photographs, first as a moody mannish butch with a cigarette in her mouth, and now in a dress, stockings and hairdo. 'I threw away the grey suit in which I had posed as a man. Then I went out and for the first time walked through a women's shop buying frocks and dainty, frilly underwear.... It meant that at last... I had turned my back on the past.' [23] Lesbianism is posed here as a problem of indeterminate and malleable female desire, lived out through masculine presentation.

But masculine appearance or personality was only sometimes highlighted as part of the psychology of the lesbian, even in crimes of violence. Indeed, the excessive emotionality of the lesbian (in medical or criminological discourse) could be seen as a disorganised form of hyper-femininity or female excess. In the widely reported 1952 murder trial of Bertha Scorse, there was little of masculinity in the visual or verbal representation of her personality. Scorse had formed an 'unnatural attachment' with a married woman whom she had met in a sanatorium while both were being treated for tuberculosis, and persuaded her to leave her husband and live with her. Scorse stabbed her lover to death with brutal force when she later ended their relationship, and the trial hinged on whether she suffered from a 'gross perversion which was an extremely powerful driving force' and which had inevitably led to insanity and murderous violence. Despite her crime and its masculine agency, the imagery of feminine weakness surrounded Scorse, represented as a sick and lonely girl who sought love. Still ill with tuberculosis, Scorse was sentenced to death as she lay on a stretcher in the dock, an image which provoked sensational headlines across the popular press.[24] The strength of her love and jealousy, and her success in seducing a married woman, carried echoes of the *femme fatale*, one image of the lesbian that had circulated earlier in the twentieth century.[25]

In this particular genre of crime stories, we can see the beginnings of one public image of lesbianism. This lesbian was 'other', existing outside conventional morality and femininity in various ways. Indeed, these more explicitly-labelled examples of criminal lesbians in the postwar press represented female homosexuality as an external threat to normal marriage and family life, as other historians have argued.[26] The violent, even murderous, attacks with weapons, made by women on their married women lovers or their husbands are a tangible example, but the threads of discussion in the lesbian stories can also be seen as reflecting doubts about the malleability of female sexuality in general. Love and sex between women (often appearing in ordinary suburbs in these reports) troubled marriage and intersected with contemporary questions about how ideal marriage and family life should be organised and women's sexual potential and responsibilities within it.

The 'Love Off the Rails' article, introduced at the beginning of this chapter, is atypical in that it was a rare in-depth opinion piece on lesbianism rather than a news report. The range and complexity of this piece indicate the reach of insecurities about the family, the aetiology of lesbianism and male homosexuality and the significance of proper parenting. It was triggered by the conviction of Juliet Hulme and Pauline Parker (15 and 16 years old) in New Zealand for the murder of Parker's mother. This was the third lesbian murder within six years to receive extended press attention in Britain, and came in 1954 at the height of press debate and reporting of male homosexual scandal. In the *People*'s opinion piece, a Harley Street psychiatrist deals with parents' concerns about 'unnatural friendships between young people'.[27] 'Love Off the Rails' directly addressed the readers of the *People* as parents of ordinary families and the millions of others like them. How could they prevent their children becoming 'morbid neurotics capable of the most monstrous crimes'? This expert reassured readers that 'there isn't really much cause for alarm' about female homosexuality, since only one in 200 adult women 'has these tendencies in a practical sense'. There is a strong emphasis on the importance of the family in bringing up the child to become sexually normal, but at the same time a good deal of scepticism expressed about the success of contemporary marriage and family life.

While it was common in this period for professional expert advice on family matters and child-rearing to be relayed in the mass media, especially in magazines and on radio,[28] it was unusual for the popular press to develop psychiatric ideas about lesbianism in such depth. Three contrasting approaches – essentialist, Freudian and Kinseyesque models – are knitted together to explain the development of female sexuality; a multiple model that was typical of the confused and diverse medical aetiologies of lesbianism in postwar British psychiatry.[29] In a child's development, the psychiatrist explains, same-sex attachment is 'the homosexual stage and it is a perfectly normal one ... a phase that should pass when adolescence arrives'. At this point, a biological essentialism also comes into play: when menstruation begins, 'her maternal feelings start and she begins to look around for a mate.' Continuing lesbian tendencies were described as amenable to medical treatment and particularly to the wise guidance of parental love:

> By far the best way of making sure that your children grow up to be sexually normal is by giving them a happy home. By that I mean a home life in which the child is shown love by both parents, and in which the parents obviously love each other, too. Believe me, that sort of home is rare.[30]

The psychiatrist also introduced a strong dose of Kinseyism into this article, raising the idea that there was a continuum of sexual orientation and the danger that *parents* may harbour same-sex desires. He warned, 'But don't let us all raise our hands in horror at the mere thought of [homosexuality] and thank God that we are "normal". Very few of us, in fact, are.' Many married men are only really happy in the saloon bar or playing cards with their male friends, while 'there are many women with a homosexual background that makes it difficult for them to get on easily with men. They marry, but their real love life is spent over the teacups with their girl friends.'[31] 'Love Off the Rails' offers an image of the female homosexual as potentially criminal, and psychiatrically abnormal. But at the same moment, the article confuses this identity by warning readers that homosexual desire was not easily distinguished from same-sex friendship and was part of the affective potential of many apparently 'normal' married women and men. This insecurity was lurking within suburban marriage – a classic media play on readers' anxieties that was applied here to all generations, parents and children.

Love between women and the divorce courts

Divorce case reports involving accusations of lesbianism also niggled at the question of marriage, love and female sexuality. After 1926, newspapers were legally restricted in the scope of their divorce court reporting, but many still used the judge's summing-up to develop titillating headlines and stories about marital and sexual wrongdoing as in this 1959 example: 'The Wife's Woman Friend Made It a Threesome'.[32]

The 1937 Matrimonial Causes Act had extended the grounds for divorce to include desertion, cruelty and insanity.[33] Unlike male homosexuality, lesbianism was not a legitimate grounds for divorce in itself, but it might be cited as a form of mental cruelty, and several plaintiffs pursued this line in 1950s divorce cases. In the 1954 case of *Spicer v Spicer*, the husband was granted a divorce on the grounds of cruelty after his wife had persisted in continuing a close friendship with another woman, causing him anxiety and ill health, although the court explicitly made no finding of a physical relationship between the two women, which both had denied.[34] The 1951–1956 Royal Commission on Marriage and Divorce considered, in passing, whether lesbianism should become a ground for divorce, but it decided there was a problem in finding a workable definition and in any case was not minded to expand the ground of 'cruelty'.[35]

Several 1950s divorce court stories raised this question of definition: what features could distinguish lesbianism as a sexual practice, in a culture in which women's friendships could be publicly affectionate? Divorce court judges were generally reluctant to agree with husbands that the close female friendships of which they complained should be seen as a matrimonial offence. A clergyman alleged to the divorce court in 1954 that his wife and her friend

> had been seen hand in hand; they called each other 'darling'; they kissed on the lips; they spent a number of holidays together; they were constantly alone in the wife's room and on two or three occasions they occupied the same bed.[36]

However, the judge found that while their friendship was extremely close, it was not close enough to entitle the husband to a reasonable belief that it was 'an improper association'.[37]

Divorce court reporting in the press aimed to sensationalise marriage breakdown and entertain readers, but between the lines we can see debates about the nature of same-sex affection and the proper roles of wives and husbands. In a 1959 case, a court heard how a couple came to what the judge described as 'a peculiar arrangement' before marrying, by which a woman friend of the wife would live with them and sleep with the wife. The husband said he had not agreed to forgo sexual intimacy with his wife (as she maintained) and had hoped to 'win her slowly'.[38] In adjudicating a maintenance order in the wife's favour, the judge declared: 'It is fair to the wife and Miss Barker [her friend] to emphasise that there was never any suggestion that there was any kind of Lesbian relationship between them, either physical or emotional.'[39] This was the first time the term 'lesbian' was used in either the *News of the World* or the *People* in this period. Of course, these judgements reflect a judicial desire not to soften the legal grounds for divorce in this period. In these and other reported divorce cases, the close female friendships were described as 'an odd business'[40] but absolved of lesbianism – yet, up to the point of judgement, and perhaps still to readers, the question remained open.

Same-sex emotional investments outside marriage were increasingly questioned in the postwar years, but these cases also open up the issue of what kinds of heterosexual behaviours, in terms of gender roles, love and affection and sexual expectations, were appropriate within 1950s marriage. A clash between older and more modern ideas about marital duties was quite stark in the 1959 case just outlined. The wife was committed to a traditional role of housekeeping and childcare: she 'always regarded it as her job to look after the husband's children by a former marriage. Beyond that she was unwilling to go.'[41] The *News of the World* report highlighted the discussion and judge's disapproval of the (contested) agreement to exclude sexual intimacy. Contemporary sex advice manuals and marital guidance organisations in the postwar period increasingly emphasised sex as a conjugal duty of wives in the building of a happy marriage.[42]

If kissing, affection, companionship and bed-sharing were being enjoyed, should this not be between husband and wife rather than between women friends?[43] In the 'Initials-only' divorce suit of 1952, the husband 'complained that the warmth and friendship between his wife and Miss H.C.M., including frequent kissing, was in marked and humiliating contrast to the coldness that his wife showed towards him'. The wife and Miss H. C. M. had been close friends since they had met in the Girl Guides. They had lived and worked together, and Miss H. C. M. later went to live with the couple as their housekeeper following the birth of their child. In dismissing the case, including the allegation that this was an 'immoral or improper' friendship the judge remarked that: 'This marriage hardly started on a high emotional level. The wife said she did not love him, and when he had made the proposal of marriage, on his own evidence he never took her into his arms and kissed her.'[44] The idea that modern marriage should include affection, sexual pleasure and companionship between spouses, in addition to their gendered roles as breadwinner and housewife, meant that such emotionally cold relationships were increasingly censured, whether in the divorce courts or problem pages or by popular press psychiatrists.

The boundaries between women's heterosexual and homosexual relationships are constructed as rather fuzzy in much of this reporting. Rebecca Jennings argues there was a shift in the postwar period away from the idea that married women might be the passive victims of lesbian seduction to a greater awareness of the potential lesbianism of married women themselves.[45] She places this change in the 1960s, but the press evidence above shows that it was already apparent in the 1950s, and I would argue that it is a reflection of a broader uncertainty about married women's sexual desires and sexual agency. The press is provocatively playing with these insecurities and doubts, through headlines such as 'Her Woman Friend Cleared',[46] and the repeated dwelling on who was constantly kissing whom. When same-sex desire appears in the debates about marital behaviour, it highlights concerns about the capacity of marriage as an institution to contain the new demands with which it was now freighted – as a sustained loving, sexually-satisfying relationship for women as well as for men, in which each could find emotional self-realisation.

Funny peculiar: queer joking about marriage

The popular Sunday press aimed to entertain its readers on many levels, including finger-wagging at transgressive others, the titillation of sexual immorality and the production of enjoyable anxiety about social problems. Many reports and articles were leavened with humour, and engaged multiple registers to involve readers. In earlier twentieth-century news reporting, the queerness of same-sex desire and gender deviance (for example, in relation to cross-dressing) was mediated through multi-layered humour, knowingness and oblique points of reference. In the 1940s and 1950s, these languages of comedy and allusion began to fall away in crime reporting involving homosexuality, as psychiatric explanations and moral condemnation grew.[47] But remnants remain in the popular media, including some mockery and joking around marriage and fifties morality.

Such comic relief might destabilise the concurrent moral message about criminality or the gravity of marriage. The 1954 divorce case discussed above, in which a clergyman and his wife accused each other of cruelty, was headlined: 'Vicar Drank Cups of Tea in Secret' and presented as a funny-peculiar type of collapsing marriage. Marital disharmony had long been a topic for popular joking, and here we have the nagging wife and the henpecked husband, together with the 'out-of-place' nature of the accusations; not only the odd female friendship but the matter of the secret cups of tea.[48] Cups of tea here (and in the 'Love Off the Rails' article) symbolise an everyday domestic stability, which could nevertheless be distorted and subverted by same-sex affection. Furthermore, the perceived high divorce rate in the 1950s meant this traditional joking now had a sting in its tail for those anxious to preserve the institution of marriage – warring couples were now no longer locked together forever.

When it appears in crime stories, humour allows the women involved to have some agency, even if they are being processed through the courts. The story of fraudsters Pearl Brown and Margaret Haworth mobilised several codes for sex between women, and different forms of performative comedy. After their release from prison in Manchester for earlier offences the two women stole a doctor's car and travelled to London. Brown, described as 'Eton-cropped', posed as a (woman) doctor, and the couple stayed in 'a Mayfair hotel, where they lived in a double room for nearly a week, and left owing £16 2s'.[49] During this time, they met a theatrical producer who let them have the run of his flat in the West End: unwisely, since they stole his chequebook and clothes and then took a train up to Blackburn, Brown now dressed as a man. Over several days of thieving and deception, they were successful in fooling other people; a perennially comic activity, especially when tricking others of a higher status. Their denouement was passing as a newly married couple. 'Covered in confetti, they posed as a honeymoon couple and stayed at a well-known hotel', before eventually being arrested in Morecambe.[50] There was no moral narrative in the story, nor psychiatric comment, just simple criminal fun. Two women getting away with it (at least for a time) was subversive, especially in their mocking of the elaborate celebration of postwar marriage.

One of the most complex queer jokes about marriage in the postwar media was the running gag fostered by contemporary personalities Nancy Spain and her close friend Gilbert Harding around whether either of them had proposed marriage to the other. Harding was the most famous television personality in Britain in the 1950s, appearing on *What's My Line?* and other panel shows, also on radio and as a columnist for the *People*.[51] Spain was a popular newspaper journalist and novelist, moving into radio and TV in the early 1950s, and described in the *Daily Sketch* in 1954, when the rumours of an engagement first broke, as 'sharp-witted bohemian Nancy, who even wears slacks to the theatre'.[52] Both were homosexual, something only 'knowing' members of their audience and readership would have been aware of. The joke was maintained on and off for 18 months during 1954 and 1955, in various newspaper gossip columns as well as on the radio. Nancy Spain revived it on one of their appearances on *Who Said That?* in 1955, as she later described:

> After the panel had gone on quite a long time about how a wise woman would let her husband have her way I said that a wise woman wouldn't marry, anyway.... 'My dear,' said Gilbert. 'I hope you don't mean that. A good marriage is a wonderful thing. I often wished that I had married...' and so on and so on.... 'You know quite well,' I said, 'that I'll marry you any time you like.' 'Ah....' said Gilbert. 'It's too late for that now.' Forthwith the telephone began to ring. The *Daily Mirror*, the *Sketch*, the *Daily Mail*, six ladies from Eastbourne who had cherished an unwholesome passion for Gilbert for years...; one or two gentlemen who said that since Gilbert wouldn't have me *they* would: all these came on the line and upset the BBC duty officer.[53]

The joke, described by Andy Medhurst as 'an extended camp trick on the great British public',[54] works on many levels, including the ambiguity of who knows what about these celebrities. This unlikely couple – Gilbert Harding was a confirmed bachelor, while Nancy Spain did not hide the fact she lived with a woman partner – invert heteronormativity in their own lives, while treating marriage with huge levity and irony on air.

Conclusions

The popular press is an important point of entry into popular culture for historians of sexuality. Press reports were selective in their content and were rapidly produced and used limited types of narrative forms, but nevertheless they can show us what languages and discourses were available to conceptualise lesbianism and how these changed. These stories from the 1950s form a relatively disorganised group of texts, but in their sometimes tangential treatment of love between women, we can unpick their modes of address and trace some patterns. Female homosexuality was gaining a public image in the 1950s. In part, this was associated with various discourses of deviance – criminality, psychological excess, gender deviance and moral transgression – but not inevitably. The lesbian was not simply figured as urban, lonely and excluded from mainstream structures of femininity and the family.[55] In the fifties, homosexuality was seen as a potential sexual hazard within the family, among wayward daughters, and particularly among unhappy wives in affectionless marriages. What's most interesting is this indeterminacy of female sexuality, and how lesbian desire is not clearly differentiated either from heterosexual alliances or homosocial affection.

These new vernacular languages of 'improper friendships' and 'perverted passions' highlighted the instability of female sexual desire and the difficulty of representing either heterosexual or homosexual love and affection as discrete forms of emotional and sexual commitment, despite the new ideals bound up in 1950s marriage. There was an undecidedness about lesbianism, even as it became more strongly delineated. These new conceptualisations of same-sex desire had a specific purchase in the mass-market press because most of the protagonists in these crime and divorce reports came from similar class backgrounds as the readers, the lower middle class or respectable working class. Unlike interwar reporting of female homosexuality, which situated it among an elite, in bohemian parts of London and on the continent, postwar lesbianism was found in very ordinary, very everyday urban or suburban locations. Sixteen-year-old factory girls fell in love in Newcastle and ran away together; women working in telephone exchanges in Catford began relationships; divorce cases citing lesbianism came from Surrey and Brighton; and criminal lesbians attacked old ladies in Lewisham, committed murder in small-town Cornwall and stole property in Marylebone and Morecambe.[56] In the sexually-fluid 1950s, same-sex desire flourished in the same suburban spaces as heteronormativity, in the frayed edges of marriage.

Notes

1. The *People*, 5 September 1954, 6.
2. The *News of the World* (hereafter *NoW*), 29 August 1954, 5.
3. The *People*, 5 September 1954, 6.
4. The *People*, 5 September 1954, 6.
5. Jeffrey Weeks, *The World We Have Won* (Abingdon: Routledge, 2007), 50.
6. Matt Cook, ed., *A Gay History of Britain: Love and Sex between Men Since the Middle Ages* (Oxford: Greenwood World Publishing, 2007), 173–174. Matt Houlbrook, *Queer London: Perils and Pleasures in the Sexual Metropolis 1918–1957* (Chicago: University of Chicago Press, 2005).
7. See, however, Rebecca Jennings, *Tomboys and Bachelor Girls: a Lesbian History of Post-War Britain 1945–71* (Manchester: Manchester University Press, 2007). Jull Gardiner, *From the Closet to the Screen: Women at the Gateways Club, 1945–85* (London: Pandora Press, 2003). Alison Oram, *Her Husband Was a Woman! Women's Gender-Crossing in Modern British Popular Culture* (London: Routledge, 2007).

8. See especially Claire Langhamer, 'Adultery in Post-war England', *History Workshop Journal* 62 (2000), 87–115. Claire Langhamer, 'Love and Courtship in Mid-Twentieth-Century England', *The Historical Journal*, 50.1 (2007), 173–196.
9. Lesley Hall, *Sex, Gender and Social Change in Britain since 1880* (Basingstoke: Palgrave Macmillan, 2000), 166. Pat Thane, 'Family Life and "Normality" in Postwar British Culture', in Richard Bessel and Dirk Schumann, eds, *Life after Death: Approaches to a Cultural and Social History of Europe during the 1940s and 1950s* (Cambridge: Cambridge University Press, 2003), 193–210. Weeks, *World We Have Won*, 39–47. Hera Cook, *The Long Sexual Revolution: English Women, Sex, and Contraception 1800–1975* (Oxford: Oxford University Press, 2004).
10. Stephen Brooke, 'Gender and working class identity in Britain during the 1950s', *Journal of Social History*, 34.4 (2001), 773–796; Jane Lewis, *Women in Britain since 1945* (Oxford: Blackwell, 1992), chapter 3.
11. Anthony Giddens, *Modernity and Self-Identity: Self and Society in the Late Modern Age* (Cambridge: Polity, 1991), 53–55, 74–79.
12. Jane Lewis, *The End of Marriage? Individualism and Intimate Relations* (Cheltenham: Edward Elgar, 2001). Langhamer, 'Adultery in Postwar England'. Thane, 'Family Life and "Normality"'.
13. These are readership, not circulation, figures. Ross McKibbin, *Classes and Cultures. England 1918–1951* (Oxford: Oxford University Press, 1998), 503–504. Adrian Bingham, *Family Newspapers? Sex, Private Life, and the British Popular Press 1918–1978* (Oxford: Oxford University Press, 2009), 19.
14. For discussion of the *News of the World*'s successful formula see Bingham, *Family Newspapers?* 127–133.
15. Chris Waters, 'Disorders of the Mind, Disorders of the Body Social: Peter Wildeblood and the Making of the Modern Homosexual', in Becky Conekin, Frank Mort and Chris Waters, eds, *Moments of Modernity: Reconstructing Britain 1945–64* (London: Rivers Oram, 1999). Houlbrook, *Queer London*. For a recent assessment see Bingham, *Family Newspapers?* chapter 5.
16. Oram, *Her Husband Was a Woman!*, chapter 6. Alison Oram, '"A Sudden Orgy of Decadence": Writing about Sex between Women in the Interwar Popular Press', in Laura Doan and Jane Garrity, eds, *Sapphic Modernities: Sexuality, Women and National Culture* (New York: Palgrave Macmillan, 2006). Bingham, *Family Newspapers*? 197–199.
17. *NoW* (24 February 1952), 7. *NoW* (6 June 1954), 7. *NoW*, (16 March 1952), 3.
18. *NoW* (13 February 1949), 5.
19. For example, to sentence offenders to psychiatric treatment if appropriate. For homosexual men, see Chris Waters, 'Havelock Ellis, Sigmund Freud and the State: Discourses of Homosexual Identity in Interwar Britain', in Lucy Bland and Laura Doan, eds, *Sexology in Culture: Labelling Bodies and Desires* (Cambridge: Polity Press, 1998), 165–179. For juvenile offenders, see Pamela Cox, *Gender, Justice and Welfare: Bad Girls in Britain, 1900–1950* (London: Palgrave Macmillan, 2003), especially chapter 6.
20. Melanie Bell, *Femininity in the Frame: Women and 1950s British Popular Cinema* (London: IB Tauris, 2010), 112–121.
21. *NoW* (1 December 1946), 3. For more detail on this case, see Oram, *Her Husband Was a Woman!*, 134–137.

22. *NoW* (4 March 1951), 2. For her earlier prosecution for posing as a man, see *NoW* (31 May 1942), 7.
23. *NoW* (2 October 1956), 2. Also see *NoW* (15 July 1956), 5; (22 July 1956), 5. Ellen Young similarly vowed to follow a normal moral path after her prosecution. *NoW* (1 December 1946), 3.
24. 'A Girl Lies dying in the Shadow of the Gallows', *NoW* (24 February 1952), 7. Also see 'Death Sentence on Stretcher Girl', *Daily Mail* (22 February 1952), 1.
25. Oram, 'Sudden Orgy'. Also see Jennings, *Tomboys and Bachelor Girls*, 83–84.
26. Jennings, *Tomboys and Bachelor Girls*, 83.
27. The *People* (5 September 1954), 6.
28. Thane, 'Family Life and "Normality"', 198, 210.
29. For changing psychiatric explanations of lesbianism in the postwar period, see Jennings, *Tomboys and Bachelor Girls*, especially chapter 1. Also see Alison Oram and Annmarie Turnbull, *The Lesbian History Sourcebook: Love and Sex between Women in Britain from 1780–1970* (London: Routledge, 2001), 95–96, 116–128.
30. The *People* (5 September 1954), 6.
31. The *People* (5 September 1954), 6.
32. *NoW* (1 March 1959), 3. Gail Savage, 'Erotic Stories and Public Decency: Newspaper Reporting of Divorce Proceedings in England', *The Historical Journal*, 41.2 (1998), 511–528.Bingham, *Family Newspapers?* 133–144.
33. Lewis, *The End of Marriage?*, 101–106. Langhamer, 'Adultery in Postwar England', 93–95.
34. *Spicer v Spicer* (Ryan intervening) 3 All ER (1954) 208. Reprinted in Oram and Turnbull, *The Lesbian History Sourcebook*, 173–174.
35. *Report of the Royal Commission on Marriage and Divorce 1951–55* (1956) HMSO. Cmd. 9678, 30–31; also see 41–42, 63.
36. *NoW* (6 June 1954), 7.
37. *NoW* (6 June 1954), 7. The husband was granted a divorce on other grounds.
38. This was the report headlined: 'The Wife's Woman Friend Made It a Threesome'. *NoW* (1 March 1959), 3.
39. *NoW* (1 March 1959), 3. Also see *NoW* (16 March 1952), 3.
40. *NoW* (6 June 1954), 7.
41. *NoW* (1 March, 1959), 3.
42. Cook, *Long Sexual Revolution*, 225–238.
43. For the exclusion of other friendships in favour of companionate marriage focused on the heterosexual couple, see Langhamer, 'Love and Courtship', 188. Langhamer, 'Adultery in Postwar England', 91.
44. *NoW* (16 March 1952), 3.
45. Jennings, *Tomboys and Bachelor Girls*, 84.
46. *NoW* (16 March 1952), 3.
47. Oram, *Husband Was a Woman!*, chapter 6.
48. *NoW* (6 June 1954), 7. The wife would not allow her vicar husband to drink tea before directing communion services on Sundays.
49. *NoW* (15 February 1948), 3. See also *NoW* (8 February 1948), 3; *Daily Mirror* (7 February 1948), 5.
50. *NoW* (15 February 1948), 3.

51. Andy Medhurst, 'Every Wart and Pustule: Gilbert Harding and Television Stardom', in John Corner, ed., *Popular Television in Britain: Studies in Cultural History* (London: BFI Publishing, 1991), 60–74.
52. Rose Collis, *A Trouser-Wearing Character: The Life and Times of Nancy Spain* (London: Cassell, 1997), 151. And see Jennings, *Tomboys and Bachelor Girls*, 94–95.
53. Nancy Spain, *Why I'm Not a Millionaire: An Autobiography* (London: Hutchinson, 1956), 243.
54. Medhurst, 'Gilbert Harding', 67.
55. As Jennings has argued, in relation to other literatures of the period. Jennings, *Tomboys and Bachelor Girls*, 80–82.
56. *NoW* (29 November 1959), 3; *NoW* (19 December 1954), 2; *NoW* (6 June 1954), 7; *NoW* (1 March 1959), 3; *NoW* (20 April 1958), 13; *NoW* (24 February 1952), 7; *NoW* (15 February 1948), 3.

Part II

Living

4
'Someone to Love': Teen Girls' Same-Sex Desire in the 1950s United States

Amanda H. Littauer

In the 1950s, Americans who read newspapers, perused paperbacks or flipped through magazines encountered a robust discussion of female homosexuality. Diverse forces inspired this discussion: anxiety about wartime disruptions of sexual norms, Cold War fears about hidden threats to American family life, the influence of Freudian psychology, women's growing social and economic mobility and Kinsey's studies of 1948 and 1953. A central claim of this literature was that women who desired other women were psychologically immature, frozen in a state of permanent adolescence.

Treating adolescence both as a demographic category and as a metaphor for female homosexuality, this chapter attempts to weave same-sex desire and female youth into the fabric of postwar society. Drawing upon oral history, memoir, fictional and social scientific literature and case studies, I claim that although mid-century social forces and institutions isolated and punished same-sex-desiring girls and women, at least some such youth recall having experienced the 1950s as dynamic, navigable, and even, at times, pleasurable. Discerning, naming and acting on desire for other girls, searching for support from heterosexual and lesbian adults, mining fictional and social scientific texts for recognition, running away from repressive homes, finding a way into lesbians bars, connecting with other girls and women through intimacy and sexuality, and crafting a sense of lesbian identity, same-sex desiring teens and young women pursued their interests and struggled to create a place for themselves in postwar society. A very few individuals even managed to articulate subjectivities as women-loving adolescents on the path toward satisfying, mature, lesbian adulthood.

In the history of postwar sexual culture, the intersection of lesbianism and adolescence is unfamiliar territory. Existing studies of lesbian culture before the gay and women's liberation movements revolve around bars and homophile organisations, which privileged adults by necessity.[1] What we as scholars and historical actors do know is that oppression plagued the lives of adult gay and lesbian Americans in the 1950s, and fragmentary evidence suggests that isolation could be even more powerful for adolescents, whose dependence on their families limited their access to outside resources.[2] Isolation appears to have affected queer youth not just in small towns and rural areas of the US but in major cities as well. One New York narrator – echoing similar statements by other women – explained that when she was sixteen in 1957, her feelings for a friend led to her realisation that she was 'queer'. 'It wasn't earth-shaking for me ... [but] I had no one to talk to about it.... I kept it inside.'[3] A Los Angeles woman recalled of her youth, 'If there were others that felt the same as I and [had] the same experiences, I was unaware of their existence.'[4] Several LGBT historians claim that this sense of isolation lessened somewhat in the 1940s and 1950s, with wartime mobilisation, nascent gay leisure communities, and the emergence of lesbian bar culture.[5] But for most adolescents struggling to make sense of same-sex attraction and/or non-normative gender identity, there was little relief in sight. Not until the 1960s did a queer youth movement begin to emerge, and not until the very end of the twentieth century did online virtual communities and Gay/Straight Alliances break the isolation of most queer youth. Even amidst oppression and isolation, however, I argue that at least some mid-century girls found ways to connect – with their own desire, with ideas about lesbianism, with trusted adults and with other girls and young women. They did so by engaging in self-fashioning, recognising their own difference, searching for language to describe that difference, relishing rare opportunities for self-expression, drawing upon the adult lesbian community's resources, and forming intimate relationships with others.

Given the limitations of the archive, this discussion of queer girls in the 1950s draws from diverse and fragmented sources, especially oral history and memoir, through which adult women have crafted memories of their own postwar youths. Though oral history interviews are more interactive, less public and usually less carefully constructed than autobiographical writing, both types of sources enable scholars to evaluate the remembered experience of historical subjects and to 'draw attention to the inextricability of that experience from its representation' in dominant discourses of the past.[6] Another key source is an unusual interview study of the sexual behaviours and attitudes of African- and Puerto Rican–American Harlem teens conducted by the American Social Health (formerly Hygiene) Association (ASHA) in the late 1950s. Lesbian-authored paperback fiction provides a glimpse of the kinds of representations of female homosexuality that girls and women found in their corner drugstores. Finally, this chapter draws upon the immense body of popular nonfiction works about homosexuality and female sexuality that were widely available in the postwar years. These journalistic forms of social science proliferated in magazines and in mass-market paperbacks, where publishers packaged freely-borrowed psychoanalytic ideas for popular consumption. Most authors of this 'popular nonfiction' were technically psychiatrists, but their publications were hardly scholarly in nature. The reliability of these texts varied considerably, and they are usually most useful as evidence of discursive representation.[7]

Childhood desires

In autobiography and oral history, adult lesbians have described erotic connections to other girls in childhood, long before they had the language to label their feelings. There are many examples to illustrate this. Koreen Phelps, for instance, claims, 'I think I was in love with other little girls or my teacher' in grade school. [8] In the autobiographical *Zami*, acclaimed black lesbian poet and writer Audre Lorde describes childhood friendships with sensual and erotic dimensions.[9] Joan Nestle, founder of the Lesbian Herstory Archives, recalls her attraction to a more masculine friend at age 13.[10] Dorothy Fairbairn in turn recalls, 'I knew at a very young age that there was something different about me. I wasn't just a tomboy, it was more than that.... I remember having crushes on girls when I was like ten, twelve years old' in the 1940s.[11] Ina Mae Murri, growing up as a Mormon child in Utah, 'knew kind of subconsciously' that she had same-sex attractions in her youth,[12] while Sarah, an African-American woman, says that she knew she was gay at the age of twelve in 1956. She received love letters from little girls and knew that she didn't like boys, even though she didn't yet know the terminology of homosexuality: 'I didn't call it gay. I didn't call it *anything*.'[13] Decades after their own youths had ended, these women remembered – and attributed lasting meaning to – childhood feelings of same-sex attraction or romance.

Gender non-conforming girls who later identified as gay women or lesbians took pleasure in masculine self-expression. A white girl's father tried to punish her for wearing out her flimsy, feminine shoes by buying her men's shoes: 'I couldn't let my father know that I liked them', she recalls. 'Inside I was elated.... I lived in those shoes'.[14] Kathy Martinez, a Puerto Rican girl, irked her mother by combing back her short hair in masculine fashion. Offering evidence of her early awareness of her 'gay' sexual identity, Reba Hudson explained that she had her hair cut short and 'boyish' when she was ten years old.[15] These girls used masculine self-fashioning to convey their early sense of sexual difference. As adult lesbians speaking about their youths, these women traced their queer sexuality back in time, privileging moments in childhood when sexual and gender difference seemed to originate.

As they aged, girls in postwar America heard about lesbianism from peers. Urban girls learned on the streets as well as in school hallways. The ASHA study reveals that many high-school girls of colour in New York were familiar with the concept of female homosexuality as well as with common words describing black lesbians, such as 'bull-daggers', 'bull-daddies', 'lesbians', 'studs' and 'broads'.[16] Forty female interviewees (16 per cent of 250) answered, 'Yes' when asked whether they had ever approached or been approached by someone of the same sex. Interviewers recorded that certain subjects were 'well aware of homosexual activity which was rampant in school' and that 'there was quite a bit of it at the all girls [sic] school' that one girl attended. A teen interviewee said that she knew a 'lot of girls like that'.[17] Even when study subjects were not personally drawn to same-sex encounters, many understood that other girls were. In this particular subculture, female homosexuality was not hidden from schoolgirls' sight.

Seeking connections

As girls grew increasingly aware of their own sexual difference, they often sought out peers and adult allies, finding them on athletic teams and in boarding schools as well as among gay boys and men and parents of their friends. Reba Hudson quickly figured out that about half of the girls who played softball were bisexual or gay; the team became her community.[18] Charlotte Thompson's oral history describes 'a very lucky homosexual thing' that she experienced as a high-school student in the late 1940s in Dallas, Texas: five or six gay boys recognised that she and her girlfriend were a couple and adopted them into what Thompson's interviewer called a 'little gay clique'. When the teens were old enough to get into bars, they started going there together.[19]

Girls also found empathy and recognition from adults, especially among parents of their peers. In the mid-1940s, 14-year-old Roberta

Bobba got a job at a local hardware store when its female proprietor recognised Bobba as 'a little boy-girl', just like her own adult daughter. That daughter and her partner became lesbian mentors for Bobba.[20] In Minneapolis, Koreen Phelps, age 15, knew not to confide in her father, whose job in the Navy was to arrest 'queers'. Phelps remembers, 'I ended up, thankfully, meeting a friend in high school whose mother was enlightened'. She spent as much time there as she could, though when her parents found out about her sexuality, they had her committed to a state psychiatric hospital, where she was abused. Like many youth rejected by their parents, Phelps later escaped her home life by running away and starting a new life in San Francisco.[21] Phelps was in good company. Kinsey's *Sexual Behavior in the Human Female* (1953) reported that among women respondents with 'extensive homosexual experience', just over one-fourth had 'gotten into difficulty because of it', often meaning rejection by parents or other family members.[22] A smaller number of young women were fortunate to be able to discuss their feelings with their parents; a few lucky ones found acceptance, or at least tolerance. Reba Hudson's mother, for instance, said that 'all she ever cared about was my happiness, and if this is what made me happy, you know, that was just fine with her'.[23]

Certain youth, such as Phelps, persisted in finding other people like them, even when doing so required running away or roaming city streets. Twenty-year-old Jackie Jones lived in New Orleans in a cheap attic apartment, which she shared with a 16-year-old lesbian teen who had run away from home.[24] Allegedly only nine years old when she had left her Boston home and taken the train to Manhattan in 1959, Catherine Odette followed around a masculine-appearing woman for days until the older woman and her lesbian apartment mates finally took her in. She lived with the women for two years until a truant officer caught her stacking bottles behind the local lesbian bar and sent her back to her parents in Boston.[25] Unlike Odette, Kathy Martinez, a Puerto Rican New Yorker, did not have to leave her hometown to search for lesbian mentors: 'I used to go down to Greenwich Village and walk around down there on the weekends by myself hoping that someone would recognise that I was gay and talk to me, you know'.[26] With mixed results, these girls attempted to alleviate their isolation by seeking connections to older women.

Occasionally, adolescent girls found a sense of community and acceptance in lesbian bars. Many of Kennedy and Davis' interviewees were under the legal drinking age of eighteen when they first entered lesbian bars or house parties. Teens came up with forged identification and worried about being exposed and thrown out.[27] Young Roberta Bobba, for example, would tell her mother that she was going to a double-feature movie and then take the train into San Francisco, where her adult lesbian friends would put her in the centre of their group. 'They'd always stick me in the middle and just sort of bustle in. And it worked.'[28] Only thirteen when she first visited a lesbian bar, another narrator recalled her discovery: 'There were so many different kinds of women in there, women I had never seen anything like before in my life, real out-and-out lesbians in men's clothing.'[29] The public culture of black lesbians revolved around house parties as well as bars, and girls and young women relied upon older friends, acquaintances and lovers to help them get in. In Buffalo, New York, Piri partied with the many women living in her building: 'I seen it as A-O.K., 'cause by me being so young. And I found out that by hanging with the older crowd I could get into places maybe I wouldn't have been able to get in by myself'.[30] Piri utilised her connections to adult black lesbians to expand her social network.

Some girls masked their interest in lesbian or mixed-clientele bars by going there with boyfriends, since many urban bars where gay men and lesbians congregated in the 1940s and 1950s also catered to heterosexual couples, often tourists, who entertained themselves by watching gay and lesbian bar-goers.[31] An oral history narrator named 'Bev', who claimed that she had 'been sexual' with other girls since junior high, asked her boyfriends to take her to gay bars. As historian Roe Thorpe explains, 'a heterosexual date was a safe way for people to experience a gay bar for the first time, and for some of these people, it was a step toward entering the bar in search of a same-sex relationship'.[32]

In San Francisco, a 1954 scandal revealed that high-school girls frequented at least one of that city's lesbian bars: 'Tommy's Place'. Ostensibly investigating parental complaints, police uncovered what newspapers called a 'sordid story' in which twelve girls, ranging in age from fourteen to eighteen, had become 'habitués' of the lesbian-owned establishment. Media reports claimed that most of the girls were from 'good families' and had recruited others from their high school. According to the lead officer, '[S]ome of the girls began wearing mannish clothing. They called themselves "Butches". Others, becoming sexual deviates, ... called themselves "Femmes"'.[33] Because of the alleged involvement of illicit drugs and because of the timing of the scandal (only weeks before the Senate Judiciary Committee investigating juvenile delinquency was set to hold hearings in San Francisco), the Tommy's Place case was quite sensational.[34] It revealed, however, that despite the risks, certain lesbian bars overlooked adolescent patrons and also that some teens experimented with the butch/femme gender identity practices that shaped lesbian bar life in the postwar years.

Erotic encounters

In addition to sensing attractions, crafting identities, finding allies, and seeking adult lesbian community, girls often acted on their desire by entering into intimate friendships and sexual relationships. Such human connection could alleviate girls' sense of alienation, even if only temporarily. Sometimes, teens entered into, and even initiated, consensual relationships with older women. Kathy Martinez, for example, carried out a two-year sexual relationship with a married friend of her mother's,[35] and Audre Lorde's first explicitly sexual relationship was with a divorced co-worker.[36] The 16-year-old runaway who shared a room with 20-year-old Jackie Jones took the lead in their brief affair. When Jones' interviewer asked whether picking up a younger girl 'scared' her, Jones emphasised the teenager's sexual agency: 'No, she led the way, are you kidding?'[37]

More common in memoirs are relationships between adolescents, many of whom skillfully camouflaged sexual relationships as normal friendly intimacy. Dr. Benjamin Morse described a woman who was pleased when her daughter ceased her 'boy-craziness' and began spending all her time with a female friend, but her daughter, Rhona, allegedly told Morse that the girls had sex 'in the privacy of my own snug little bed'.[38] In a memoir, 'Alison' remembers, 'I had my first real love affair when I was sixteen. I fell in love with another girl in class. I'd never felt so excited being around anyone before.... I didn't have any name for it. I just knew it was wonderful.' Making the most of available social opportunities, the two girls went out on dates together – with their steady boyfriends in tow – and then enjoyed overnights at one another's houses.[39] Dorothy Fairbairn remembers that she would 'kiss and make-out' with girlfriends in high school, though they would 'never talk about it'.[40] Through sexual and romantic intimacy, girls not only expressed and satisfied non-normative desires, but they also alleviated feelings of loneliness and isolation in favour of connection and excitement.

Perhaps unsurprisingly, ASHA interviews from the 1950s themselves are less sentimental than retrospective accounts by adults and convey African-American teen girls' struggles to articulate their same-sex desires to interviewers who held considerably more socioeconomic and racial power than did interviewees themselves. Nonetheless, several black youth reported past and present sexual encounters with other girls and young women. One 19-year-old who had recently immigrated with her mother from St. Thomas to New York reportedly 'seemed shocked' when her interviewer asked about same-sex experience but described a sexual relationship with a close friend that she had just ended out of fear of others' attitudes toward homosexuality. 'They don't understand', she explained.[41] A 12-year-old African-American girl reported a first 'homosexual relation' at the age of seven with a school friend and current sexual activity with both girls and boys, because she liked the people involved. She reported no sense of shame or regret, although when asked what kind of person she was, she said, 'I'm bad, I don't listen to my mother'.[42] There was less conflict in the interview of an 18-year-old black woman who claimed her interest in same-sex sexuality directly and unapologetically. She reacted to her first homosexual encounter with a 'friend of a friend' a year earlier with a sense of satisfaction. Since then, she had been sexual with women 'once or twice a month'. When asked why 'your sex relations usually take place', she selected the answer of physical attraction. Her interviewer carefully recorded her boldest claim: 'I prefer women to men.'[43] Although these girls strained against social norms in their relationships and possibly also in their interviews, they articulated their interest in same-sex sexuality and their ability to fulfill their desires for other girls and young women.

Discursive engagement

For certain girls, perhaps especially in rural areas, texts were easier to find than role models, lesbian bars or girlfriends. For better and for worse, there were hundreds of books and articles for them to find, because in the late 1940s and 1950s, psychiatric authorities scrambled to assert their expertise over homosexuality.[44] 'Liza', whose story appeared in one of the many popular works on lesbianism, allegedly read 'every word on sexual deviation that she could find' after first sensing her attraction to other girls in early high school.[45] One of the same-sex-desiring Harlem girls interviewed by the ASHA reported that she regularly read popular sexology.[46] Edith, an African-American woman who had a serious girlfriend as a teenager, remembered, 'I bought every book that they ever printed about gays trying to sort out my feelings.'[47] Similarly, Toni, an oral history narrator from Buffalo, New York, struggled to 'put a concept or a word' to her early awareness of sexual difference. 'When I looked up that word at about ten or eleven, I was looking for some confirmation of my identity, and all I found was something that was very derogatory.... I knew I was what they were talking about.'[48] Once girls found useful texts, they shared them with selected others, creating shared reading practices that helped to build micro-communities.[49] At school, kids passed around books about male homosexuality that helped one girl identify her own same-sex desire.[50] Another narrator was shocked to find a group of ostensibly heterosexual acquaintances discussing lesbian sexual practices as described in Frank Caprio's widely-distributed *Female Homosexuality*.[51] Like a funhouse mirror, psychiatric discourse reflected a partial and warped image of the self – as a girl and a lesbian – that could be appalling and legitimating at the same time.

Young female readers picked up on something in the vast postwar literature on homosexuality that many historians have since overlooked: experts' persistent association of female homosexuality with childish immaturity.[52] During and after World War II, psychiatrists reoriented their focus from illness to 'mental health', turning psychiatry into a 'growth industry' according to historian Ellen Herman.[53] As part of this process, psychiatric and psychological authorities reshaped the cultural meaning of adulthood. While the definition of adulthood varies across time, region, culture and subculture, its common denominators in the mid-twentieth-century West were (heterosexual) marriage, parenthood, and economic self-sufficiency, especially for men. In that context, experts insisted that true maturity required psychological health and 'adjustment' and, furthermore, that homosexuality represented a failure of psychological maturation. In addition to being heterosexual, ideal American adulthood was also implicitly white; advocates of desegregation argued in *Brown v. Board,* for example, that only through quality education would infantilised black people be able to achieve psychological equality with white adults.[54] When psychiatric experts depicted homosexual men and women as neurotic, immature and emotionally disturbed, they guarded the status of American adulthood from incursions by social outsiders.[55]

Though the association of lesbianism with immaturity took on a life of its own in postwar America, it originated with Freud himself. Analysing Freud's seminal essays on female homosexuality, feminist psychoanalytic scholar Adria Schwartz explains that '[t]rue femininity, a feminine sexuality that is embedded within a heterosexual matrix, became a developmental achievement. Failures along this path left a girl at risk for masculine/(homo) sexuality'.[56] During the postwar years, Freudian ideas about female homosexuality leapt from the pages of rarefied medical journals and into mainstream consciousness.

A selection of evidence conveys the construction of lesbian immaturity. In *Female Homosexuality,* Frank Caprio explained, 'Psychoanalysts are in agreement that all women who prefer a homosexual way of life ... betray their emotional immaturity in their attitude towards men, sex and marriage.'[57] Elsewhere, Caprio referred to lesbians' 'arrested development of the libido'.[58] Other popular psychiatrists described lesbianism as indicating an 'extreme pathological immaturity' and 'artificial childishness'.[59] A 'veteran analyst' from the *Washington Post* answered a letter from a lesbian reader with the claim that the lesbian 'is handicapped by failure to mature, emotionally'.[60] In an especially blunt statement, author Henry Galus wrote, 'All females go through a psychosexual evolution whose final goal ... is a willing acceptance of a heterosexual kinship with a male. NO other female concept of sex may be called mature.'[61] According to these texts, young women who chose not to build their lives on the cornerstones of postwar social life – marriage and motherhood – were stunted in their psychosexual development, frozen in a kind of permanent adolescence.

This message was not lost on young women who confronted the notion of lesbian immaturity as they searched for information about their own same-sex desire. Autobiographical accounts of women's encounters with this construction highlight the tension between discursive representations of the immature lesbian and the lived experience of youth – and of adults reflecting back upon and thereby recasting their own adolescent perspectives. As George Chauncey has explored in analysing gay men's lives in the early twentieth century, queer readers did not uncritically internalise pathologising discourses about homosexuality.[62] In an oral history interview, for example, a British woman named Diana Chapman reflects on the interplay between her sense of sexual subjectivity and expert discourses: 'Every psychological book said how immature it was to be homosexual. If there was one thing I didn't want to be it was immature.' Chapman initially absorbed the stigma of immaturity, leading her to 'try and become normal' by dating and being sexual with men, but she ultimately denied the power of this stigma when she returned to lesbian relationships.[63] Similarly, an American named Jacqueline Byer initially succumbed to family pressure to see a psychiatrist but quickly decided 'to hell with this ... My life is my life,' and stopped treatment. [64] With the benefit of hindsight, these women contested not only the association of female homosexuality with immaturity but also the very authority of so-called experts to define women's psychological and sexual status.

In addition to popular scientific texts, fictional works also became important sources of connection, identification (and disidentification) and imagined community for same-sex-desiring youth. *The Well of Loneliness* was (and long remained) a staple for girls and women seeking a literary mirror of their own desires in the mid-twentieth century. Published in Britain in 1928 and in the US in 1929, Radclyffe Hall's novel, in the words of literary critic Rebecca O'Rourke, 'render[ed] lesbianism visible' to girls and women on both sides of the Atlantic for decades thereafter. [65] A 1986 survey of lesbian readers revealed how influential the book was for its many readers. One woman who read the book in 1946 claimed that 'it suggested to me that somewhere I might find a community, if only a small and beleaguered one–someday.'[66]

Lesbian paperbacks were accessible and visible in postwar consumer culture and became a resource for young women. Lesbian mystery writer Katherine Forrest recalls her first encounter with Ann Bannon's *Odd Girl Out* when she was 18 years old, in 1957:

> I did not need to look at the title for clues; the cover leaped out at me from the drugstore rack.... Overwhelming need led me to walk a gauntlet of fear up to the cash register. Fear so intense that I remember nothing more, only that I stumbled out of the store in possession of what I knew I must have, a book as necessary to me as air.... It opened the door to my soul and told me who I was.[67]

Although most lesbian paperbacks were written and published by men for male readers, a small number were written by (secretly) lesbian authors and portrayed lesbian characters with more nuance. Available in drugstores, grocery stores and even some gas stations, lesbian paperbacks attracted the notice of teen girls, like Forrest, and offered labels, stories, characters and imagery with which readers could craft a sense of self-recognition. As Yvonne Keller points out, outside of psychology and the occasional scandal magazine, this genre offered the only medium through which women and girls could access images or representations of gay women.[68] The books were constrained by publishers' repressive requirements, but reader response theory and studies of girls' contemporary reading practices suggest that readers of such texts may, nonetheless, have used 'active reading strategies' to resist the 'ideological effect' of the novels' negative depictions and tragic conclusions.[69] In fact, *Odd Girl Out* was the first lesbian paperback to adopt a hopeful ending.

In most fiction and nonfiction alike, the stigma of lesbian immaturity gave rise to the related claim that lesbians could never sustain healthy intimate partnerships. Caprio, for example, regarded lesbians as doomed to unhappiness because their sexual relationships were necessarily unstable and ephemeral. [70] Despite this construction, some queer girls and women claimed that they sought what all women in the 1950s were supposed to want: romantic love and domestic life. One memoirist, for example, recalled her youthful desire for a butch lesbian with whom she could make a home, settle down, and even adopt a child. [71] 'Paula', a fictional character in *First Person, Third Sex*, which was published in 1959, is unusually optimistic about lesbian partnerships: at the novel's close, she says, 'All I was sure of was that someday, somewhere, I would find the woman who would love me as I loved her.' While this ending affirmed the hegemony of marriage and monogamy, it broke with publishing and psychiatric norms that denigrated all lesbians as unstable, immature, and ultimately alone.[72] Finally, the 18-year-old ASHA interviewee who boldly stated her sexual preference for women over men also described herself in strikingly positive terms, telling her interviewer, '[I] try to be independent,' that she wanted 'a steady job, to work at something interesting and worthwhile' and planned to go to business school after graduating from high school, and most significantly, and that what she 'wanted out of life' was a home, a good job, and 'someone to love'. [73] Although limited by the interview format, this 18-year-old young woman portrayed her sexuality as a quality of her self rather than as a phase, or sickness, or a sin. She also envisioned a future that included a stable home, employment and a (presumably female) life partner. She thus dismissed the white, middle-class experts' portrayal of female homosexuality as immature and of lesbian relationships as ephemeral. She also rejected long-standing white supremacist associations between black female sexuality and immorality, excess and pathology. In so doing, this teenager staked a critically important claim to queer female adolescence: a subject position that did not exist in public discourse of the time.

This historical archive shows, then, that although alienation and homophobia caused incalculable suffering in the postwar years, some female youth resourcefully created a sense of lesbian subjectivity and possibility by pursuing opportunities for self-expression and for social, sexual and discursive connection. For a lucky few, young queer womanhood in the postwar years even had its moments of exhilaration, such as when Reba Hudson first encountered members of the Daughters of Bilitis, the pioneering, mostly middle-class lesbian homophile organisation; she recalls thinking that although the women were attractive, 'none of them had an ounce of respect or a smile on their face.' Satisfied with her proud, working-class bar-based community, she wondered, 'What did we need an organization like that for? We had the world by the tail.'[74] Despite living in what Weeks describes as the 'heterosexual dictatorship' of the 1950s, Hudson and other same-sex desiring girls and young women attempted 'to live as if their sexual difference did not, in the end, matter'.[75] Queer life existed and persisted in this repressive decade, illustrating that postwar society was rife with tensions, contradictions and possibilities amidst which girls and young women could explore their sexuality and forge a sense of identity.

Notes

1. Elizabeth Lapovsky Kennedy and Madeline D. Davis, *Boots of Leather, Slippers of Gold: The History of a Lesbian Community* (New York: Penguin Books, 1993); Roe Thorpe, 'The Changing Face of Lesbian Bars in Detroit, 1938–1965', in Brett Beemyn, ed., *Creating a Place for Ourselves* (New York: Routledge, 1997); Marcia M. Gallo, *Different Daughters: A History of the Daughters of Bilitis and the Rise of the Lesbian Rights Movement* (Jackson: Seal Press, 2007). Studies of desire between young women in nineteenth-century Britain and the U.S. – in boarding schools, for example, or between intimate friends – rarely consider youth or age as analytic categories and usually regard girls as nascent women rather than as a distinct social group. In part, this is because the very notion of an age-based peer culture did not emerge in the West until the early twentieth century. On nineteenth-century intimacy, see Lillian Faderman, *Surpassing the Love of Men* (New York: Harper, 1998) and Martha Vicinus, *Intimate Friends: Women Who Loved Women, 1778–1928* (Chicago: University of Chicago Press, 2004). On the rise of adolescence and peer culture, see Paula Fass, *The Damned and the Beautiful* (Oxford: Oxford University Press, 1979).
2. Marcy Adelman, ed., *Lesbian Passages: True Stories Told by Women over 40* (Los Angeles: Alyson Publications, 1986), 14.
3. Kathy Martinez, interview by JoAnn Castillo, 25 September 1981, transcript, Oral History Project #81–004, GLBT Historical Society (hereafter GLBTHS), San Francisco, CA.
4. Bernice Miller, interview by Marie Dulcini, n.d., transcript, Oral History Project #95–44, GLBTHS.
5. John D'Emilio, *Sexual Politics, Sexual Communities* (Chicago: University of Chicago Press, 1998); Esther Newton, *Cherry Grove Fire Island* (Boston: Beacon Press, 1995); Kennedy and Davis, *Boots of Leather*; Thorpe, 'The Changing Face.'
6. Regina Kunzel, 'Pulp Fictions and Problem Girls: Reading and Rewriting Single Pregnancy in the Postwar United States', *American Historical Review*, 100 (1995), 1470.
7. On the growing influence of popular social science about homosexuality, see Donald Webster Cory, *The Lesbian in America* (New York: Citadel Press, 1964), 131, and Jeffrey Escoffier, 'Popular Sociology, Reading, and Coming Out', in Kathy Peiss, ed., *Major Problems in the History of American Sexuality* (Boston: Houghton Mifflin, 2002), 397.

8. Martinez interview.
9. Audre Lorde, *Zami: A New Spelling of My Name* (Freedom: Crossing Press, 1982).
10. Joan Nestle, *A Restricted Country* (Ithaca: Firebrand Press, 1987), 23.
11. Dorothy Fairbairn, interview by Elise Chenier, 25 April 2011, transcript, 1, Archive of Lesbian Oral Testimony, Simon Frasier University.
12. Ina Mae Murri, interview by Lee Jenkins, 22 August 1993, transcript, 4, Oral History Project #95–011, GLBTHS.
13. Edith and Sarah, 'We Have Each Other', in Adelman, ed., *Lesbian Passages* (Los Angeles: Alyson Publications, 1986), 72–73.
14. Elizabeth Lapovsky Kennedy and Madeline D. Davis, 'I Could Hardly Wait to Get Back to That Bar', in Beemyn, ed., *Creating a Place for Ourselves* (New York: Routledge, 1997), 31.
15. Martinez interview; Reba Hudson, interview by Jim Breeden, 23 August 1995, transcript, Oral History Project #95–112, GLBTHS.
16. Kennedy and Davis, *Boots of Leather*; Thorpe, 'The Changing Face.'
17. American Social Health Association, *Teen-agers and Venereal Disease: A Sociological Study of 600 Teen-agers in New York City Social Hygiene Clinics*, Celia S. Deschin, ed. (U.S. Department of Health, Education, and Welfare, 1961) in Records of the American Social Health Association (SW045), Social Welfare History Archives, University of Minnesota (hereafter ASHA Study).
18. Hudson interview, 31. On lesbianism in women's sports, see Susan Cahn, *Coming on Strong: Gender and Sexuality in Twentieth-Century Women's Sports* Boston, MA., (Harvard University Press, 1998).
19. Thompson interview, 9–11.
20. Roberta Bobba, interview by JoAnn Castillo, 22 October 1981, transcript, 9, Oral History Project #81–001, GLBTHS.
21. Koreen Phelps, interview by Scott Paulsen, 5 November 1993, transcript, 1–2, Oral History #42.3, Minnesota Historical Society, Minneapolis, MN.
22. Alfred Kinsey et al., *Sexual Behavior in the Human Female* (Philadelphia: W.E.B. Saunders, 1953), 479. For a discussion of Kinsey's findings on lesbianism, see Donald Webster Cory, 'Lesbianism', in Ellis, ed., *Sex Life of the American Woman and the Kinsey Report* (Greenberg, 1954).
23. Hudson interview. For a useful new discussion of parental responses to their children's queer disclosures, see Heather Murray, *Not in This Family: Gays and the Meaning of Kinship in Postwar North America* (Philadelphia: University of Pennsylvania Press, 2010), especially chapter 1; see p. 16 for specific examples of maternal sympathy in the 1950s and early 1960s.
24. Jackie Jones, interview by Emily Miller, 12 October 1994, transcript, 14–15, OHP #95–67, GLBTHS.
25. Catherine Odette, 'New York, 1959', in J. Penelope and S. Valentine, eds, *Finding the Lesbians* (Freedom: The Crossing Press, 1990), 239–249.
26. Martinez interview, 7.
27. Kennedy and Davis, *Boots of Leather*, 79. For another account of juvenile girls using fake IDs, see Nan Boyd, *Wide Open Town: A History of Queer San Francisco to 1965* (Berkeley: University of California Press, 2003), 66.
28. Bobba interview, 9.
29. Kennedy and Davis, *Boots of Leather*, 105.
30. Kennedy and Davis, *Boots of Leather*, 124.
31. Boyd, *Wide Open Town*.

32. Thorpe, 'The Changing Face', 167.
33. 'Bar facing ban in dope, sex ring for minor girls', *San Francisco Examiner* (10 September 1954), 1.
34. 'Sex Deviate Ring Here', *San Francisco Examiner* (24 September 1954), 1. Local police leaders later contended that the Tommy's Place incident was isolated and had been blown out of proportion. 'Sex Deviate Problem in S.F. Detailed', *San Francisco Examiner* (29 September 1954), 11; US Congress, Committee on the Judiciary, *Hearings before the Subcommittee to Investigate Juvenile Delinquency* (24 and 27 September and 4–5 October, 1954), 261. For a more thorough discussion of the Tommy's Place situation, see Boyd, *Wide Open Town,* 94–95.
35. Martinez interview.
36. Lorde, *Zami*, 136–140.
37. Jones interview, 51.
38. Benjamin Morse, *Adolescent Sexual Behavior* (New York: Monarch Books, 1964), 131.
39. Alison, 'It's Not Any Worse Than Alcoholism', in Adelman, ed., *Lesbian Passages*, 58–59.
40. Fairbairn interview, 1.
41. ASHA Study Interview #331.
42. ASHA Study Interview #43.
43. ASHA Study Interview #82.
44. Ellen Herman, *The Romance of American Psychology: Political Culture in the Age of Experts* (Berkeley: University of California Press, 1995), 83, 241.
45. Cory, *The Lesbian in America,* 60–61.
46. ASHA Study Interview #82.
47. Edith and Sarah, 'We Have Each Other', 75.
48. Kennedy and Davis, *Boots of Leather,* 355.
49. Suzanne Neild and Rosalind Pearson, eds, *Women Like Us* (London: The Women's Press, 1992), 97.
50. 'A Diet of Green Salads: An Interview with Whitey', Bennett L. Singer, ed., *Growing Up Gay, Growing Up Lesbian: A Literary Anthology* (New York: New Press, 1994), 45.
51. Marilyn, interview by JoAnn Castillo, 22 October 1981, transcript, Oral History Project #81–000, GLBTHS.
52. An exception is Kate Adams, 'Making the world safe for the missionary position: images of the lesbian in post-World War II America', in Karla Jay and Joanne Glasgow, eds, *Lesbian Texts and Contexts: Radical Revisions* (New York: NYU Press, 1990).
53. Ellen Herman, *The Romance of American Psychology: Political Culture in the Age of Experts* (Berkeley: University of California Press, 1995), 83, 241.
54. Paula Fass, personal communication; Herman, *Romance*, chapter 7.
55. Miriam G. Reumann, *American Sexual Character: Sex, Gender, and National Identity in the Kinsey Reports* (Berkeley: University of California Press, 2005), 168, 173–174. For a discussion of psychological understandings of maturity in the early 20th century, see Don Romesburg, 'Arrested Development: Homosexuality, Gender, and American Adolescence, 1890–1930', PhD Dissertation, (Berkeley: University of California, 2006).
56. Adria E. Schwartz, *Sexual Subjects: Lesbians, Gender, and Psychoanalysis* (New York: Routledge, 1998), 18.

57. Frank Caprio, *Female Homosexuality: A Psychodynamic Study of Lesbianism* (New York: Citadel Press, 1954), 170.
58. Frank Caprio, *Variations in Sexual Behavior* (New York: Grove Press, 1955), 164.
59. Edward A. Strecker and Vincent T. Lathbury, *Their Mothers' Daughters* (Philadelphia: J.B. Lippincott, 1956), quoted in Jennifer Terry, *An American Obsession: Science, Medicine and Homosexuality in Modern Society* (Chicago: University of Chicago Press, 1999), 319; Benjamin Morse, *The Lesbian* (Derby: Monarch Books, 1961), 20.
60. 'Trying to Build After Tragedy', *Washington Post* (24 September 1952).
61. Henry S. Galus, *Unwed Mothers: A Penetrating Study of the Alarming Rise of Illegitimacy in America* (Derby: Monarch Books, 1962), 93. The exception here was John McPartland, *Sex in Our Changing World* (New York: Rinehart and Co, 1947), 152.
62. George Chauncey, *Gay New York*: *Gender, Urban Culture, and the Making of the Gay Male World, 1890–1940* (New York: Basic Books, 1994), 4–5.
63. Neild and Pearson, *Women Like Us*, 98.
64. Jacqueline Byer, interviewed by Alan Berube, December 1984, transcript, 19–20, OHP# 84-001, GLBTHS.
65. Rebecca O'Rourke, *Reflecting on The Well of Loneliness* (London: Routledge, 1989), 114, cited in Martin Meeker, *Contacts Desired: Gay and Lesbian Communications and Community, 1940s–1970s* (Chicago: University of Chicago Press, 2006), 26. On the ubiquity of *The Well*, see also Kennedy and Davis, 'I Could Hardly Wait', 32.
66. O'Rourke, *Reflecting*, 119, as quoted in Meeker, *Contacts Desired*, 27.
67. Katherine V. Forrest, ed., *Lesbian Pulp Fiction: The Sexually Intrepid World of Lesbian Paperback Novels 1950–1965* (Berkeley: Cleis Press, 2005), ix.
68. Yvonne Keller, 'Pulp Politics: Strategies of Vision in Pro-Lesbian Pulp Novels, 1955–1965', in Patricia Juliana Smith, ed., *The Queer Sixties* (New York: Routledge, 1999), 2. On readers' 'disidentification' with derisively portrayed lesbian characters, see Jose Munoz, *Disidentifications: Queers of Color and the Performance of Politics* (Minneapolis: University of Minneapolis Press, 1999), introduction.
69. Angela E. Hubler, 'Can Anne Shirley Help "Revive Ophelia"? Listening to Girl Readers', in Sherrie A. Inness, ed., *Delinquents and Debutantes: Twentieth-Century American Girls' Cultures* (New York: New York University Press, 1998), 269.
70. Caprio, *Female Homosexuality*, xvi.
71. Ruth Allison, *Lesbianism: Its Secrets and Practices* (Los Angeles: Medco Books, 1967), 48.
72. Sloane Britain, *First Person, Third Sex* (Chicago: Newsstand Library Books, 1959), 182, 191.
73. ASHA Study Interview #82.
74. Hudson interview.
75. Weeks, *World We Have Won*, 9.

5
Cross-Generational Relationships before 'the Lesbian': Female Same-Sex Sexuality in 1950s Rural Finland

Antu Sorainen

Finland's role on the edge of Europe was a complicated one in the 1950s. World War Two had split the Scandinavian community, and the Nordic countries had ended up on different sides during the war. Finland not only was attacked by the Soviet Union in 1939, but it also attacked the Soviet Union itself and fought with and against Germany from 1941 to 1944, whereas Sweden had remained neutral; Denmark and Norway had been occupied by the Nazis; and Iceland, the Faroes and Greenland had been controlled by American and British troops. The two lost wars against the Soviet Union meant that Finland had to comply with harsh armistice demands and had lost ten per cent of its territory. Twelve per cent of the entire population were displaced and resettled within the new borders in 1944 and 1945. The bloody civil war in 1918 left a deep mark on the national psyche, and the urbanisation process only took place from the late 1950s onwards. Finland also differs sharply from other Nordic countries in regard to its language, culture and history. The distinctiveness of Finland's national history shaped the development of sexuality debates in the country, which, unlike other European contexts, are distinguished by the fact the language of sexology had not yet entered the Finnish public sphere in the 1950s.

This chapter aims to develop understanding of the complicated ways in which female sexuality came to be part of a wider public discourse in 1950s Finland, focusing in particular on the question of how women's queer desires were recognised in a penal code that was not influenced by sexology. It explores some of the issues at stake in these debates by focusing on two specific court cases that concerned a group of women who lived and worked in the Herb Grove orphanage in rural Eastern Finland in the 1950s. The orphanage was also known as 'Sisterhome', reflecting the fact that it had been founded by a religious sect by and for women. This sect was led by a charismatic headmistress named Helka. Her female followers were called 'sisters in faith'. In the early 1950s, allegations of sexual relationships between female employees of the Herb Grove orphanage as well as with some of their foster girls emerged, leading to a series of trials, between 1951 and 1954, that proceeded from the Lower Court through the Court of Appeal and to the Supreme Court.[1] The result of these trials was that eight female employees of the orphanage were convicted of same-sex fornication with each other, and some were also sentenced for same-sex fornication with under-age girls.

The Herb Grove court case gained national and front-page media coverage and was preceded by another separate trial of one of the 'sisters in faith', a woman named Eeva, who in 1950 was imprisoned for long-term sexual relations with a number of women as well as with a 17-year-old girl.[2] The similarity between the two trials is evident. Both took place in small villages in the eastern part of Finland, were geographically and otherwise closely interconnected and concerned female members of the same religious sect. Furthermore, both court cases enforced the Finnish penal code on 'haureuden harjoittaminen toisen samaa suku-puolta olevan kanssa' [fornication with a person of the same sex] and 'haureuden harjoittaminen 15 mutta ei 17 täyttäneen henkilön kanssa' [fornication with a person between 15 and 17 years'].[3] Together, these two trials reveal a fascinating glimpse into the world of women's queer desires for each other and sexual relations with each other in a rural and religious context, in a country that recognised women's non-normative sexual acts in its penal code but that had not yet developed a popular language and discourse of female same-sex sexuality. These trials allow us to trace how the modern category of the 'homosexual' was taking shape in Finland by the 1950s. During that decade, profound shifts took place in medical, psychiatric and criminological discourses. In what follows, I will explore the meanings attached to the legal concept of 'same-sex fornication' in this distinct rural and religious context, and how these meanings intersect with the women's own understanding of sexuality and subjectivity. I argue that the Herb Grove case shows that we still need to explore further women's religious communities as social spaces which (not 'that have often') offered and created an opportunity for practising and negotiating women's same-sex desires that at a time when they were not politically recognised, openly visible or publicly categorised.[4]

Herb Grove and its role in rural society

The Herb Grove orphanage was located in a small, isolated village in the wilderness of rural Eastern Finland and was very much part of that local community. It provided employment, education, accommodation, dental care and general nurturing for almost one hundred people, including both adults and children.[5] These included war veterans, orphans, the mentally ill, elderly people, widows and divorced mothers and their children. The orphanage relieved a substantial burden of the social duties of the village, which, like many rural communities, was economically fragile following the devastation of the war. Therefore, it was in the interest of the local community and the county authorities to prevent allegations about sexual misconduct from going to court after they were reported to the police. Indeed, an interviewed member with a member of the village's 1952 social board said that the 'village was not willing to take the responsibility of the Herb Grove orphans even after the trials, not until the Ministry of Social Affairs gave instructions to do so'.[6]

The religious sect that founded Herb Grove was formed in 1940, calling itself the 'apostolinen seurakunta' [Apostolical Congregation].[7] In 1941, it established its first two orphanages, also located in the Finnish countryside. The sect gained a reputation as a social space where women's queer desires might be explored soon after its founding when, according to court documents, their landlady, a certain Salme, discovered the headmistress having sexual relations with a 15-year-old orphan girl. While it is difficult to ascertain what actually happened between the landlady and the 'sisters' (according to the headmistress, the landlady was simply envious and jealous), the episode had two tangible effects: the sisters were thrown out of their first home;[8] and gossip spread in religious circles around the country spread the sect's female same-sex practices.[9]

From 1889 to 1971, the Finnish penal code decreed that 'fornication with a person of the same sex', including both sexes, was punishable by imprisonment for a maximum period of two years for both parties. This law was rather particular in that in most European countries only fornication between men was criminalised under sodomy legislation, whereas fornication between women was usually not decreed to be punishable.[10] In Finland, women's same-sex sexual practices were criminalised without further societal or legal debate on the issue. Indeed, the wording of the clause criminalising homosexual acts in the Finnish penal code was gender-neutral:

> Jos joku harjoittaa haureutta toisen samaa sukupuolta olevan kanssa; rangaistakoon kumpikin vankeudella korkeintaan kahdeksi vuodeksi [If someone fornicates with a person of the same sex, may both parties be punished with imprisonment, for a maximum of two years].[11]

In those cases involving an underage party, priority was given to the law on 'fornication with a person between 15 and 17 years', even when it was a question of a homosexual act.[12]

The Apostolical Congregation of Herb Grove was officially part of the dominant Christian Lutheran Church, but it had its own particular features, which reflected outside influences. For example, the headmistress and the other leaders of the sect visited the Maria Sisters in Switzerland and in Germany and maintained a particularly close contact with one Maria community in Darmstadt, Germany. From those contacts, the Herb Grove leaders had adopted a special style of that was eventually also adopted by the 'sisters' of Herb Grove. The headmistress referred to herself as the 'vihkimätön naispappi' [non-inaugurated High Priestess] of the congregation.[13] The 'sisters' also wrote more than 400 religious songs, which were published as a book and then used in the religious rituals of the sect.

The doctrines of the sect differed in other ways from the dominant, rather stern and bleak Finnish Lutheran Church rituals. For instance, the Herb Grove members emphasised dancing and bodily rejoicing for the Lord's praise [karkelo eli iloitseminen ja kiittäminen koko olemuksella].[14] The everyday encounters in the orphanage also differed from the conventions of Finnish culture: at Herb Grove, physical touching was common and recommended, which was in contrast to the conventional rural way of life, where touching was very rare, even between family members. Yet, life in the Sisterhome was full of embraces and kisses between members of the community, on both their cheeks and on their mouths, whereas in Finnish culture generally, friends did not kiss at all but shook hands instead. It was also common for women and girls to sleep together in the same bed – this was a general norm in rural life, where large families lived in small village houses. The headmistress told the police that the encouraging of all kind of physical touching at the Sisterhome was a compensation for her own deprived childhood which had been full of abuse. She further explained the physical encounters between the 'sisters' through a rather queer interpretation of Paul's letters in the Bible, saying that the genital embraces were not meant to satisfy sexual drive but to 'recreate Spiritual Love' [henkisen rakkauden virkistys].[15]

One of the distinctive rituals of this sect consisted of an oil anointment. This ritual was meant to spiritually strengthen the 'Brides of Christ'. In the course of it genitals, breasts and other body parts were oiled in order to see whether religious devotion had made a 'sister' resistant to secular or 'abnormal' lusts. Oiling often involved penetration with fingers as well as the kissing of breast and genitals. If the person was sexually aroused during oiling, the ritual could be repeated later. The main objective was that there be no sexual reaction to the penetration, as proof that the body of the 'sister' had died in terms of secular lusts. Penetration with fingers that could last for several minutes was also thought to help those 'sisters' who were tempted by the 'sin' of masturbation. The woman who was acting as the oil-provider was seen as the mediator between Jesus Christ and the object of oiling. Moreover, not only the headmistress but also the other inaugurated sisters were allowed to perform as 'holy priests' [pyhä pappeus].[16] The headmistress had, for example, penetrated a 15-year-old girl to check whether her hymen was intact after a childhood rape, and another young woman who had been engaged to marry a man, to teach her what she should request from her fiancé regarding sexual matters.[17]

Documentary evidence suggests that heavily charged bodily activity had taken place between a number of sisters of faith, as well as between some under-age girls and adult 'sisters'. The first step leading to legal action was an incident of whistleblowing that occurred in April 1951. One of the members of Herb Grove, Eeva, alerted the authorities that 'indecent sexual acts' took place in the orphanage.

Eeva's trials

Eeva was a 31-year-old unemployed mother of four and a 'sister in faith'. In early February 1951, she herself had been reported to the police for committing perjury. One of the female witnesses in the perjury interrogation told the police that she had known Eeva from childhood and had noticed that she was 'an abnormal person' [epänormaali ihminen].[18] A dean of the local parish told the police that 'there was something dishonest in Eeva's character and that sometimes, when Eeva was giving religious speeches in the parish gatherings, some women were attracted to her'[19] [luonteessa oli jotakin vilpillistä ja että tämän pitäessä joskus hartauskokouksissa puheita, jotkut naishenkilöt olivat hurmaantuneet Eevaan]. During these interrogations for false perjury, it was revealed that Eeva had 'continually fornicated with persons of the same sex' [jatkuva haureuden harjoittaminen samaa sukupuolta olevien kanssa]. The provincial police inspector then ordered that these crimes be investigated.[20]

A week before this new series of new police interrogations, on 20 February, Eeva had moved with her children to live in Herb Grove, but she was promptly arrested two days later. At a police hearing on 26 February, Eeva revealed that the religious rituals practiced in Herb Grove were also 'weird' [kummallista toimintaa]. She mentioned several names and addresses and revealed how she had practiced same-sex fornication in Herb Grove with one of the 'sisters' on 20 February.[21] Eeva was taken into custody on 28 February and given a medical examination. The Provincial Chief Physician concluded that it was obvious that Eeva's 'sexual drive' [sukupuolivietti] was intense and passionate and that it was directed much more towards the female sex than to the male sex. According to the doctor, Eeva was 'not very inventive or rapid intellectually, but she may be such a soft character that she might admit even such acts that she never has committed' [mitään erityistä keksimiskykyä ja ajatuksen kiihkeää rientoa en ole hänessä havainnut, mutta saattaa olla että hän on siksi taipuvainen luonteeltaan, että saattaa myönnellä sellaisiakin asioita, joita hän ei ole tehnyt].[22]

One of Eeva's alleged liaisons had been with a 17-year-old girl, who, when interviewed by the police, described intimate details of their encounters. She said that Eeva had explained 'her methods as a true love between the "spiritual mother" and a child and had said that it was not a sin' [menettelynsä hengellisen äidin" ja lapsen väliseksi todelliseksi rakkaudeksi ja ettei se ollut syntiä]. The girl still regarded Eeva as her 'sister in faith'.[23] The girl was taken for a medical examination where the district doctor examined her genitals and explained to the police that she had 'observed obvious marks of violence in there' [todenneensa niissä ilmeisiä väkivallan merkkejä].[24]

Eeva herself vividly described long-term intimate relations with eight 'sisters in faith' between 1943 and 1951. With one of these women, she had formed what she called 'a deep love relationship' [syvällinen rakkaussuhde].[25] Eeva further recounted that she had started to give speeches in religious gatherings since she was 17-years-old, and on those occasions, she had noted that some women 'fancied her in some queer way' [kiintyivät jollakin kummallisella tavalla].[26] However, she married at age 17, but noticed then that she had an extremely intense sexual drive, which her husband was not able to satisfy. She had not, though, been aware that 'women together can satisfy their sexual lust' [naiset saattoivat keskenään tyydyttää sukupuoliset halunsa]. Later, in her twenties, she met a resettled woman from the territory that Finland had lost to the Soviets in the war, Carelia. This woman had taught her how to make love with women, and after that, she had become aware that she could get sexual satisfaction with women as well as with men.[27]

Eeva was very talkative in her interrogation, and many of Eeva's lovers, even those who were older than her, told the police that Eeva had called herself 'a spiritual mother' and explained that love-making between such a 'mother' and a 'child' was not a sin. All of the interrogated women described the alleged sexual acts in a similar way, using the same terminology – 'sexual drive' [sukupuolinen vietti], 'touching or kissing of genitals' [kosketella ja suudella sukupuolielimiä], 'fondling of breasts' [hyväillä rintoja], 'satisfaction of lust' [sukupuolinen tyydytys], 'passionate embraces' [intohimoiset hyväilyt].[28] This may be more of a signal about the form of questions asked by the police than about the meanings that the accused women themselves actually gave to their alleged sexual acts and relationships. It is noteworthy that it was the same chief constable who conducted almost all of the interrogations with the suspected 'sisters'.

On 3 April, 1951, Eeva was charged with committing false perjury and eight counts of continued fornication with persons of the same sex in the Lower Court and sentenced to four years hard labour and had to forfeit her civil rights for five years. The case seemed to provide conclusive evidence that Eeva had had long-term sexual relations with several women around the country between 1943 and 1951. Two of her female lovers were also sentenced for the same crime to six months suspended for a three-year probation period. Three of the other accused women were released for various reasons.[29]

Considering the wording of the law – 'both parties may be punished', no matter who might have been the active and who the passive partner – it remains unclear why the 17-year-old girl was not accused at all. The girl had requested a discharge based on her 'young age, inexperience and lack of understanding' but legally, these were not valid reasons for discharge. She asked for Eeva to be blamed, telling the police that 'if the Doctor could clarify that she had been "corrupted" in Eeva's hands, her father would then be free to consider charging Eeva on her behalf'. Her father did indeed demand that Eeva be tried, because a 17-year-old girl was legally responsible; it was not appropriate for her father to intervene in the legal proceedings.

The Herb Grove case: police proceedings, interrogations, sentencing

In spite of the doctor's questioning of Eeva's reliability as a witness, the police officer who had interrogated her reported her revelations to the chief inspector. Because Herb Grove was doing valuable social work, and 'so as to avoid undue publicity' [julkisuutta karttaen hiljaisudessa], an unofficial gathering was organised on 23 February.[30] Those present were the chief inspector, the police officer, the headmistress and two other sect leaders. The headmistress failed to acknowledge this diplomatic gesture from the police because she firmly believed that a competing religious Pentecostal sect was spreading false gossip about her having penetrated a 15-year-old girl. A perhaps deliberately misguided eyewitness, the above-mentioned landlady Salme, had then spread gossip about the headmistress being a 'lady-lover' [naisrakastaja].[31] In the police narrative of Herb Grove, it seems to have been worse that the Head Mistress had touched another woman than the fact that this woman was an under-age girl.

The police officer subsequently sent a letter to the County Government on 5 March 1951, in which he wrote that it was to be suspected that in the Sisterhome – where, to his knowledge, 50 women currently lived, most of them young, almost 10 young men, and about 30 children, and where there was an elementary school and a sister school which officially functioned on religious grounds – the education, nurturing, and personal relationships 'offend[ed] decent manners and prevailing sexual morals' [hyviä tapoja ja sukupuolikuria loukkaavia].[32]

The provincial county police inspector ordered a criminal examination to be set up on 20 April 1951. The interrogations of various 'sisters' and other witnesses started on 7 May and lasted until 5 June. As a consequence, the headmistress was held in custody for seven days. Finally, the police invited the leaders of the Herb Grove association to a gathering on 8 June. In August, additional interrogations were conducted. Some of the sisters then returned to the police and wanted to change their stories, probably after they had received legal advice. During the first interrogation, many of them had talked quite freely about the life and rituals at Herb Grove. The oiling ritual was taken up and interpreted as a crime of fornication in the legal proceedings.

Once the police interrogation began, the police officers translated the religious meaning behind the oiling ritual into the language of the criminal law. Legally speaking, 'fornication' [haureus] comprised of acts that were taken up for the 'purpose of satisfying or arousing one's sexual drive' [sukupuolivietin tyydyttämisen tai kiihdyttämisen tarkoituksessa].[33] If anyone had been aroused during the oil-anointment ritual, and if there had been touching of genitals, that constituted a proof of fornication. Apparently, the police officers were not aware that for lawmakers in the 1950s, the criminal act of same-sex fornication also entailed a person being made to expose her genitalia and, by doing so, to get her 'induced to be an object of indecent observation' [epäsiveellisen tarkastelun alaiseksi].[34] The penetration by fingers was legally not even necessary for the crime of fornication to have been committed, whatever the religious rationale behind it was.

Moreover, in a legal sense, the activity or passivity during the act was irrelevant, if the deed was consensual.[35] Nevertheless, in the police interrogations the most crucial question to the 'sisters' was to ask which one of the accused woman had been on top and which one underneath during the sexual act. By attempting to determine this information, the police officers attempted to define who the seducer was and thus who was the active party. They also, as a rule, inquired as to whether the women's 'liquid had run' [sukupuolinesteen vuotaminen].[36] The police officers – who were, in practice, local men hired without education in the police force – revealed an everyday knowledge of female anatomy, ejaculation and sexuality. Their conceptualisations of female sexuality and cross-generational relationships constituted a mixture of common village lore, the medical and psychoanalytic inventions that were referred to in the discussions at that time, and some random information from police training textbooks. The rare textbooks that did exist were predominantly translated from Swedish or German.

The police officers tried to combine their diffuse knowledge with the prosecutor's alleged need to be able to demonstrate in court that the quality of the evidence that they had gathered was sufficient to prove that one's 'sexual drive' had been aroused or satisfied. In police interviews, meanwhile, the suspected women – even when they confessed to detailed sexual acts – spoke in terms of their religious doctrine and freely described the course of the oil-anointment ritual. The court proceedings worked as a kind of language laboratory, where the accused women and their religious lexicon met medico-forensic terminology.

The women themselves explained their acts in terms of the rationale of their religious doctrine. For example, one of the convicted women appealed to The Law of God instead of secular law. She wrote for the Supreme Court in a 28-page handwritten letter of appeal, stating that the matter in question could not be solved according to the human law, and, citing the Bible, argued that everything is pure for the pure. She further stated that the sentence had been given based on the human rationale and that if her motive would have been criminal, she could have never done anything like this. She wrote, 'The matter has been so much holier and high-minded than the filthy-labelled homosexual' [kysymys on ollut paljon pyhemmästä ja korkeammasta asiasta kuin saastaiseksi leimatusta homoseksualista].[37] This was one of the rare occasions when the word 'homosexual' was mentioned in the Herb Grove case. In the documents of Eeva's court proceedings, this word was never mentioned. Whereas Eeva and her lovers discussed the possible 'sinful' [synti] or 'criminal' [rikollinen] nature of their relations, they never associated with any identity-based concepts with themselves.

The concept of 'lesbian' was not used either by the women or by the police officers. The women were obviously aware of the existence of a category of people identified by same-sex interests, as the term 'homosexualist' [homoseksualisti] was mentioned occasionally. However, the interrogated women always excluded themselves from this category. Only Eeva had internalised the medical discourse to some degree. She said in the court proceeding documents that she had "became accustomed to homosexuality" [homoseksuaalisuuteen tottuneena].[38] However, she never explicitly stated that she *was* a homosexual. From a legal point of view, this was officially of no importance as only the acts were significant. The language of homosexuality haunted the police interrogations and the courtroom as an apparition that never fully materialised.

Two of the Herb Grove women were suspected of having sexual relations with under-age girls: the 49-year-old headmistress, Helka, and another of the founding members of the orphanage, a 38-year-old dentist, Kreetta, who worked and lived in the Sisterhome. They responded to the police officers' questions by using language of spiritual love that was similar to Eeva's manner of discussing these matters. They said that they had nurtured the girls with a Christ-like love, emphasising that they had been acting like 'mothers' for their 'children'.[39] They also pointed to the religious meaning of the oil-anointment ritual. As for the two underaged girls who were involved in these alleged acts, they were submitted to a rather harsh medical examination by doctors, in which the central concern was whether or not their 'maidenhood had been corrupted'.[40]

On 19 December 1951, eight of the Herb Grove women were convicted in the Lower Court of fornication with persons of the same sex. Most of them were granted a suspended sentence with a three-year probation period. Those women who received the most severe punishment were the ones who were tried not only for same-sex fornication but also for fornication with under-aged girls. The headmistress received an

18-month prison sentence for two counts of same-sex fornication with foster girls who were 15–16-years old, and three counts of fornication with a person of the same sex (between 1943 and 1951). She was the only one who was actually imprisoned.

The second founding member, Kreetta, was convicted in the Court of Appeal for continued same-sex fornication with a person of the same sex and for fornication with a foster girl of 15–16-years old between 1944 and 1950. She was sentenced to ten months in prison, suspended for three years. This meant that if she were to 'commit any crime, binge-drinking, or otherwise indecent life' [tekemällä koetusaikana rikoksen taikka antautumalla juoppouteen tai epäsiveelliseen tahi muutoin pahantapaiseen elämään] during that period, she would be imprisoned.[41]

After the trials

Those women who faced the most severe punishment for same-sex fornication in the 1950s were, as a rule, sentenced for their alleged sexual acts with under-aged girls. In this respect, Herb Grove was the most spectacular of these two 1950s court cases. On the one hand, the police suggested that Herb Grove was a sanctuary for widows, single mothers and orphans. On the other, they suspected that Herb Grove was an intergenerational community for women whose sexuality they pathologised as 'sexually sick' [sukupuolisesti sairaiden kokoontumispaikka][42] and which existed in the shadow of religion. It seems inevitable that a number of young women deliberately moved into that community, as it not only provided a possibility for education, employment and nurturing but allowed same-sex sexual exploration in patriarchal postwar Finnish society. In the 1950s, there were only a few public places where women could act on their own: for example, before 1967, women were not allowed to go to restaurants or bars without male company.

The media coverage of Herb Grove case was extensive, but it was perhaps more confused than morally aggressive. Neither the concept 'lesbian' nor 'paedophilia' was used in the media. The media attention concerned not so much adult-child relations but 'wayward' [harhautunut] religious women, 'sexual offences' [seksuaalirikokset] and 'fornication' [haureus]. It was also discussed whether the accused women were martyrs in a religious sense:

> Ovatko tuomitut teidän mielestänne marttyyreitä?" kysytään käytävällä todistajina olleilta sisarkodin asukkailta, mutta nämä eivät

anna suoraa vastausta, vaan alkavat puhua hengenasioista. ... Muuan toinen uskonsisar etsi lohtua "pyhän rakkauden opista", ja kertoi jo 20 vuoden ajan valmistautuneensa näihin kärsimyksiin: – Ensimmäinen aste on nyt vankila, sitten seuraa kuolema [Are the convicted women martyrs, in your opinion?" Sisterhome members who had been called as witnesses were asked by journalists in the courtroom corridor. They refused to give a direct answer but began to talk about biblical matters. ... Another sister in faith was looking for comfort from "the doctrine of Holy Love" and stated that she had been, for twenty years, preparing herself for these sufferings: – The first degree is now prison, then death]

Only three of the Finnish papers used the word 'homosexual'; just one in the headline: 'Yrttilehdon homoseksualistit tuomittu' [The homosexualists of Herb Grove convicted].[43]

After the Second World War, starting in the late 1940s and culminating in the early 1950s, public outrage against child sexual abuse became manifest in many Western countries. The campaigners turned to criminal law; harsh punishments were demanded as a means of solving a social problem that was deemed to be utterly dangerous.[44] The main concerns in Finnish society and in Parliament in the late 1940s and early 1950s were not only the protection of children from sexual predators through harsher punishments and castration, but also the protection of society from the reproduction of undesirable classes: the poor, the feeble-minded and the pathological.

In Finland, the moral campaigning for harsher punishments against child sexual abusers occurred simultaneously with an increase in same-sex fornication trials concerning both men and women, starting in 1948 and culminating from 1951 to 54. In 1950, law reforms were introduced in Finland against free abortion (the abortion law), unwanted reproduction (the sterilisation law) and sexual pathologies (the castration law). In Finnish parliamentary debates of 1949 where the government bill for the castration law was debated, it was quite clear that the law was understood as an attack on heterosexual male offenders. The chairperson for the national Finnish organisation *Pelastakaa Lapset* [*Save Our Children*] stated in Parliament that children have no power or experience to defend themselves against candy-men, who often are 'seductive in extremely calculative ways' [useimmiten erittäin laskelmallisesti houkuttelevia], or to save themselves from the abhorrent vice of these men who seduce them into crimes.[45] In the *travaux prepatoires* of the castration law, it is apparent that it was considered appropriate that the definition of the offender was gender-neutral. The Finnish government and, accordingly, the Finnish penal code thus acknowledged, recognised and constructed matters that were not debated in Parliament. The concept of the 'candy-man' referred to in the Parliamentary debates was not only gendered but also heterosexualised and classed: a heterosexual man seducing little working-class girls. For example, one of the right-wing MPs argued the following:

> Useimmat näistä lapsista ovat suomalaisten työläiskotien herttaisia päivänpaisteisia lapsia...Pienet tyttöset...tuskin itse edes tajuavat, mitä heille on tapahtunut, mutta heidän kokemansa kipu ja myöhemmin heidän kärsimänsä väkivallan aiheuttamat tuskalliset vahingoittumat riittävät lyömään kauhun leiman heidän kasvoilleen [Most of these children are sweet sunny kids from working-class homes...Small girls hardly realise what has happened to them, but the pain and later the severe injuries that has been caused to them are enough to attach the stigma of horror on their face].[46]

The tone of debates changed after the Herb Grove trials in 1954 when the public prosecutor tried to have the headmistress castrated. Under the new castration law, the prosecutor claimed that the headmistress, together with her accomplices, had directed her 'lust' [himo] to very young girls and had tried to seduce them to enter into same-sex fornication by lying that the Bible approved certain activities. The castration application was, however, halted at the National Board of Health. The 1950 law was gender-neutral in theory, but not in practice. In the era of castration, between 1950 and 1958, only four women were prosecuted for castration, but none of them was actually castrated, whereas 91 men were operated on. By castration, what was referred to was the attempt to eliminate 'sexual drive' by surgically removing the sexual glandulas.[47]

According to Heike Bauer, in early sexology, 'female inversion' was largely linked to issues of social differences rather than sexual differences, at least initially, and to the mapping of distinctly configured roles for men and women. The discourse of male inversion, she argues, was tied to the emergence of sexual identity, coined to describe male same-sex practices, and overtly politicised in discourses of the emerging modern state.[48] It is worth noting that same-sex fornication was criminalised between adult women only in four remote European countries – Sweden, Austria, Greece and Finland – and in some cantons of Switzerland. In the Netherlands, 'fornication with an under-age person of the same sex' was decreed punishable from 1911 to 1971; acts between women were included in this section. The Herb Gove case allows us to trace some of the complex intersections between legal, social and religious discourse that characterised the emergence of female same-sex visibility in 1950s Finland.

The Finnish medical profession was influenced by German Idealism and publications in German, or it used Nordic legal scholarly literature until the 1950s.[49] The concept of 'paedophile' first appeared in a legal context in 1956 in a criminological study but only entered everyday language in the 1990s. That of (male) 'homosexual' was introduced into everyday language around the early 1950s, but the concept of 'lesbian' became commonplace only after the mid-1970s. The Herb Grove women, then, were not paedophiles in the current sense of the word, nor were they lesbians: the community-based, politicized concept of 'lesbian' was simply not available as a cultural or social category in Finnish village life in the 1950s.

It is striking that the largest proportion of men and women who were convicted of same-sex fornication in Finland took place directly after the 'castration law' was put into force in 1950.[50] Through to the castration law, the concept of 'sexuality' was introduced for the first time into Finnish legislation.[51] Finland was the only European country in the 1950s where castration against one's will was legal. To my knowledge, no such castrations were executed after 1958 in Finland, even though the law remained in force until 1971. Between 1950 and 1957, castration orders were often given to male offenders who had been convicted of homosexual acts with minors.[52] Thus, what was really frowned upon was the alleged seduction or corruption of youth. So, during the time in question, concepts such as 'women's same-sex fornication' [naisten keskinäinen haureus], 'fornication with under-age persons' [alaikäisiin sekaantuminen] and the 'protection of children' [lasten suojelu] existed and were familiar to almost everyone as ideas, even though the concepts that would make sense to us now, such as 'lesbian', 'paedophile' and 'sexual abuse', were not yet associated with them.

Notes

Many thanks to Heike Bauer, Matt Cook, Tuula Juvonen, Satu Lidman, Salla Peltonen and Kathleen Moore for valuable comments on the draft. A large part of the archive materials was gathered jointly with Eve Hirvonen, and I thank her for sharing some of the research history.

1. Lower Court decision 19 December 1951; The Court of Appeal 20 June 1952; The Supreme Court 26 April 1954.

2. For the sake of anonymity, I have changed all the names and have not given precise location of documents consulted.
3. *Penal Code of Finland*, 39/1889, chapter 20; 7,2.
4. See, for example, A. Sankar, 'Sisters and Brothers, Lovers and Enemies: Marriage Resistance in Southern Kwantung', in E. Blackwood, ed., *Anthropology and Homosexual Behavior* (New York: The Haworth Press, 1986), 69–81.
5. Herb Grove court proceeding documents: Helka's appeal letter for the Supreme Court 18 August 1952.
6. Interview with a 1952 social board member (12 December 1995); Minutes of the social board 1949–1954.
7. Herb Grove court proceeding documents: Helka in the police interrogation 20 August 1951.
8. Herb Grove court proceeding documents: Helka in the police interrogation 22–28 May 1951.
9. Herb Grove court documents: interrogations of a number of witnesses from religious communities from all over Finland, 22 May–6 June 1951.
10. J. Löfström, 'The Social Construction of Homosexuality in Finnish Society from the Late 19th Century to 1950s' (Unpublished PhD thesis, Department of Sociology: University of Essex, 1994); K. Mustola and J. Rydström, 'Women and the Laws on Same-Sex Sexuality', in K. Mustola and J. Rydström, eds, *Criminally Queer*, 41–60; A. Sorainen, 'The Power of Confession: The Role of Criminal Law and Court Practices in the Production of Knowledge Concerning Sexuality between Women: Finland in the 1950s', in J. Löfström, ed., *Scandinavian Homosexualities,* 117–138; A. Sorainen, 'Foreign Theories and Our Histories: The Emergence of the Modern Homosexual and Local Research on Same-Sex Sexualities' in *Journal of the Finnish Anthropological Society,* 24.3 (1999), 61–74.
11. *Penal Code of Finland*, 39/1889 chapter 20; 12,1. In Swedish: 'någon'. In Finnish, there exists no feminine or masculine forms of words, but the gender-neutral formulation here is obviously deliberate, not accidental.
12. *Penal Code of Finland*, 39/1889 chapter 20; 7,2 and chapter 20;12,1. A total of 51 women and 1,036 men were sentenced for same-sex fornication from 1894 to 1971, the time when the law was enforced (Löfström, *Social Construction*, Appendix C; J. Rydström, *Criminally Queer*, 24, 52). The number of women convicted of same-sex fornication was only five per cent of the total number of sentences ('General Courts of First Instance. Offences and persons prosecuted and convicted according to the nature of crime, 1950–1959', *Official Statistics of Finland*, XXIII: 36–88; XXIII B: 89–106). Most of the convictions that were not suspended were convictions of those women and men who had had sexual relations with under-age persons of the same sex (*Official Statistics of Finland*, XXIII: 36–88; XXIII B: 89–106).
13. Herb Grove court proceeding documents: the police officer in his letter to the County Government 5 March 1951.
14. Herb Grove court proceeding documents: Kreetta's letter to the Lower Court 19 December 1951.
15. Herb Grove court proceeding documents: Helka in the police interrogation 28 May 1951.
16. Herb Grove court proceeding documents: Helka in the police interrogation 20 August 1951.

17. Herb Grove court proceeding documents: Helka in the police interrogation 22–28 May 1951.
18. Eeva court proceeding documents; Lower Court injunction 29 May 1951.
19. Eeva court proceeding documents; police interrogation 22 February 1951.
20. Eeva court proceeding documents; the police officer 26 February 1951.
21. Herb Grove court proceeding documents; Eeva in the police interrogation 20 February 1951.
22. Eeva court proceeding documents; medical certificate 26 February 1951.
23. Eeva court proceeding documents; police interrogation 2 March1951.
24. Eeva court proceeding documents; the police officer 2 March 1951.
25. Eeva court proceeding documents; Eeva in the police interrogation 26 February 1951.
26. Eeva court proceeding documents; Eeva in the police interrogation 26 February 1951.
27. Eeva court proceeding documents; Eeva in the police interrogation 26 February 1951.
28. Eeva court proceeding documents; police interrogations 2 February–5 March 1951.
29. Eeva court proceeding documents; Lower Court decision 3 April 1951.
30. Herb Grove court proceeding documents; the police officer 5 March 1951.
31. Herb Grove court proceeding documents; Helka in the unofficial meeting 23 February 1951.
32. Herb Grove court proceeding documents; the police officer 5 March 1951.
33. Sorainen, 'Foreign Theories', 121; B. Honkasalo, *Suomen rikosoikeus, yleiset opit II osa [Finnish Criminal Law, general part II]* (Helsinki: Suomalainen Lakimiesyhdistys, 1960), 71.
34. Honkasalo, *Finnish Criminal Code*, 71.
35. Honkasalo, *Finnish Criminal Code*, 47, 71.
36. Herb Grove court proceeding documents; police interrogations 22–28 May 1951.
37. Herb Grove court proceeding documents: a handwritten letter of appeal to the Supreme Court by one of the convicted women 18 August 1952.
38. Herb Grove court proceeding documents: Eeva in the police interrogation 20 February 1951.
39. Herb Grove court proceeding documents: Kreetta in the police interrogation 1 June 1951.
40. Herb Grove court proceeding documents: police interrogations 22–28 May 1951. See also Sorainen, 'Foreign Theories', 122–124, 136.
41. Herb Grove court proceeding documents, the Supreme Court decision 24 April 1954.
42. Herb Grove court proceeding documents: police interrogations 22–28 May 1951.
43. Savon Sanomat 20 December 1951; Kansan Sana 22 December 1951.
44. A. Sorainen, 'Moral Panic! The Figure of the Paedophile and Sexual Politics of Fear in Finland', in S. V. Knudsen, L. Löfgren-Mårtenson and S. Månsson, eds, *Youth, Gender and Pornography* (Copenhagen: Danish University of Education Press, 2007), 189–203.
45. *Finnish Parliamentary Minutes 1949*, 22 April 1949.
46. *Finnish Parliamentary Minutes 1949*, 22 April 1949.

47. I. Anttila, *Alaikäisiin kohdistuneet siveellisyysrikokset ja niiden tekijät. Kriminologinen tutkimus* [*Sex Offences on Minors and their Perpetrators. A Criminologicial Research*] (Helsinki: Suomalaisen Lakimiesyhdistyksen julkaisuja A-sarja, No 50, 1956), 30–31.
48. Bauer, H., 'Theorizing Female Inversion: Sexology, Discipline, and Gender at the Fin de Siècle', *Journal of the History of Sexuality*, 18.1 (2008), 85.
49. English was generally not comprehended amongst academics or the majority of the Finns until the 1960s or 1970s. See A. Sorainen, 'Siveellisyys ja seksuaalisuus Suomen rikosoikeustieteessä' ['Decency and Sexuality in the Finnish sexual criminal science'], in T. Pulkkinen and A. Sorainen, eds, *Siveellisyydestä seksuaalisuuteen – poliittisen käsitteen historia* [*From Decency to Sexuality – History of a Political Concept*] (Helsinki: Finnish Literature Society, 2011).
50. *Penal Code of Finland*, 84/1950.
51. Sorainen, *Decency and Sexuality*, 219–220.
52. I. Anttila, *Sex Offences*, 30–31; Löfström, *Social Construction*, 185–188.

6

Moral Panic or Critical Mass? The Queer Contradictions of 1950s New Zealand

Chris Brickell

The New Zealand of the 1950s, we are usually told, was no dynamic place. These complacent and conservative years epitomised everything that was static and settled about the postwar world. Although the Second World War temporarily disturbed the social order, some historians suggest it ultimately changed little.[1] Michael King argues that 'the 1950s were dull, grey, conformist years in New Zealand – the calm before the storm that was the 1960s', while Paul Millar laments the period's 'unforgiving puritanism'.[2] Indeed, King goes as far as claiming that 'stodginess permeated national life', 'clothes were drab', 'there was little variety in food', citizens looked to 'material comfort, suburban lifestyle and conformity', and 'there was still little tolerance of diversity'.[3] Matthew Wright in turn suggests that this 1950s New Zealand was 'a quintessentially white, blokeish and conservative society'.[4] Back in 1960, visiting American scholar David Ausubel was even more condemnatory. He claimed that New Zealanders' 'apparently mild exterior' barely disguised a 'strong undercurrent of repressed hostility' and a 'punitive attitude toward personal inadequacy'.[5]

Many historians agree, then, that postwar New Zealand society settled into a uniform pattern. Women returned to the home from their work in factories and on farms, and embraced domesticity and family. The male breadwinner worked for pay during the week and played sport on the weekends. Heterosexual familialism reigned supreme. There were white weddings aplenty and the visible signs of a baby boom: suburban washing lines with cloth nappies drying in the sun. Evoking the iconic US wartime woman factory worker, historian James Belich observed that

'Rosie the Riveter doffed her overalls for a wedding ring and a maternity dress'.[6]

What space could there have been for those who rejected prevailing social mores? Writer Bill Pearson, himself homosexual – and temporarily living in England – was pessimistic. In 1952, in the literary magazine *Landfall*, he wrote with evident sadness: 'There is no place in normal New Zealand society for the man who is different. The man with the cleft palate, with a stutter, with short sight, will suffer.'[7] That man – clearly intended as an analogue for the homosexual – could find no peace. 'There will always be jokes behind his back; he will find it hard to make honest contact with other men because once he has been isolated, most men will talk to him only with tongue in cheek, humouring him at best, saving up a report for the boys in the bar.'[8] In the following pages, I suggest that New Zealand in the 1950s was a more complex place than these descriptions imply. There was, in Redmer Yska's words, an 'insistent undertow of new cultural forces'.[9] Like the recent work of Nick Thomas and Frank Mort, this chapter challenges the idea that the 1950s were conservative years sandwiched between the relative upheavals of World War Two and the 'permissive society' of the 1960s.[10] This was no 'calm before the storm that was the 1960s', as King would have it. Instead, new modes of sociability and resistance took shape during the 1950s, and these laid the groundwork for the social movements of the years that followed.

The decade's contradictions manifested themselves on a number of fronts. Some articles in women's magazines – with titles like 'Prison Without Bars: Home Life for the Married Woman' and 'Three Reasons Why Mothers Go to Work' – questioned the apparent consensus over domestic heterosexuality, and told of women yearning to escape from a regimented suburban existence.[11] The rapidly expanding cities were home to another transgressive group, too: young rebels out to test the status quo. The 'bodgies' were noisy motorbike boys with tight trousers, ducktail hairstyles and loose sexual morals. Their female counterparts, the 'widgies', were jiving, loudmouthed girls who refused to sit quietly in conformity's corner. The challengers sparked controversy. Independently-minded women were pathologised as 'Amazons' who 'reject their own sex and ape the other',[12] while the 1954 government 'Mazengarb inquiry' frothed over teenage 'milk bar gangs', seedy sex in darkened picture theatres, and underage 'orgies'.[13] The newspapers told their readers that 'police figures show a big increase in sex crimes' and that such crimes 'are at an all-time high', especially among the young.[14]

Debates about gender and sexuality were fertile grounds for social anxiety during the 1950s. This chapter explores such anxieties in relation to homoeroticism, but it sets out to do more than that. It argues that these anxieties were not all-encompassing and all-determining. Through their expressions, especially in the news media, we glimpse a postwar queer culture, something that no moral panic could suppress. The chapter examines only male culture in any depth, while recognising the importance of the detailed lesbian histories currently being written by other New Zealand scholars.[15] Evidence emerges through insider and outsider narratives. Oral history interviews allow men to look back at the decade retrospectively and evaluate their pasts afresh, while photographs reveal queer sociability and challenge preconceptions of misery, isolation and pathology.[16] These sources reveal that urban life also enabled the development of increasingly large and complex networks among homosexually inclined men. The 1950s were important years in the consolidation of the homosexual male subculture. A rich and variegated queer world took hold in New Zealand's cities and paved the way for the collective activism of the decades that followed.

Panicking

The moments of anxiety set the scene. Sociologists identify a moral panic when a given social group or particular social patterns are defined – and denounced – as a threat to the established social order.[17] In New Zealand, challenges to a conservative vision of postwar society – the vision so forcefully described by Pearson, King and others – were condemned, and some hyperbolic claims were made. One event generated considerable heat. Christchurch teenagers Juliet Hulme and Pauline Parker set out to 'moider mother' (Parker's, that is) in a local park one afternoon in 1954, with a brick wrapped in a stocking. It seemed the girls would be separated, and Hulme sent to live abroad, a possibility the teenagers tried to forestall. The newspapers reported the subsequent trial under lurid headlines – 'Girls in Dock: Crown Says Crime was Cold-blooded', 'Brutal Killing of Mother with Brick', and 'Girls Never Will be Sane' – and contended that the girls were 'abnormally homosexual' in character.[18] Throughout the trial and its reporting, the crime – and the homosexuality presumed to underpin it – were declared to be pathological. 'There was evidence...that the relationship between the accused rapidly became a homosexual one', declared a prominent psychiatrist, only to add: 'homosexuality and paranoia are very frequently related'.[19]

In other examples, commentators declared male homosexuality a moral menace. In a 1949 piece on goings-on aboard a ship moored in Auckland harbour, Roger Fulton, a journalist for the *Observer*, reminded his readers that 'normal, healthy, heterosexual New Zealanders regard "queers" with amused scorn or outright distaste... It is high time for the community to take a determined stand against this offensive behaviour'.[20] Six years later, the best-selling tabloid *Truth* newspaper told of a 'cell of indecency' in the small city of Whanganui – involving a music master, a warehouseman and other professionals – and warned that the 'contamination' was liable to spread.[21] Meanwhile, the *New Zealand Pictorial* complained: 'There are gangs of homosexuals who live together for the sake of perversion. You can see these warped-brain men – and women too – wandering about the streets or sitting idly in night cafes. Auckland has too many of them.'[22]

These reports were not without their contradictions. While the journalists railed against 'this offensive behaviour', they also provided voyeuristic detail for those who wanted to know more, and rendered homosexuality publicly visible in the process. Chris Waters, writing in the British context, calls this a 'tabloid discourse of homosexuality', 'a strategy dedicated to uncovering, naming and codifying homosexual lives for popular consumption'.[23] Others have identified similar discourses in Australia and the US.[24] The *Observer*'s Roger Fulton told his astounded readers about 'a certain coterie of Aucklanders, commonly known as "queers"', 'effeminates' who clambered aboard visiting ships and drank and danced with visiting seamen. Fulton added that 'anyone who frequents the Auckland waterfront when an overseas ship is sailing is liable to see groups of effeminate-looking men calling shrill farewells to seamen aboard a departing ship.' '"Goodbye, darling", called the "wharfie", who by this time was nearing the bottom of the gangway. "Gooooodbye. Come and get me dearie – if you can!"'[25]

There were more revelations. In 1957, *Truth* described a house in Seatoun Road, Wellington, the headquarters of a 'homosexual circle'. There a former police sergeant, a salesman, two shop assistants and a taxi driver took their own erotic photographs 'under floodlights in the lounge', invited others to their 'orgies', and one of the men – 'The Country Girl' – paraded in dresses, earrings and brooches.[26] This was a 'house of depravity', *Truth* mumbled, but keen readers – including those who shared these men's erotic interests – learned more about these new urban cultures. Indeed, homosexual men across the country read such reports with great excitement and passed the newspapers from hand to hand.[27]

The *New Zealand Pictorial* provided more details for those who wanted them:

> Homosexuals have a strict code of their own and on no account will they sexually associate with women. Oddly enough they fight among themselves like kilkenny cats. For this reason a group of homosexuals is always controlled by the "queen bee" whose word is absolutely final. Others in the sect are "marthas," who dress as women; "arthurs," who adopt the normal male role, and "butchs" who stand in either way. At times they stage mock weddings and have been known to fool ministers of religion into actually performing marriage services in churches. Another group who pad the city's streets are the ambisexuals, a comparatively new sect of men who are not particularly fussy which sex they pick up as long as it's company.[28]

Never a newspaper to be left out, *Truth* added its over-excited shilling's worth:

> Many of these men affect a style of haircut which is thick and peaked at the nape of the neck. There are those among them who are not above using a touch of rouge to improve their complexions. They are usually neatly dressed, though some of them favour bright colours and "zoot suit" styles...One of the sights of Auckland last year was the arrival in the city of a blond, permanent-waved young male, dressed in shorts and wearing heavy gold earrings. He was a member of the crew of a visiting vessel and quickly made himself acquainted with other known perverts.[29]

As the Parker-Hulme murder case shows, the anxieties over homosexuality sometimes overlapped with worries about young New Zealanders. The left-wing Auckland magazine *Here and Now* reported that 'Teddy boys', named for their Edwardian clothing, were associated with effeminacy as well as petty crime.[30] The 1954 'Mazengarb inquiry' complained that school pupils were involved in 'depravity, both heterosexual and homosexual', and considered it 'wise to remind parents that sexual misbehaviour can occur between members of the same sex'.[31] In his 1958 book *The Bodgie: A Study in Psychological Abnormality*, New Zealand psychologist A.E. Manning summarised his interviews with thirty self-identified 'bodgies' and 'widgies': fourteen divulged 'homosexual tendencies', and seven admitted 'homosexual experiences'. A few, Manning noted, 'were frankly libidinous in their opinions'.

He concluded: 'if the group represented in any degree a reasonable cross-section of "youth in revolt", then homosexuality is becoming more and more a serious social problem, one for the most urgent research and treatment, and not for punishment.'[32]

These postwar accounts exhibit the typical features of a moral panic. Homosexuals were identified as a threat to the established order, as they occupied coffee bars, beseiged visiting ships and hosted 'depraved' parties in suburban living rooms. Commentators set themselves up in judgement, insisting that 'contamination' was a clear possibility (*Truth*) and that the country had to 'take a determined stand against this offensive behaviour' (*Observer*). Some, like Manning, urged 'research and treatment'. At the same time, the visible signs of this panic, the newspaper and magazine articles published up and down the country, were more revealing than condemnatory. In many ways, the voyeurism was stronger than the outrage that framed it, and readers learned a lot about homosexual cultures in the process. When all was said and done, the newspaper reports generated more light than heat.

Amassing

John Joliffe stepped off the boat from England one day in 1956. In a recent interview, he described his new society in new-familiar terms: 'New Zealand seemed a very narrow, conservative country. I'd been aware of being gay for most of my life, but society was very different back then and I married a few years after arriving here.'[33] Auckland man Ron Mark, in contrast, did not marry. He built a gay life for himself in this time of 'double lives and double standards'. Mark's was something of a 'cloak and dagger' existence, but he began a relationship with another man that would last for 14 years, and immersed himself in Auckland's expanding homosexual world.[34]

Urbanisation bought new opportunities as it did elsewhere. In Sydney, Australia, the nearest metropolis, new bars were established, and drag show clubs emerged during the 1950s.[35] In New Zealand, the larger centres – Auckland, Wellington and Christchurch – grew rapidly after the war. More and more of the inner-city cafés and bars catered for a bohemian clientele, many of whom were homosexual. Auckland's queerer pubs included the Shakespeare, the Star and the Occidental, while the Lilypond in the Great Northern Hotel was a good place to meet stewards off visiting British ships. Trevor Rupe, who would later change his name to Carmen and become an icon of the Wellington scene, held court there in chiffon and silk, 'like a prettier version of

Carmen Miranda'.[36] In Wellington, the capital city, the Grand and the back bar of the Midland served the queer crowd. So, too, did the Royal Oak. The downstairs bar was the most popular among the queer crowd, while the upstairs one catered for the arty and genteel. Visiting actors and dancers gravitated there. Christchurch men enjoyed Warners and the United Services Hotel, both on Cathedral Square.

These establishments were located right in the middle of town. In some overseas cities – Sydney, Australia, and Jackson, Mississippi, for instance – most queer-oriented bars occupied the fringes of the central business district.[37] The British Hotel, at the nearby port of Lyttelton, was an exception to the New Zealand pattern. The establishment was home to 'Marilyn', a resident piano-playing drag queen who hailed her fellow travellers as 'beautiful belles'. 'The mix was about half local and half homosexuals', recalled one regular, noting that many queer men travelled from the city to the port to drink.[38]

In the coffee shops, city dwellers could relax until well after the pubs' closing time of 6 o'clock. Auckland had the Ca D'Oro and the cosy, almost living-room-like Blake's Inn, a Vulcan Lane coffee bar patronised by the temperamental and the artistic. Men enjoyed the tearooms at department stores Milne & Choyce and Smith & Caughey, along with the Regent Theatre teashop on a Friday night. 'It was all cake stands and starched pinnies', one regular recalls.[39] Christchurch men went to the Coffee Pot, Dunedin locals to the Sirocco and the Savoy, and two establishments were especially popular among Wellington's queer crowd: the Picasso and the Man Friday. The news media, with their complaints about brightly-coloured 'gangs of homosexuals' loitering in 'night cafes', documented something very real: the emergence of a publicly-visible subculture.

These visible elements formed the tip of a much larger iceberg. Further investigation reveals the concentrations of more-or-less openly queer men in particular occupations. Two examples stand out: the catering sections of ships, and the display, drapery, soft furnishings and menswear sections of the inner-city department stores. One university study noted the popularity of the *Maori* and the *Hinemoa* – the ferries that plied their way between the North and South Islands – on the grounds that 'you can get away with more at sea'.[40] One 20-year-old steward, with 'good looks, effeminate mannerisms, soft voice', a prominent 'love bite' on his neck, and 'beefcake pictures on the wall above his bunk', told a researcher about the attractions of shipboard life. 'Was attracted to working on ships because of the fact that homosexuals were present', jotted the researcher as the pair chatted. 'Feels at sea everyone is very tolerant which is just the opposite situation to that ashore.'[41] Conversely, as the *Observer* noted, seamen were popular among the 'Shipboard Suzies' (or 'shippies'), enthusiastic locals with a penchant for sailor trade.[42] In Dunedin, Trevor Rupe discovered quite a few sailors were 'up for it': a blowjob followed by a visit to a tea shop.[43] Ron Mark figured shipboard men 'didn't give a damn, they were only in port for a few days'. While it was well-known that 'the ships' cooks and stewards were mainly gay', a nice muscly stoker could be had 'if the time was right and nobody was watching and they were horny enough'.[44]

Mark was a display artist in Auckland's Milne & Choyce department store, and he found the management tolerant 'as long as you weren't blatantly gay'. After all, he remembers, 'you were fulfilling a function that was needed'.[45] William Campbell told an interviewer the same store's display department 'was just a whole mass of gays. Gay guys worked in display departments you see'.[46] Mark describes Smith & Caughey, another store, as 'a gay old men's home', and John Court and Rendells were similar. He knew quite a few lesbians in the department stores too, especially in corsetry and cosmetics.[47] In 1957, John Croskery left school at fifteen and went to work as a window dresser at the Drapery and Importing Company (DIC) in Wellington. There he had his 'first introduction to gay people'. 'I thought they were delightful, they were different, not your usual type of male, rather fairyish. It was said that they were camp, they like each other. And I thought "that's what I must be."'[48]

The department stores functioned as entrees into the gay life, and those with a contact could establish their networks. Croskery went to a few camp parties in Wellington, 'that's when I first saw it all, wide-eyed'. Of his fellow store-workers and partiers, Croskery recalls 'Clara Bow, and there was Eva Gabor and Za Za, I can't remember the others'.[49] Similarly, William Campbell's Milne & Choyce connections 'gave me entry into that sort of life and from then on that's the sort of life I'd lead'. Campbell and his Auckland friends went out on Friday nights to peruse the parks and 'bogs' to see who was there, cruised down Queen Street in Campbell's car and went out for supper. 'It wasn't threatening', he remembers. 'The cops were a threat, but as long as you used a bit of common sense you didn't have to worry very much.'[50] Men assumed the male prerogative to occupy public space; some, like Laurie McIlroy and Derrick Hancock, donned sunglasses and stylish shirts and became flâneurs on the streets (Figure 1).

Parties, like the coffee shops, were popular in the years when the pubs closed at 6 o'clock. Hancock and his partner Ron Hawley hosted parties

Figure 1 A street photographer recorded friends Laurie McIlroy (left) and Derrick Hancock (right), flâneurs in the provincial city of Napier in 1952. PA-Coll-9297, Alexander Turnbull Library

at their place on the outskirts of Christchurch. On Saturday night, a crowd left the British Hotel in Lyttelton or the Coffee Pot café in town and went off to a party at Derrick and Ron's. Others spent hours getting frocked up before heading out. The relative seclusion of the house was a boon in a time of suspicious neighbours, and men could come and go without being noticed.[51]

There was a two-way traffic between the parties in Christchurch and those in Wellington, an overnight journey away on the *Maori* or the *Hinemoa*. Sometimes a frocked-up welcoming party waited on the wharves, the locals primed and ready to whisk the visitors off to the weekend's events. Neville Sole remembers his first Wellington party, at John and Paul's place. This was highly significant for him:

> It was a screaming, mad gay party, and I had a wonderful time, and for the first time in a great many years, probably forever, I felt at home, I somehow felt I'd found my people. It was a wonderful breakthrough, I had discovered my sexuality, if you like. I don't think I had fully realised up until that point that I was truly gay. I knew I was different, I knew I had a certain attraction for men, but I wondered often if it was so much attraction for men as disaffection for women that drove me to men, that sort of thing. After this first party at John

> and Pauls' I knew undoubtedly that I was gay. The people there were my people. Everything seemed to come together from that time.[52]

There were other Wellington party venues, too, including a house in inner city Abel Smith Street. 'We used to have parties there two or three times a week sometimes', Sole told an interviewer, 'and it was a wonderful meeting place to meet people of the same ilk, you know. I'd go home with them or take them home or arrange to meet them later, or whatever'.[53]

Wellingtonians visited Auckland for weekends – this time an overnight trip by express train – but Ron Mark remembers his fellow Aucklanders were 'quite cliquey', and wary of letting the Wellington men into their circles. Still, queer Auckland was 'very social' during the 1950s, and 'ninety percent of the entertainment' took place in private homes. Hosts would compete with each other to present the best supper or dinner, there would be intellectual conversation, 'gay banter and a lot of bitchiness', and someone always played the piano.[54]

There were outings, too, and weekends away. Auckland friends decamped to the beachside settlement of Piha for weekends. There they spent days on the sand, and nights in a holiday house with plenty of 'charades and camp numbers'. 'You were suppressed so long', Mark recollects, 'that on the weekend you'd throw caution to the wind and drop your curlers, as you'd say' (Figure 2). In 1954, when the camp movie *Carmen Jones* came out – the tale of a wartime parachute factory worker who tried to seduce her soldier acquaintance – 'everybody wanted to be Carmen' and 'you trotted about with a rose in your mouth and an old shawl'.[55]

The beachside escape was a common theme across the country, as groups of friends sought the holiday vibe – not to mention the semi-privacy and freedom – of the coastal settlements. Dunedin men had fun at nearby Mapoutahi, in a railway ganger's house perched high above the sea. 'It was full of rats, but it was just something, it was a getaway. It was really like a valve, that you could let yourself be yourself', one man remembered.[56] Queer Christchurch men enjoyed the public reserves and nearby beaches. Groups of friends – couples among them – hung out under the pine trees and posed together in their bathing trunks (Figure 3). As the decade drew to a close, their 'togs' shrank in size and sometimes disappeared entirely, suggesting a loosening of rules around male public nudity – in certain circles at least (Figure 4). Like their Auckland counterparts, the Christchurch crowd enjoyed inside spaces, too. In a holiday house at Scarborough, an amateur photographer snapped one

Figure 2 On the beach, location unknown, mid-1950s. S10–571a, Hocken Collections

Figure 3 A group of friends spends time out-of-doors near Christchurch, c.1949. Note the two couples. Chris Brickell's collection

couple lounging with their dog, accompanied by a friend or two and a bottle of gin (Figure 5). These parallel private worlds ran alongside the public lives lived most of the time. Still, 'they were fun times', recalls Aucklander Ron Mark with an evident air of nostalgia.[57]

The stage offered another realm of freedom and escape. Mark got to know a great many gay men – and sympathetic women – through Auckland theatre groups. Robert Erwin found the Christchurch scene amenable, too. 'The Repertory Theatre provided some kind of outlet for my sexual activities, with the people who were there', he told an interviewer. 'People who were connected to it seemed to be vaguely gay.'[58] Derrick Hancock and Ron Hawley met at the same theatre in 1952.[59] They quickly became stalwarts of the Christchurch queer scene and were together as a couple until Ron's death in 2005. Theatre contacts were valuable in the smaller centres, too. William Campbell met his lover, John, in a theatre in the provincial city of Hastings, and their relationship became a sexual one during a trip to the Morere Hot Pools further up country. This was 1953: the year of the Coronation of Queen Elizabeth II, as Campbell proudly pointed out to an interviewer many years later.[60]

Figure 4 At the beach, near Christchurch, c.1959. The men show a little more flesh than their predecessors ten years earlier. Chris Brickell's collection

Figure 5 Ferrars, Lloyd, Brian, Bo the poodle and a bottle of Gordon's Gin, Scarborough, Christchurch, mid-1950s. Chris Brickell's collection

Theatricality and its correlate – drag – spanned the spectrum, from the amateur to the highly professional. Repertories and amateur theatres were somewhere on the middle of the scale. On one flank were the men who got together with their friends and dragged up at the beach or made an impression at parties. Memorable Auckland characters included 'Scotch Annie', who turned up at parties with a 'drag bag' with dress, wig and dance pumps and quickly transformed himself into a waitress, and 'Cleopatra' who danced as the famous Egyptian queen.[61] Some men offered informal cabaret acts. Derrick Hancock's pal Fred Newton took his queer friends and performed drag numbers at a Christchurch workingmen's club. Fred made himself up as Mary Martin or Ethel Merman, depending on his mood, and his rendition of 'No Business Like Show Business' was especially popular.[62]

The early 1950s were the heyday of professional drag, too, exemplified by the Kiwi Concert Party (Figure 6). This began as the New Zealand equivalent of the British 'Soldiers in Skirts' and ran in a postwar civilian guise until 1954. Queer men ably carried off the female roles, among them soprano Wally Prictor (with a 'gorgeous sense of humour, quick wit' and 'extraordinarily useful voice'), Ralph Dyer (a glamorous and accomplished dress designer) and John Hunter (with 'high heels, a clinging frock and a bust line right out of Hollywood').[63] Prictor, Dyer,

Figure 6 Members of the Kiwi Concert Party photographed during the early 1950s. Phil Jay is on the left, Wally Prictor on the right. The queer connotations were clear to those 'in the know'. AAYO 3120 2, Archives New Zealand

Hunter and their friends sang soprano, danced in the most elaborate frocks they could stitch together, and performed romantic scenes with their male co-stars. John Hunter's balcony scene from Noel Coward's 'Private Lives', performed in a stunning full-length black dress accessorised with pearls and lace, often stole the show. The female impersonators were stars. Hunter – 'the shy young man who becomes a glamorous lass on the stage' – became a household name and an advertising icon.[64] In the pages of the newspapers, under a photo that showed off his coiffed hair, mascara-ed eyelashes and reddened lips, he extolled the virtues of 'Club Razor Blades': 'I've tried all types of razor blades but have never found one to give me as smooth a shave'.[65]

This truly was queerness in plain sight. While the impersonators donned frocks and added glamour to the stage, the unquestioning 'square' (heterosexual) audiences lapped it up. Of course, the homosexual men in the Kiwis' audiences reveled in the sumptuous drag played out before their eyes and interpreted it in its queerest sense. Older men bought tickets and went along in groups, while teenagers experienced the shows during family outings. Everybody on the gay party circuit knew sassy Ralph Dyer and John Hunter – 'the belle of the Kiwis' – during the early 1950s. These lynchpins of the queer community threw house parties while they toured around New Zealand and made friends with many of the locals along the way.

When the Kiwi Concert Party broke up in 1954, its members moved on to other things. Dyer went into cabaret in Auckland, Hunter joined a touring theatre company (the New Zealand Players), and Wally Prictor returned to a retail job. While it lasted, though, the revue encapsulated the complexities of its age. It was simultaneously a public and a private phenomenon. Beyond the footlights, cultural assumptions were suspended: a man in a dress was 'just acting', and the better the act, the greater the acclaim. Stage femininity, it was assumed, ought not be confused with subcultural effeminacy. In private, however, these were pretty much the same thing, and this fact made the Kiwis' performances so appealing to queer audiences. Subculture and mainstream culture flowed backwards and forwards but, ultimately, the joke was on 'square' society.

Conclusion: the queer fifties

These were complex times. Cautionary tales, woven into broader moral panics, alerted New Zealanders to the sanctity of traditionalism, familialism and heteronormativity. Unsurprisingly, some men and women found life in the 1950s to be conformist and conservative. Writer Bill Pearson felt the disapproval of his sexuality most acutely and revealed his desires only reluctantly – even to his closest friends.[66] But this was not the same for everyone. As Nick Thomas writes of the British context, this period demands a more 'subtle and more convincing analysis' than has been advanced thus far.[67] This was a more dynamic time than we might think, a decade of new possibilities and slow transformations as well as hostile judgmentalism. Across a range of spaces and spheres of influence, some New Zealanders confounded the attempts to limit their lives, and they contributed to new social worlds in the process. More than a few married men sneaked out to queer parties, nudging the boundary between normativity and transgression.

In New Zealand – and elsewhere, as the other chapters in this book demonstrate – these were years of critical mass for the growing homosexual world. A range of urban locations – workplaces, wharves, parties, pubs and cafés – fostered patterns of association and leisure. A sustaining queer culture developed, with its rituals, symbols and shared reference points: drag (Carmen and her shawl; Hunter's 'Private Lives'), language ('Shipboard Suzy'; 'queer' and 'square') and creative and leisure spaces (department store windows, parties and bars). As the cities grew, the friendship groups of earlier decades became larger and more complex, and, as the news media coverage indicates, private cultures were increasingly visible in public spaces.

We ought not to bestow too much power to the moral panics. These were rear-guard actions in many respects. Worried doctors and indignant news reporters responded anxiously to social change, and proffered a defence against Yska's 'undertow of new cultural forces'. Ultimately, though, these new forces continued to exert their presence. Not everyone fell into line with the consensus of 'meat and two veg suburbanism', to borrow a phrase from Thomas' piece on 1950s Britain.[68] Importantly, the regulation of homosexuality was not as marked in 1950s New Zealand as it was elsewhere. There were no McCarthyist purges, no media-orchestrated witch-hunts, and a gradual loosening, rather than a tightening, of the penalties for those convicted of homosexual offences.[69] We must not ignore the legal strictures and restrictive attitudes of this small society, but still, gaily-coloured flowers managed to grow among the cracks in the social pavement.

This tension is clearly visible in the nature of the media reporting. In many ways, the moral panic reflected the expansion of queer subculture the urban centres. Many commentators saw 'queer male behaviour' as 'a contemporary urban problem', as did their British counterparts.[70] The horrified newspaper journalists whipped up a degree of public concern, that is true, but they were responding to a growing homosexual culture. In the process, the newspaper reports described a scene and a culture for their audience. Some audiences were themselves homosexually inclined and keen to see their friends' lives in print. For those just beginning to realise their feelings for other men, the newspaper articles exercised a performative function; they helped to coalesce feelings and desires into meaningful form. As John D'Emilio points out in the US context, 'political and moral conservatives unwittingly helped weld that subculture together'.[71] Moral panics and critical mass constantly rubbed up against one another.

What about queer men's resistance to the social mores of their time? It would be wrong to suggest that the urban 1950s cultures were crucibles of organised and explicit political activity. Instead, men's resistance was quiet, informal and implicit. By creating their own cultures, and defying prevailing notions of heterosexual familialism – some of the time, at least – queer men constructed spaces and identities that sustained them. They met and forged connections with those with similar interests. Some friendships and intimate relationships, like

Derrick Hancock's and Ron Hawley's, would last a lifetime. Culture-building was a form of resistance in itself and provided the seed-bed for more formal organisations in later years. Many of the 1950s men would, in turn, take part in these new endeavours.

By the end of the decade, the increasingly complex and extensive friendship networks allowed more formal kinds of organisation and paved the way for the reformist and liberationist moves of later decades. In 1962, Wellington men established the Dorian Society, a private club that a year later set up a subcommittee to challenge the illegality of sex between men. Initially known as the Wolfenden Association, after the British parliamentary committee of the same name, this was the first salvo in a campaign that eventually resulted in decriminalisation in 1986. Without the consolidation and expansion of the 1950s, this movement would not have happened. Socially and politically, the 1950s were pivotal years.

Notes

1. For instance, Deborah Montgomerie, *The Women's War: New Zealand Women 1939–45* (Auckland: Auckland University Press, 2001).
2. Michael King, *After the War: New Zealand Since 1945* (Auckland: Hodder and Stoughton, 1988), 45; Paul Millar, *No Fretful Sleeper: A Life of Bill Pearson* (Auckland: Auckland University Press, 2010), 253.
3. King, *After the War*, 45, 91.
4. Matthew Wright, *Reed Illustrated History of New Zealand* (Auckland: Reed, 2004), 368.
5. David Ausubel, *The Fern and the Tiki: An American View of New Zealand: National Character, Social Attitudes and Race Relations* (Sydney: Angus and Robertson, 1960), 6, 18.
6. James Belich, *Paradise Reforged: A History of the New Zealanders* (Auckland: Penguin, 2001), 298.
7. Bill Pearson, 'Fretful Sleepers', *Landfall*, 23 (1952), 206. On Pearson, see Millar, *No Fretful Sleeper.*
8. Pearson, 'Fretful Sleepers', 206.
9. Redmer Yska, *All Shook Up: The Flash Bodgie and the Rise of the New Zealand Teenager in the Fifties* (Auckland: Penguin, 1993), 16.
10. Nick Thomas, 'Will the Real 1950s Please Stand Up? Views of a Contradictory Decade', *Cultural and Social History*, 5.2 (2008), 227–236; Frank Mort, *Capital Affairs: London and the Making of the Permissive Society* (New Haven: Yale University Press, 2010), 4.
11. Sandra Coney and Margie Thompson, 'Signs of Rebellion against the Back-to-the-Home Movement of the 1950s: Housewife or Human Being?', in Sandra Coney, ed., *Standing in the Sunshine: A History of New Zealand Women since They Won the Vote* (Auckland: Viking, 1993), 80–81; *New Zealand Truth* (12 June 1950), 37.

12. J. Dassent, 'Rejectors of Their Sex', *NZ Woman's Weekly* (8 January 1948), 10, 37–38.
13. Oswald Chettle Mazengarb et al., 'Report of the Special Committee on Moral Delinquency in Children and Adolescents', AJHR, 1954, H-47, 7. I provide more detail of the 'Mazengarb Report' in Chris Brickell, 'Sexuality, Morality and Society', in Giselle Byrne, ed., *The New Oxford History of New Zealand* (Melbourne: Oxford University Press, 2009), 465–486.
14. *New Zealand Truth* (7 August 1956), 3 and (6 March 1956), 20.
15. See, for example, Alison Laurie, 'Lady-husbands and Kamp Ladies: Pre-1970 Lesbian Life in Aotearoa/New Zealand', PhD thesis, Victoria University of Wellington, 2003.
16. For a pioneering example of the use of oral histories, see Jeffrey Weeks and Kevin Porter, eds, *Between the Acts: Lives of Homosexual Men, 1885–1967* (London: Rivers Oram, 1998). I offer further discussion of photographs as evidence of homoerotic sociability and subjectivity in Chris Brickell, 'Visualizing Homoeroticism: The Photographs of Robert Gant, 1887–1892', *Visual Anthropology*, 23.2 (2010), 136–157.
17. Stanley Cohen, *Folk Devils and Moral Panics: The Creation of the Mods and Rockers* (Oxford: Martin Robertson, 1980), 9.
18. *New Zealand Truth* (25 August 1954), 1; (1 September 1954), 21; 22; Julie Glamuzina and Alison Laurie, *Parker & Hulme: A Lesbian View* (Auckland: New Women's Press, 1991), 84; James Bennett, 'Medicine, Sexuality and High Anxiety in Peter Jackson's *Heavenly Creatures* (1994)', *Health and History*, 8 (2006), 147–174.
19. Reginald Medlicott, cited in Glamuzina and Laurie, *Parker & Hulme*, 89. The term 'lesbian' appeared in several New Zealand newspapers during a well publicised 1936 court trial, but the extent of the term's use during the 1950s remains unclear. See Dianne Haworth and Diane Miller, *Freda Stark: Her Extraordinary Life* (Auckland: HarperCollins, 2000); Laurie, 'Lady-husbands and Kamp Ladies', chapters 6; 18.
20. *New Zealand Observer*, 'Two of Tamaroa's Crew Depart' (13 April 1949), 11.
21. *New Zealand Truth* (24 November 1955), 9.
22. *New Zealand Pictorial* (12 December 1955), 36.
23. Chris Waters, 'Disorders of the Mind, Disorders of the Body Social: Peter Wildeblood and the Making of the Modern Homosexual', in Becky Conekin, Frank Mort and Chris Waters, eds, *Moments of Modernity: Reconstructing Britain 1945–1964* (London: Rivers Oram, 1999), 134–151, esp. 139. See also Richard Hornsey, *The Spiv and the Architect: Unruly Life in Postwar London* (Minneapolis: University of Minnesota Press, 2010).
24. Garry Wotherspoon, *City of the Plain: History of a Gay Subculture* (Sydney: Hale & Iremonger, 1991), 110; John D'Emilio, *Making Trouble: Essays on Gay History, Politics, and the University* (New York: Routledge, 1995), 68.
25. *New Zealand Observer*, 'Tamaroa's Crew', 11.
26. *New Zealand Truth* (23 July 1957), 5; (30 July 1957), 5, 7; (6 August 1957), 19.
27. Chris Brickell, *Mates & Lovers: A History of Gay New Zealand* (Auckland: Random House, 2008), 203.
28. *New Zealand Pictorial* (12 December 1955), 36.
29. *New Zealand Truth* (8 June 1955), 11.
30. Scrutineer, 'The Teddy Bogey', *Here and Now* (March, 1956), 13–18.

31. Mazengarb et al., 'Report',10, 20, 29.
32. A.E. Manning, *The Bodgie: A Study in Psychological Abnormality* (Wellington: Reed, 1958), 15.
33. John Joliffe, cited in Mark Beehre, *Men Alone – Men Together* (Wellington: Steele Roberts, 2010), 224.
34. Ron Mark (pseud.), interview with Chris Brickell (18 February 2010).
35. Wotherspoon, *City of the Plain*, 155.
36. Mark, interview.
37. Wotherspoon, *City of the Plain*, 155; John Howard, *Men Like That: A Southern Gay History* (Chicago: Chicago University Press, 1999), 95.
38. Tony Stanley, 'The Life and Times of Derrick Hancock', Sociology Research Essay, University of Canterbury, Christchurch (1996) 28.
39. Mark, interview.
40. H.E. Williams, 'Homosexuality: Aspects of This Problem Aboard Ships', *Preventive Medicine Dissertation* (Dunedin: University of Otago, 1962), 41.
41. Williams, 'Homosexuality', 22.
42. Mark, interview.
43. Carmen Rupe, interview with Chris Brickell (22 March 2010).
44. Mark, interview.
45. Mark, interview.
46. William Campbell (pseud.), interview with Robin Duff, no date, Oral History Centre, Alexander Turnbull Library, Wellington.
47. Mark, interview.
48. John Croskery, interview with Gary Bedggood (1992), Oral History Centre, Alexander Turnbull Library, Wellington.
49. Croskery, interview.
50. William Campbell (pseud.), interview with Robin Duff, no date, Oral History Centre, Alexander Turnbull Library, Wellington.
51. Stanley, 'Life and Times', 28.
52. Neville Sole, interview with Tony Nightingale (2 December 1992), Oral History Centre, Alexander Turnbull Library, Wellington.
53. Sole, interview.
54. Mark, interview.
55. Mark, interview.
56. Eli Gray-Smith, interview with Chris Brickell (12 September 2005).
57. Mark, interview.
58. Robert Erwin, interview with Gary Bedggood (6 June 1992), Oral History Centre, Alexander Turnbull Library, Wellington.
59. Stanley, 'Life and Times', 20.
60. Campbell, interview.
61. Mark, interview.
62. Derrick Hancock, interview with Chris Brickell (13 January 2006).
63. Brickell, *Mates & Lovers*, 183–192.
64. Quoted in unattributed, undated newspaper clipping in author's possession.
65. Quoted in unattributed, undated newspaper clipping in author's possession.
66. Millar, *No Fretful Sleeper*.
67. Thomas, 'Will the Real 1950s', 228.

68. Thomas, 'Will the Real 1950s', 227.
69. I offer a more extensive comparison between New Zealand, Australia, the UK and the US in Brickell, *Mates & Lovers*, 266–268. In terms of punishments, the provision for flogging had been removed when the Crimes Act was amended in 1941, and hard labour was abolished in 1954.
70. Hornsey, *The Spiv and the Architect*, 26.
71. D'Emilio, *Making Trouble*, 68.

7

Warm Homes in a Cold Climate: Rex Batten and the Queer Domestic

Matt Cook

> *Home is the basis of the family, just as family is the basis of the nation*
>
> *British Prime Minister Harold Macmillian, 1952*[1]

'Home', writes Richard Hornsey, was 'one of the most contested sites in the concerted drive for social reconstruction and renewal' in Britain in the 1950s.[2] As a material place and as an ideal, it represented what could go right for the nation. It alluded to a companionate and nuclear form of family to which men and women brought their respective and highly gendered skills, and to a coming generation reared with a clear set of values aligned with respectability and good citizenship.[3] The new welfare state was based on presumptions about the tight form and functioning of this unit, further ingraining it as the obvious and ideal base for domestic life.[4] Home had long held this pivotal status in British culture, but it was given a fresh impetus in this period in ways that we can trace through novels, films, the media, popular psychology and the words of politicians, lawyers, medics and more.[5] Those without a home, those who did not take care of it, or who took care of it a little too frivolously, meanwhile, boded ill. The upsurge in discussions about the homosexual, the prostitute and the immigrant conjured these figures especially as the threatening 'others' to the 'normal' home and 'normal' family. Whilst the latter were figured as intrinsic to a civilised, modern and forward-looking culture, this threatening triumvirate was an apparent link to primitive realms and/or to earlier scandals borne of a supposedly very different city and era.[6] Retired teacher Rex Batten, the focus of this piece, wrote that for his first lover Ashley, 'the heady years of his teens when anything went...had given way to something very different. It was called normality, and that was returning with a vengeance.... His ilk had no place in the new planned economy racing headlong to Utopia.'[7]

Such powerful articulations of normal and abnormal, insider and outsider, family and non-family, homely and homeless had a very real impact on people's lives and expectations in the 1950s and have come to characterise that decade since. We do not have to dig very deep, however, before we see the extent to which they fail to map straightforwardly on to the realities of people's lives. Recently, historians have given an account of the low levels of home ownership, of the chronic housing shortage, of the shared and cramped conditions many people lived in, and of mundane everyday domestic life.[8] If people clearly paid attention to domestic fashion, to home and family, and to what they could signify, relatively few were in a position to do very much about their own living conditions or about whom exactly they lived with and alongside. It was thus in the interstices between a set of cultural fantasies and ideals on the one hand, and material realities and pragmatic circumstances on the other, that people muddled through in the everyday with varying amounts of resentment, shame, anger, fun and love.[9] And muddling through amongst them, of course, were 'queans' [*sic*], homosexuals, and queer men.[10] Far from 'stand[ing] apart' as one contemporary commentator had it,[11] these characters lived with and alongside other men and women who had similar, and also rather different, troubles and joys. 'Even the most scandalous gay lives had a domestic component',[12] observes Sharon Marcus, and these men had to negotiate the practicalities of finding somewhere to live, sustaining a home in the context of illegality, and also navigating consciously and less consciously those potent cultural fantasies of what home and also homosexuality meant.

Using home as a prism for the analysis of the queer past troubles some of the cultural separatism touted in writing from the period and in subsequent histories of homosexuality which tend to focus on the 1957 report of the Wolfenden Commission, on trials and scandals, and on exclusive clubs, downbeat pubs and notorious cottages and cruising grounds. These various events and sites were crucial in the orientation and experience of (homo)sexual subjectivity. But they were necessarily supplemented in queer experience by other less sensational happenings, by the places where men lived and had neighbours and families and interfering, supportive or indifferent landlords and landladies. So, if London was a draw for queer men in this period and seemed to offer some common experience, local and particular living circumstances once they arrived in the capital made for markedly different lives there. In this sense, home in its material reality and its freshly reinscribed cargo of meanings was key, and if queer men were rhetorically excluded from, or differentiated through, the domestic, that did not mean they were actually distant from it or its meanings. Michael Schofield – the pioneering sociologist who worked on homosexuality in the 1950s and 1960s – suggested something similar when he sketched out his research methodology: 'Wherever possible', he wrote, 'the research worker preferred to visit the contact at his home, as much can be learnt from noting his home background and he would feel more at ease in his own surroundings.'[13] Typically, Schofield presumed that home would provide clues to character and selfhood, and be a place of comfort and retreat.[14]

Though in this piece I am not seeking to read identity off the home in any direct way, I am seeking to give credence to the importance that Schofield, his homosexual 'contacts' and queer men more broadly accorded to it. I do this by tracking home in the testimony of Rex Batten who recalled his life in the 1950s in a fictionalised memoir, *Rid England of this Plague* (2006) and in an interview I conducted with him in 2010.[15] Analysing such 'evidence of experience' is a way of (cautiously) recouping aspects of queer life for which there is little material in the textual archive.[16] It is valuable for what it suggests about the 1950s and about the complex dance men like Rex had to perform in living out their daily relational, social and sexual lives. But what is especially telling in Rex's testimony is the way home is writ large in his accounts and carries multiple meanings and associations. It is, I argue, one of the key ways in which he oriented himself then and remembers that period in his life now.

Homeward bound

When Rex was 20, he moved from his family home in Dorset into his lover's house in a nearby village. He lived with Ashley (not his real name) for a year and then in the same house with his subsequent lover, John. Rex moved to London when he got a place at the Royal Academy of Dramatic Art. He and John lived first in a bedsit near Russell Square and then in another in Camden. In 1957, the couple moved into a house in East Dulwich in South East London and lived there together until John's death on Christmas Eve 1994. Rex still lives in the same house and has a new partner, also called John, to whom his novel is dedicated. Rex's account in *Rid England of this Plague* stops at the move to East Dulwich and the greater sense of security that marked the subsequent period for him, and for him and John as a couple. He took up that part of his life story more fully in interview. His account in both media, however, hinges and returns again and again to his family home in Dorset. This comes as a tacit repudiation of common narratives of homosexual becoming emerging in the postwar decade. Schofield describes theories in which dysfunctional homes – with absent or weak fathers and overbearing mothers – produced homosexual sons who subsequently distanced themselves from their families.[17] In *Rid England of this Plague*, meanwhile, concerned calls and letters from Dorset provide the key narrative markers in Rex's account of the fearful months after Ashley's arrest on indecency charges. They were 'a good accommodating family', and whilst he never 'came out' in a post-liberationist sense, and his parents never directly asked, they accepted Rex and also his relationship with John. As Heather Murray convincingly shows in her examination of familial relations between parents and their gay and lesbian children in the US in the 1950s, this pattern of support was relatively common and constructive in ways that a later generation schooled in the liberatory rhetoric of openness and visibility tended not to grasp or to see as repressive.[18] The experience of family and of the family home brace Rex's account of himself and his close ties. They represent for him some of those broadly understood values – of safety, support and retreat especially.[19] As they are figured in the novel, they also represent a time before: before London, before his brush with the law, before the drive to normalcy in the 1950s' drive to normalcy. Rex's sexual awakening when he was living with his parents was not clouded by guilt or that dangerous underworld of the city. His parents were unruffled when he moved into Ashley's cottage. In Rex's fictionalised account, this simplicity, naiveté even, was indelibly linked to 'this idyllic, quintessentially English setting' and to a pre-fifties moment.[20]

This then comes up against a new era and also Ashley's more sophisticated, urbane middle-class world and persona which Rex conjures in his novel through a rendition of his lover's cottage. Looking back, Rex identified something 'almost theatrical' about it:

> Ash's cottage, in common with all the other dwellings, had neither running water nor mains drainage, though it did have electricity and could boast a telephone. When they arrived Ash seemed far more interested in showing Tom [the Rex character in the novel] his house than getting him into bed. Tom knew only too well what cottages

> were really like to live in. He had known nothing else. A rural slum was an apt description.... Here in Lower Budleigh was another world. Tom was impressed.... The transformation Ash had worked moved the man into a realm well beyond simple sex. He had created a show-piece...the perfect recreation of the archetypal cottage that never existed.[21]

Rex marks the difference in perspective of his younger and older selves here, and conjures too his 'authentic' family home through a contrast with Ashley's mock-up of the rural cottage. The latter is surface, show and pretention, furnishing 'simple sex' with some cultural identity and identification. Ashley's interior transformation is an adjunct to, and partial articulation of, Ashley's homosexuality – and of a particular upper-middle-class and self-consciously tasteful homosexuality at that. Whilst Rex characterises his parents' home primarily through the people who live there, and so the associated emotional bonds (this is the first time we get a direct description of it in the novel), he describes Ashley's home materially and in ways which produce and frame its owner. 'The cottage', Rex writes, 'had flair and style, as did the man who lived there'.[22]

Ashley had an eye for quality and value. When he divorced, it had been the 'better pieces of furniture' he had clung to tenaciously, hiding them in a barn 'to prevent her family getting their hands on them'.[23] Rex's description of Ashley resonates with the self-depiction of Mass Observation diarist B. Charles around the same time. B. Charles – an antique collector – relished beautiful things and was proud of the way he had put his home together, comparing himself favourably on that score to his heterosexual neighbours and acquaintances.[24] Hearing of a move to instruct working-class 'lads' in 'cultural matters', B. Charles wrote 'to say that if there is any organisation in Edinburgh interested in giving working class lads instruction in interior decoration or antique furniture, I shall be pleased to receive visits from lads for chats on old furniture, etc.'[25] B. Charles and Ashley aligned themselves with a loosely queer tradition of culture, good taste and antiques in the home.[26] Richard Hornsey suggests that as a result of the upsurge in discussion and debate about home and homosexuality in the postwar period, this association had been consolidated; there was, he argues, a heightened sensitivity to the domestic signs of queerness.[27] Novelists at this time – Mary Renault in *The Charioteer* (1953), Rodney Garland in *The Heart in Exile* (1953) and Michael Nelson in *A Room in Chelsea Square* (1958) – each signalled particular and different queer types through careful descriptions of their homes. In Renault's novel, for example, the flamboyant and self-consciously modern homes of the histrionic Bunny are contrasted with the domestic simplicity and restraint of the respectable homosexual, Ralph.[28]

For Ashley, as for B. Charles, the queer tasteful domestic twist was also associated with elitism and an investment in class position. Ashley 'would casually mention country house parties in the days before the second world war', writes Rex.[29] At these parties and in these homes, queer lives were determinedly and flamboyantly classed as a cut above. At one, 'the footmen served dinner nude with their cocks and balls painted gold'.[30] There is in this a flavour of what the 1950s media feared might be going on at *louche* queer gatherings in luxurious Mayfair apartments where working-class men and guardsmen might (it was feared) be corrupted.[31] These contemporary activities and Ashley's recollections of a decadent queer past structured around class difference and decadence seemed out of kilter with postwar austerity, a new social democrat pulse and a reorientation of queer identifications.[32] Ashley's time had passed. He 'could no longer afford to mix with the real landed gentry'; 'the war had blown the smart world of the 1930s into the past'.[33] These privileged, privatised and elite domestic affiliations mark Ashley out from Tom and Michael (Rex and John) and signal his anachronism.

Tom's new boyfriend, Michael, is, meanwhile, shown in the novel to be more equal in terms of age, class and money, and the companionate domestic relationship is apparently more in tune with the new era. Michael moved into the cottage with 'no consultation' and ostensibly 'no great plans' – the move to cohabitation itself signalling the desire for a relationship with Tom (he did not want to 'risk being turned down').[34] Ashley, meanwhile, went to 'take care of his ailing widower father' and left the two younger men to it.[35] Rex characterises this time as 'a simple domestic period' with little intrusion from the outside world. He emphasises repeatedly the equality of the partnership in terms of sex and domestic chores especially, and in the novel and in interview the home is pivotal to the way Rex describes the initial and subsequent stages of their relationship. At moments of crisis, the domestic represents normality and continuity and comes as a mode of reassurance. When they received news of Ashley's arrest after their move to London:

> They both sat looking at each other not knowing what to do. "There's the washing up to finish." That prosaic domestic task seemed to break

> the tension. "You always do so well with our meals and I know it isn't easy." Michael said. Tom smiled.[36]

Further down the same page, the narrator remarks that 'both, in their different ways, had been bought up to conform'.[37] Their shared experiences and understandings of home provide a means of speaking to each other and to family, friends and neighbours about their relationship and intimacy in ways which might not have been easy to articulate directly. For Tom and Michael/Rex and John the domestic space offered a haven in which discretion was not a burden, and the unspoken was not seen as oppressive or repressive. The men were held by the benign inarticulacy of those around them and the ongoing ordinariness of the day-to-day. In the novel, when Tom returned to Dorset in the wake of Ashley's arrest, 'his mother was waiting'; 'She cooked him breakfast. His father was at work. Everything was fine. Vic wagged a welcome... [and] jumped and barked insisting he would take Tom for a walk'.[38] After their brush with the law, he turned more to his family because 'support was there without having to ask or explain'.[39] Rex and John didn't tell any of their London friends about what had happened to them; the wartime slogan 'careless talk costs lives' perhaps found new meaning and resonance for them and for queer men more broadly in the early to mid-1950s. In turn, and precisely because of this pernicious climate and the escalating arrest and prosecution rate (reaching an all-time high in 1955),[40] Tom/Rex took care not 'to put [his family] in the line of homophobic abuse'; he 'valued [them] far too highly' for that.[41] Rex speaks here and in interview of a felt need to accommodate and protect his family, and this seems relatively easy for him to do, partly because of his own domestic circumstances and his validation of home and what it represented. This engagement with the domestic and familial, which tugs against wider press characterisations of those 'evil men'[42] haunting street corners and public toilets, resonates with a 1950s reformist discourse which stressed domestic accord as a way of legitimising homosexuality. This, Hornsey, Waters and Houlbrook suggest, can be observed in Garland's *The Heart in Exile* and in Renault's *Charioteer*, and we also see it in Andrew Salkey's *Escape to an Autumn Pavement* (1959) in which the relationship between Jamaican immigrant, Johnny, and Englishman, Dick, is articulated and normalised through their co-residence and domesticity. 'We [Johnnie and Dick] took a flat in Whitcomb Street, quite near Leicester Square. We shared the rental, which was exorbitant. We cooked for each other, and when that was becoming a bore, we decided to employ a woman who'd cook our evening meal and hover over us on Sundays.'[43] In this way, their partnership is set apart from the one Johnny has with Fiona, whose 'sexuality' is 'depressing'. An agonised Dick ultimately asks Johnny to choose between him and Fiona 'for our sake, for the pleasant memories we've stored up through the months of partnership in the flat and before at Hampstead'.[44]

Safe as houses

The relationship between Johnny and Dick in *Escape to an Autumn Pavement* and the way it is conducted, first in a bedsitter house in Hampstead and then under the eye of their domestic help, reflect the local acceptance or toleration some queer men describe in that period. London's status as a city of incomers ('half the population were born elsewhere')[45] made conjunctions of difference common for those who could not afford more secluded homes. Schofield's contacts felt that 'homosexuality was regarded with greater toleration by Londoners than by many others'; 'two men living together', were, moreover, 'less noticeable among the millions of Londoners'.[46] If real caution was needed by many men (and the flip side is Schofield's statistic showing that 50 per cent of his contacts who had their own rooms felt unable to take partners there),[47] the mixed bedsit rental market facilitated, or perhaps necessitated, a strand of live-and-let-live toleration, indifference and sometimes solidarity between people living cheek-by-jowl. Alan Louis, another oral history interviewee, shared lodgings amiably, and sometimes passionately, with new Afro-Caribbean immigrants around Notting Hill and Ladbroke Grove when he moved to London in the 1950s. The area was becoming known both for its new immigrant population and for its 'large concentrations of homosexuals',[48] and there seems to have been a countercultural solidarity between the two.[49] Landladies and landlords there and elsewhere in London could, moreover, be actively supportive. Schofield found that about 10 per cent of his contacts lived in houses where the landlord was 'homosexual'; those in mixed houses, meanwhile, often found landladies and landlords to be welcoming and appreciative of the cleanliness and tidiness of their queer tenants. One described his landlady as 'a sweetie'.

> The boy in the next room was having an affair with another boy, and this boy's ex-boyfriend, if you understand me, came to the door and showed a photograph of Martin to the landlady and asked if he visited this house. The landlady said: 'sure enough he does. They're

two very nice boys. They make no secret of what they are and they're no trouble at all. They like their bit of fun the same as everyone else but they keep the place nice and clean so don't you be interfering with them. They're very respectable and have women up there and all. So be off with you.'[50]

Domestic propriety and respectability were key there, and it was in these ways that queer men might earn the support of their landlords and landladies. They tended to be less trouble than 'normal' men, who had a greater sense of entitlement.

This all resonates with Rex's experience. His first bedsit near Russell Square had a potentially tell-tale double bed (though with only one comfortable side; they took it in turns).[51] People came and went very quickly in that house, and the fact they were two men sharing brought no trouble. 'In bedsitter land who would bother to look?...who would know or care what happened next door?'[52] The landlady in Camden ejected an intolerant man upstairs, and there was a general sense of in-house solidarity here and also in the bedsits of friends.[53] The couple in the room next to Rex and John were each married to other people but lived 'in sin' – a matter of indifference to the tenants in the house but not, they felt, to the world beyond; under the weight of that pressure, the couple committed suicide.

Though in Rex's accounts, home is again figured as a place of relative safety, at the bedsit in Camden there is for Tom and Michael in the novel a similar sense of pressure and encroachment from outside – when the phone rings in the corridor, when letters are delivered, and when the police finally come knocking. Their domestic habits are shaped in part through such potential intrusion. Rex describes changing gender in signing off letters and talks of destroying photographs (as Ashley had failed to do; it was partly such evidence that had incriminated him). In the novel, Tom feels his heart sink when he spots a physique magazine on the table while the police are interviewing him. His pipe, on the other hand, apparently acted as a decoy. These were the day-to-day conventions of domestic caution for queer men in the 1950s. It was essential to be carefully attuned to such signs and also (as I suggested earlier) to keep the landlord or landlady onside. 'I seldom seem to be off my guard', wrote one of Schofield's case studies:

Even living with my friend – and neither of us go chasing others – I realise I'm in danger. It can happen in many ways. Perhaps a quarrel with the landlord and so he reports us to the police. The law must

> have an effect on all friendships and will hinder their development. If a person is on his guard, or feels insecure, he will be more difficult to live with.[54]

Rex echoes this in his testimony, and though he values a certain safety and support from his landlady and neighbours, there is still an inherent instability and uncertainty with bedsitter living. He talks about the way the couple's sex life suffered during the Camden period and of their 'escape' to the fantastical Orientalist cinema at Finsbury Park and to the high Anglican church they began to visit together. Later, in their own home in East Dulwich, 'one was safe ... because it was private, it was our home we were living in'.[55] This move to south east London marked the end of their troubles with the law, the close of the 1950s and the end of the novel.

What Rex and John sought in their East Dulwich home was the space to conduct their relationship without standing out from those around them. They 'just wanted to be accepted in the new street'. The two felt a sense of local community which did not stop at a bedsit next-door. 'It was very much a south London working class [street]', he said. Within a week, 'half a dozen bread puddings' had arrived from neighbours who doubted the ability of two men to look after themselves, and the couple were subsequently invited to local parties together. Deliberately or not, their home was not flamboyantly different from those of other postwar couples with limited disposable income. 'All the furniture when we moved in was second hand, pre-war', Rex said. They bought *Homes and Gardens*, ripped out the Victoriana ('it was old fashioned, past a joke: you did not take it seriously'), covered a door with orange formica (the new wonder substance – now removed; fashions change) and, like others of their generation, did not only use the parlour for 'best'.[56] But these innovations were part of a modern and modernising domestic fashion, and though this provided a link to what Rex (and also Richard Hornsey) identifies as a queer taste in the modern,[57] they did not constitute the kind of queer departures in interior décor flagged in Ronald Firbank's interwar novels, more parodically in Nelson's *The Room in Chelsea Square*, and in the contemporary interior design work of J. Ronald Fleming and Ralph Lamprell. Whatever local knowledge there was about Rex and John remained tacit, and only in 1967 – a full ten years after they had moved in – did they buy a double bed. 'That was a hell of a statement to make! Because everybody would know what came in..... We never had any comment about it ... we just wanted to fit in with the street, and we were accepted.'[58]

Aside from continuities with the local community, there were ongoing connections with Rex's Dorset home and village. The East Dulwich house belonged to a close family friend who had moved to Dorset, so allowing Rex and John to move in. This was not only a piece of good fortune but a sign of the importance of familial networks. That Rex had this connection might also have helped in their integration into the neighbourhood; there was a sense of continuity. Maps of his home county still hang on the wall. These west country links embraced both Rex and John, and once, when Rex visited Dorset alone, his mother berated him for not bringing John with him: 'he IS family', she had said, 'and don't you ever do that again'.[59]

Idealised homes

Whilst we can draw some obvious divisions between rural and urban life, and among the parental, bedsitter and East Dulwich homes, what is striking in Rex's testimony are the *lack* of disjunction and rather the emotional continuities between these different spaces. They each in different ways provided a sense of safety, security and reassurance, and the domestic served as a lodestone for Rex in these respects. It consolidated, articulated, and perhaps partially obscured and normalised Rex's relationship with John. They were the kind of couple addressed by the Wolfenden recommendations and the Sexual Offences Act of 1967 (relating to the permissibility of sex between two men over 21 in private) and they fitted into a refashioned postwar domestic culture which was seeing more and more (though far from all) couples living independently together. This was, Frank Mort suggests, 'a more distinct and privatised version of homosexual identity' than had been apparent, common or possible before – especially for men without much money.[60] Rex observed that 'the great thing moving here [to East Dulwich] was you had a house you could make a home out of, I think that was it, we found somewhere we could make a home. We didn't discuss it but I'm sure we felt we were both making a home'.[61] What other oral histories and Schofield's contemporary work highlights is the aspiration to this kind independent coupledom for many men in this postwar period – even if it was an actual or seeming impossibility. 'Sometimes', Schofield wrote:

> The contacts have become resigned to living alone because for social reasons it would be difficult or impossible to live with another man. A man who holds a position where he is expected to entertain business

> associates in his home would be in a difficult situation if he shared a flat with another man. A man would require courage to set up house with another who has any mannerisms, or who is known to have been arrested for homosexual offences. A man living with his parents would find it difficult to explain why he wishes to leave and share a flat with another man. Above all, the gossip of neighbors, of friends, and of people at work discourages many homosexuals from pairing up.[62]

The broader shift towards expectations (if not the realities) of companionate marriage and domestic togetherness informed the hopes of queer men and the presumptions of commentators more than ever before. This had the effect of creating single status or living alone as part of the queer tragedy whilst quiet coupledom and domesticity was the marker of success and of normalisation. Yet, as Schofield suggests, sexual, relationship and domestic lives did not necessarily converge in the way they increasingly did in later years. If in Garland's novel *The Heart in Exile,* Anthony Page and his housekeeper-turned-lover, Terry, achieve home-based togetherness by the end, this was not the usual fictional pattern. In *Escape to an Autumn Pavement,* Johnny leaves the flat he shares with Dick and walks across the West End and 'on to Piccadilly Circus. Into Piccadilly': 'Fiona was waiting. Dick was waiting. And in another way, London also was.'[63] In Gillian Freeman's *The Leather Boys* (1961), Dick, his relationship with Reggie over, rides into Ludgate Circus, where he catches sight of new potential: a young man astride a 'new and powerful motorbike'.[64] These fictional endings open the novels out to new beginnings and also take them into more familiar queer territory: the centre of the metropolis. Whatever the rhetoric and whatever the hopes and experiences of queer men, it was these spaces alongside the cottages, pubs and clubs which continued to define them more broadly and which have attracted our analytical gaze since. It was in these contexts that queer difference might be more clearly observed and charted – difference that was central to ensuing commentary on gay life and a developing associated politics. And yet, homes were spaces for self-making, too, and, I have argued here, had a key place in the emotional and aspirational lives of queer men in the first full postwar decade.

* * *

Rex and John marked their fortieth anniversary in 1990 with a stained glass window set into their front door and so into the fabric of the home they shared. The dates are there, the names are not. Only those in the know can understand their significance, and when Rex gave me permission to photograph it, he asked that I did not include the door number for fear someone might come and smash the glass. In *Rid England of this Plague,* Rex fictionalises his story, renders it in the third person, and uses pseudonyms. He thus preserves a distance between himself and the events he describes and so replays what was a felt necessity for many men in the 1950s who were queer themselves or who were writing about queer men. (Schofield, for example, initially wrote under the alias Gordon Westwood.) Rex's narrative choices differentiate his work from the confessional 'coming out' stories and AIDS memoirs of the 1970s, 1980s and early 1990s. They also resonate with the novel's themes of caution and (non) revelation; knowledge and lack of knowledge. Rex himself describes not having the language to describe himself or the subcultural 'type' he encountered as a younger man whilst at the same time 'knowing' what he wanted and was. He did not 'come out' to neighbours or his parents, but they knew and exercised those values of discretion, respectability and propriety which were, Murray argues, prized by the postwar generation and did not necessarily signify a lack of care, interest or love.[65] Such discretion was important in what was in many ways a cold climate for queer men (vividly signalled in the title of Rex's novel, a quote from the then Home Secretary, David Maxwell Fyfe). The sense of anxiety and fear that Rex documents was real and warranted. And yet, running alongside this in Rex's testimony is another set of memories: of prolific sex; of intimacy; of support; and, the clincher, of home – a pivot in Rex's sense of belonging and identity. It was, I have suggested here, a place of safety; a linking thread to a wider cultural and social imperative; and a building block and communicative tool in his relationship. It provided a connection to the outside world and a mode of achieving legitimacy within it, and yet also functioned as a place of retreat as it did for a wider public. These understandings intersect and run together in Rex's final comments in my interview with him. 'Well', he said, 'you can't buy a home, you've got to make it, ... and I think home means to me a place you can be together and you feel not cut of from the world outside but you are part of it and that great mass can do what they want outside.'[66] Rex's 'evidence of experience' brings us into close touch with the resources and identifications of one queer man and one queer couple in the 1950s. These are unique to them, but they also help us to draw out broader circulating ideas and experiences about queer affiliation, identification and aspiration – and indicate the ways in which they often cling to home, to family and to the domestic.

Notes

This chapter is dedicated to Rex Batten with sincere thanks for his time, comments and insight.

1. Cited in David Kynaston, *Family Britain, 1951–1957* (New York: Walker & Co, 2009), 54.
2. Richard Hornsey, *The Spiv and the Architect: Unruly Life in Postwar London* (Minneapolis: University of Minnesota Press, 2010), 201.
3. Kynaston, *Family Britain, 1951–1957,* 165.
4. See Hornsey, *The Spiv and the Architect*, 77.
5. On these points, see especially, Deborah Cohen, *Household Gods: The British and Their Possessions* (New Haven: Yale University Press, 2006).Sophie Leighton, *The 1950s Home* (Oxford: Shire, 2009); Shirley Echlin, *At Home in the 1950s* (Harlow: Longman, 1983).
6. Frank Mort, 'Scandalous Events: Metropolitan Culture and Moral Change in Post-Second World War London', *Representations*, no. 93 (1 January 2006): 106–137; Hornsey, *The Spiv and the Architect*, 83. Kynaston observes the 'anti-Victorianism' of post war society. Kynaston, *Family Britain*, 96.
7. Rex Batten, *Rid England of This Plague* (London: Paradise, 2006), 95.
8. Frank Mort, *Capital Affairs* 109; Kynaston, *Family Britain*, 46, 54–55.
9. Carolyn Steedman vividly captures existence at the juncture between circulating ideals and lived realities in the 1950s in her *Landscape for a Good Woman: A Story of Two Lives* (London: Virago, 1986).
10. Matt Houlbrook describes the multiple though diminishing queer identities and identifications available in the 1950s in his *Queer London: Perils and Pleasures in the Sexual Metropolis, 1918–1957* (Chicago: University of Chicago Press, 2005), part 3.
11. John Tudor Rees, *They Stand Apart: A Critical Survey of the Problems of Homosexuality* (London: Heinemann, 1955).
12. Sharon Marcus, 'At Home with the Other Victorians', *South Atlantic Quarterly* 108.1 (2009), 120–145.
13. Michael Schofield, *A Minority: A Report on the Life of the Male Homosexual in Great Britain* (London: Longmans, 1960), 3.
14. On the genesis of meanings of home in the British context, see especially: Cohen, *Household Gods,* 'Introduction'.
15. I hold the audio interview, interview transcript and release form from 2010. These are henceforth referenced as 'Rex, Interview'.
16. Joan Scott importantly problematises the truth value often accorded to such evidence; it is, though – and as she also acknowledges – too important to dismiss. Joan W. Scott, 'The Evidence of Experience', *Critical Inquiry* 17.4 (1 July 1991), 773–797.
17. Schofield, *A Minority*, 95.
18. Heather A.A. Murray, *Not in This Family: Gays and the Meaning of Kinship in Postwar North America* (Philadelphia: University of Pennsylvania Press, 2010), chapter 2.
19. Sharon Marcus and Deborah Cohen see these values inhering in the domestic especially from the mid-nineteenth century. See Sharon Marcus, *Between Women: Friendship, Desire and Marriage in Victorian England* (Princeton: Princeton University Press, 2007); Cohen, *Household Gods.*

20. Batten, *Rid England*, 65.
21. Batten, *Rid England*, 74–75.
22. Batten, *Rid England*, 76.
23. Batten, *Rid England*, 78.
24. Section of B. Charles diaries appear throughout Simon Garfield's, *Our Hidden Lives, The Everyday Diaries of a Forgotten Britain, 1945–1948* (London: Ebury, 2004). For comment on his own and others' homes, see especially 214, 400, 406, and 414.
25. Garfield, *Our Hidden Lives*, 409–410.
26. See Matt Cook, 'Domestic Passions: unpacking the homes of Charles Shannon and Charles Ricketts' in *Journal of British Studies* (forthcoming (2012)).
27. Hornsey, *The Spiv and the Architect*, 208–210.
28. See Matt Cook, 'Homes Fit for Homos: Joe Orton, Masculinity, and the Domesticated Queer', *What Is Masculinity? Historical Dynamics from Antiquity to the Contemporary World* (Oxford: Palgrave Macmillan, 2011); Horney, *The Spiv and the Architect;* and Matt Houlbrook and Chris Waters, 'The Heart in Exile: Detachment and Desire in 1950s London', *History Workshop Journal*, 6 (2006), 142–163.
29. Batten, *Rid England*, 80.
30. Batten, *Rid England*, 80.
31. Hornsey, *The Spiv and the Architect*, 99–101.
32. Houlbrook, *Queer London*, 193.
33. Batten, *Rid England*, 82.
34. Batten, *Rid England*,116.
35. Batten, *Rid England*, 108.
36. Batten, *Rid England*, 123.
37. Batten, *Rid England*, 123.
38. Batten, *Rid England*, 168.
39. This from Rex when he commented on a draft of this piece in March 2011.
40. Court cases involving sodomy, gross indecency and indecent assault had risen from 719 in 1938 in England and Wales to 2,504 in 1955. Jeffrey Weeks, *Coming Out: Homosexual Politics in Britain, from the Nineteenth Century to the Present* (London: Quarter, 1977), 158.
41. Batten, *Rid England*, 168.
42. Douglas Warth, 'Evil Men', *Sunday Pictorial*, 25 May 1952, 6 and 15.
43. Andrew Salkey, *Escape to an Autumn Pavement* (Leeds: Peepal Tree, 2009), 150.
44. Salkey, *Escape*, 211.
45. Schofield, *A Minority*, 181.
46. Schofield, *A Minority*, 180.
47. Schofield, *A Minority*, 181.
48. Schofield, *A Minority*, 181.
49. Alan Louis (interviewed by Matt Cook, 2009); see also Houlbrook, *Queer London*; Mort, *Capital Affairs*.
50. Schofield, *A Minority*, 175.
51. Rex, Interview.
52. Batten, *Rid England*, 140.
53. Batten, *Rid England*, 194–195.
54. Schofield, *A Minority*, 147.

55. Rex, Interview.
56. Rex, Interview; Kynaston, *Family Britain*, 122, 138.
57. Hornsey, *The Spiv and the Architect*, 212–213.
58. Rex, Interview.
59. Rex, Interview.
60. Mort, *Capital Affairs*, 17.
61. Rex, Interview.
62. Schofield, *A Minority*, 115–116. What the testimonies gathered by Schofield make clear is that whatever value was accorded to domesticity and to living independently with a partner or queer friend, the realities were markedly different and varied. In his sample of 127 men, Schofield found: 17 per cent of men lived in the parental home; three per cent with wives; one per cent in a hostel; 11 per cent in his own property; 29 per cent in rented accommodation in which the landlord or lady was absent; 36 per cent in rental accommodation with landlord/lady on the premises. 36 per cent lived on their own; 24 per cent lived with their own or landlady's family; seven per cent shared with men not homosexual; 32 per cent shared with other homosexuals. Schofield, *A Minority*, 178.
63. Salkey, *Escape*, 212.
64. Gillian Freeman, *The Leather Boys* (1961; London: New English Library, 1972), 125–126.
65. Murray, *Not in This Family*, chapter 2.
66. Rex, Interview.

Part III

Thinking

8
Sexology Backward: Hirschfeld, Kinsey and the Reshaping of Sex Research in the 1950s

Heike Bauer

In histories of modern sexology, the 1950s commonly figure as a point of rupture. The decade is seen to mark a shift in sexological research from the medico-forensic and gay rights debates of turn-of-the-century Europe, which had culminated in Magnus Hirschfeld's founding of the world's first Institute of Sexual Sciences in Berlin in 1919, to the large-scale studies of 'American' sexual behaviour conducted by Alfred Kinsey and his colleagues at Indiana University.[1] Critical histories of different national sexological traditions have productively examined the pre-war German and postwar American sexologies separately,[2] reflecting the fact that where Hirschfeld was concerned with the subcultural and the transgressive in studies such as *Die Transvestiten* [The Transvestites] (1910) and *Die Homosexualität des Mannes und des Weibes* (1914) [Homosexuality of Man and Woman], Kinsey, in *Sexual Behavior in the Human Male* (1948) and *Sexual Behavior in the Human Female* (1953), popularised and mainstreamed sex research by focusing on issues of the 'normal' and the average.[3] But if the postwar period is indeed the moment in which the centre of sexological knowledge production changed direction as it shifted across time and space, then this process is marked as much by its continuities with the immediate past as it is by our retrospective reading of sex research in the 1950s in terms of newness, change and anticipation. If the postwar years are today often conceptualised in relation to their future, as the period in which the 'sexual revolution' of the 1960s had not yet happened, sex research after the war was oriented as much towards the past as it was forward-looking. How, then, did Kinsey himself locate his work in relation to Hirschfeld's project? And what do their textual encounter and its reception reveal about the way in which sexual discourse in the 1950s both troubled and retained existing assumptions about male homosexuality?

This chapter turns to Kinsey's fleeting references to Hirschfeld in *Sexual Behavior in the Human Male* (1948), making them its sites of 'deconstructive contestation' – points of access to normative discourses in the past – to think afresh about the textual politics of sexology in the postwar period.[4] Prompted by recent queer scholarship which, to borrow the words of Valerie Rohy, 'has sought to explore the blind spots of historical narrative, expose the fantasies at work here, and probe the affective and figural investments that inform views of the past', my own investigation uses the postwar references to Hirschfeld to address what remains a central paradox in critical evaluations of the impact of sexology more broadly: the fact that the *scientia sexualis,* while multiplying ideas about sexuality, was also instrumental in helping to entrench new cultural expectations about gender and sexual behaviour that nevertheless retained many existing norms and stereotypes.[5] The difficulty of assessing the effects of sexology is reflected in the diversity of critical responses to Kinsey's work, which range from Lillian Faderman's point that the popularisation of the distinction between 'heterosexual' and 'homosexual'[6] supported the persecutory politics of the McCarthy era to the opposing argument that Kinsey was a 'sex crusader'[7] whose 'research and the public debates it stirred in the United States helped to legitimize discussion of homosexuality and spur the growth of a gay political movement'.[8] In a compelling recent reassessment of American sexology, Janice Irvine has further complicated the picture by shifting the focus to Kinsey's own 'refusal to take stands on political or social issues of the day', arguing that his avowedly apolitical scientific stance fashioned a particular 'white, middle-class, heterosexual' sexology.[9] My own investigation expands the boundaries of historical discussion, reading critically for debts of influence within Kinsey's work to gain a better understanding of how a transnational homophobic discourse was articulated in the postwar years in relation to the study of sex. It seeks out points of contact between Kinsey's American sex research and Hirschfeld's German sexology specifically to consider the process by which homophobic ideas are transmitted, even in projects such as that of Kinsey which overtly sought to challenge sexual norms. While Kinsey's work is undoubtedly part of a particular American discursive and social sphere, I argue that his references to Hirschfeld also provide textual markers that locate the national 'transformation of sex into discourse'[10] within what Laura Doyle and Laura Winkiel have identified as the wider 'global horizon of modernism'.[11]

Reading sexology backward

My concern with issues of intertextuality in the history of sexology is sparked by recent debates in queer, post-colonial and translation theory, which have returned the historical project to a focus on issues of language and the politics of meaning to explore further what is made to count within particular discourses of the past and present, and how this is done. Literary critic Heather Love, in her study *Feeling Backward* (2007), has made a forceful case for what she calls 'the backward turn' in queer history, proposing a new reading strategy which deliberately seeks out hitherto marginalised, 'difficult' subjects in the queer past to reassess the current boundaries of queer scholarship.[12] 'Backwardness', for Love, describes that which is 'excluded, denigrated, or superseded', and by reading for backwardness Love aims to insert what she calls 'texts that insist on social negativity' into the queer archive because they describe, in her words, 'what it is like to bear a "disqualified" identity, which at times can simply mean living with injury – not fixing it.'[13] Love's concern is with 'the relation between queer historians' (in the present) and 'the subjects of their study' (in the past).[14] But the scrutiny of 'backwardness' also draws attention to the fact that certain historical moments such as the 1950s have remained relatively unfashionable in the modern history of sexuality precisely because they sit uneasily within progressive narratives of sexual liberation. This is not to deny the homophobic damage caused in the McCarthy era, nor is my focus here on the important recuperation of the many queer lives lived affirmatively, and often collectively, in the 1950s.[15] Instead, I want to scrutinise the subtler processes of producing 'disqualified identity' through a particular kind of encounter: the textual disavowals *within* the sexological past that have slipped off the critical radar but whose effects continue to resonate to this day. I argue that Hirschfeld was a difficult subject for Kinsey, because while Kinsey saw in Hirschfeld a pioneer of sociological sex research, he rejected the homosexual focus of Hirschfeld's sexology. Indeed, as I will show, for Kinsey Hirschfeld's own homosexuality disqualified the German from scientific authority, revealing that while Kinsey made a case for apolitical scientific objectivity, his work was underpinned by his own assumptions about sexuality and science. Postwar responses to Kinsey's work in turn picked up on the conflation between Hirschfeld's sexuality and his science. This provides further insights into the role of the discourses about sexology in the constructions of homophobic discourse at the moment when Kinsey's 'American science of sex' replaced Hirschfeld's 'homosexual' 'German' sexology.

Disavowing Hirschfeld

Hirschfeld's life story serves as a poignant reminder of the close relationship between the textual and the experiential, as well as introducing the key issues with which his sexology was identified in its early phase. Born in the late 1860s, Hirschfeld began his work at a time when the *scientia sexualis* had already gained a recognisable shape in the European scientific and legal landscape, built around publications such as Richard von Krafft-Ebing's *Psychopathia Sexualis,* the first edition of which was published in German in 1886. Hirschfeld overtly politicised sexology when he entered the scene in 1896 with the publication of a pamphlet on female and male same-sex sexuality entitled *Sappho and Sokrates.* The work was followed shortly afterwards by his founding of the *Wissenschaftlich-Humanitäres Komittee* [Scientific-Humanitarian Committee], which campaigned for the decriminalisation of homosexuality in Germany, and the *Zeitschrift für Sexuelle Zwischenstufen* [Journal for Sexual Intermediaries], which provided a scholarly forum for the study of same-sex sexuality and attracted an international readership. While anchored in German contexts, Hirschfeld's work was deliberately international in outlook including collaborations such as the *World League for Sexual Reform,* over which he co-presided with Havelock Ellis and Norman Haire. In 1919, he founded the *Institut für Sexualwissenschaften* [Institute of Sexual Sciences] in Berlin, which provided a hub for international cultural and scientific exchange and attracted visits from a considerable number of homosexual men and women and other 'sexual deviants' who came assured that they would find a sympathetic reception. In disciplinary terms, the founding of the Institute marks the formal establishment of sexology. On a more personal level, it cemented Hirschfeld's reputation and public visibility. In 1930, ten years after having survived a hate attack during a visit to Munich that had left him hospitalised and mistakenly prompted reports of his death in the international press, Hirschfeld left Germany.[16] He spent the last years of his life on an international lecturing tour, which he began in the US. In May 1933, Hirschfeld's Institute was destroyed during a Nazi raid, following which most of its holdings were set alight in front of the Berlin opera house in the first of a series of public book burnings by the Nazi regime. Hirschfeld died in French exile in 1935.

It is not my concern here to unpack and critique the ways in which Hirschfeld's own thinking, despite its progressive aims, often touched on the very assumptions about gender, race and sexuality that he tried to dismantle. Instead, I want to single out the fact that he came to be seen as the figurehead of early twentieth-century sexology in discourses that in their German contexts in particular tended to conflate (his) sexology and (his) homosexuality (and sometimes also his Jewishness) to discredit each individual component. It is worth noting that Hirschfeld's American reception during his visit in 1930 and 1931 differed considerably from the tone of debate in Germany as it focused much more closely on what was seen to be Hirschfeld's expertise in 'love, romance and matrimony'.[17] Historian Vern Bullough has made the case that 'American sex research differed from that in England or on the continent [because of] its concentration on basic heterosexual problems',[18] which is supported by the newspaper reportage in 1930s North America that celebrated Hirschfeld as the 'Einstein of Sex'.[19] This public discourse may have played a role in the way Kinsey subsequently situated himself both in relation to, as well as against, his predecessor. While Kinsey himself says little about the direct influence Hirschfeld may have had on the direction of his work, it was not long after Hirschfeld's visit to the US that Kinsey refocused his research from zoology to human sexuality. What is striking is that when Kinsey subsequently turned his attention to Hirschfeld in *Sexual Behavior of the Human Male,* his words were less an echo of the most recent American discourses about Hirschfeld's work. Instead, Kinsey resurrects the pre-war German conflation of Hirschfeld and sexology in ways that align both the man and the discipline with homosexuality.

Kinsey's first real engagement with Hirschfeld appears some 600 pages into *Sexual Behavior of the Human Male* in chapter 21, entitled 'Homosexual Outlet'. 'Hirschfeld deserves considerable credit for having tried on a larger scale than anyone had before to ascertain the facts on a matter that has always been difficult to survey', writes Kinsey, affirming that there exists a positive link between their projects.[20] While the 'difficult matter' under discussion is homosexuality, Kinsey's reference to the scale of Hirschfeld's contribution emphasises their methodological connection, alluding to the fact that Hirschfeld anticipated Kinsey by pioneering the use of a questionnaire to map how homosexuality manifests within society. By Hirschfeld's own account, the questionnaire gathered information on the life of around 10,000 homosexual men and women, their families and those who surrounded them, using interviews to glean a fuller insight into what he called the 'Quelle des Lebens' [source of life].[21] Hirschfeld's introduction of this large-scale survey work had prompted the fallout between sexology and the fledgling psychoanalytic movement, as it privileged the study of larger groups over the individual case study which had hitherto been a shared source of analysis for both sexologists and psychoanalysts. Indeed, it was the questionnaire itself that prompted the break between Hirschfeld and Freud and his followers, providing an opportunity for Freud to distance himself publicly from Hirschfeld, whom he privately called a 'flabby, unappetizing fellow, absolutely incapable of learning anything' and suffering from characteristic 'homosexual touchiness'.[22]

When Freud wrote these words in a letter to Jung in 1911, sexology dominated both scientific and popular discourses of sex. In contrast, by the time Kinsey turned to sex research 'Freudianism in its American guise', to borrow the words of historian James Gilbert, 'exercised a powerful sway in the psychological community and, perhaps more importantly, flourished in simplified translation as a model explanation of sexual conduct pumping through the heart of popular culture'.[23] With this in mind, it is not difficult to make a case for why Kinsey, who competed with and was highly critical of what he considered Freud's 'dogmatic' approach to sexuality that lacked 'supporting data', would align himself more closely with Hirschfeld.[24] For despite the fact that he accused both Hirschfeld and Freud of being guilty of gathering data 'from the miscellaneous and usually unrepresentative persons who come to their clinics',[25] Kinsey clearly emphasised the link between his own work and that of Hirschfeld, stating unequivocally that 'down to the beginning of the present study no more serious attempt [than Hirschfeld's study of homosexuality] has been made'.[26]

The endorsement of Hirschfeld lends extra force to the ensuing scathing critique by which Kinsey continues his argument. Taking issue with the fact that Hirschfeld's questionnaire was aimed at identifying homosexuality specifically – rather than sexual behaviour more generally – Kinsey claims that

> the uncritical acceptance of these inadequate calculations has delayed recognition of the magnitude of the medical, psychiatric, social and legal problems involved in homosexuality, and delayed scientific interpretations of the bases of such behavior.[27]

Here we find a subtle shift in emphasis from the discussion of method to that of readership, as Kinsey suggests that Hirschfeld's work delayed sex research by causing a particular, 'uncritical' audience response which perpetuated his 'inadequate calculations' within a non-scientific sphere. This critique goes beyond the usual conventions of the sexological genre, whereby an author's acknowledgement of earlier contributions to sex research functions to stake a claim for the emerging discipline while the rejection of the specific contents of the earlier work serves to establish their own sexological authority. Instead, Kinsey's words draw an overt link between writer, text and reader, problematising the assumed intersections between textual, experiential and social spheres. In the opening pages of *Sexual Behavior in the Human Male,* Kinsey makes the case that he aims to provide an account of 'the man on the street', by 'the accumulation of a body of scientific fact that may provide the bases for sounder generalisations about the sexual behavior of certain groups and, some day, even our American population as a whole'.[28] But his rejection of an audience response in relation to Hirschfeld's work suggests that it was important for Kinsey that the 'man on the street' did not set the research agenda. This point is reinforced further by Kinsey's reference to what he somewhat dismissively calls Hirschfeld's 'Sex Institute in Berlin', arguing that the Institute is the source of, and the reason for, the fact that Hirschfeld's data is 'uninterpretable', because the patients and visitors who filled out the questionnaire do not constitute, in Kinsey's view, a representative part of society.[29] Ironically, Kinsey's later study of *Sexual Behavior in the Human Male* would be subject to similar criticism of 'methodological inadequacies', because, as one commentator argued, 'almost all [women interviewed] came from urban white collar or professional families'.[30] For Kinsey, Hirschfeld's work was bound up with assumptions about the *milieu* in which it was produced, which raises questions about his conceptualization of the sexologist. It suggests that while Kinsey may have advocated greater acceptance of homosexuality, he remained suspicious of the idea of the homosexual as scientist.

Kinsey's turn against Hirschfeld invokes Freud's earlier private dismissal of the sexologist's work on the grounds of Hirschfeld's homosexuality rather than his methodology. Kinsey's collaborator and co-author of *Sex in the Human Male,* Wardell Pomeroy, in a later account of their work supports the argument that methodology was not the main divisive factor between Kinsey and Hirschfeld because, as Pomeroy points out, their findings were in fact remarkably similar. While Kinsey's provided more varied data on homosexuality, for instance in relation to age, class and religion,[31] overall, according to Pomeroy, his findings chimed with that of Hirschfeld, whose 'famous questionnaire on homosexuality had produced an estimate of 27 per cent of such behavior in the population, not far from Kinsey's own figure'.[32] Pomeroy goes on to explain that Kinsey objected specifically to the-homosexual-as-scientist, claiming that Kinsey was 'offended by Magnus Hirschfeld's open proclamation of homosexuality – not because of the behavior, but because he thought Hirschfeld was a special pleader in his work and not an objective scientist'.[33] This helps to explain the paradoxical position Hirschfeld occupied in Kinsey's work, acknowledged both as the American's most important predecessor in the study of homosexuality and as someone who 'delayed' science because of a flawed methodology that drew its conclusions from what Kinsey believed to be a biased data base.

Kinsey's complex relationship with Hirschfeld shows, then, that here the issue was not primarily about the policing of the sexual boundaries within society, but about the establishment of particular assumptions about 'the scientist'. It makes clear that, for Kinsey, heterosexuality was both the norm and an implicit condition of scientific objectivity. This reading concurs with observations by some of Kinsey's own homosexual subjects of study who reflect on their role in his survey of homosexuality. In an oral history project by the Gay, Lesbian, Bisexual, Transgender Historical Society of Northern California conducted in 1983, historian Len Evans interviewed one of Kinsey's unofficial informants, Samuel Steward, whose account of his working relationship with Kinsey is revealing. On the one hand, Steward emphasises Kinsey's positive attitude towards homosexuality, recalling with great fondness Kinsey's 'liberating influence' and explaining that 'we [homosexuals in the 1940s and 50s] looked upon [Kinsey] as a savior. He was the liberator. He was our Stonewall'.[34] One the other hand, however, Steward also indicates the boundaries of Kinsey's work. Steward explains that he was not the only homosexual working for Kinsey but that the sexologist 'had a lot of unofficial collaborators whom he depended upon to a very large extent'.[35] Steward provides his own explanation for why these collaborators remained 'unofficial' in the sense of not being publicly acknowledged, claiming that Kinsey 'felt he couldn't have any homosexuals on his staff or officially connected with him, because he thought it would taint the study'.[36] Steward's choice of words implies that Kinsey's rejection of any official collaboration with homosexuals was not simply a response to the repressive political climate of his time but that for Kinsey the homosexual 'taint' would tarnish scientific authority.

Queer damage

Kinsey's disqualification of homosexual authority through the figure of Hirschfeld shows how what Love calls the process by which 'the history of queer damage retains its capacity to do harm in the present' is played out in the past.[37] Kinsey recycled a particular homophobic discourse of the pre-war years which discredited Hirschfeld's authority through its emphasis on the sexologist's homosexuality. Overtly, Kinsey set out to challenge norms, arguing, for example, in his later work on female sexuality that 'somehow, in an age which calls itself scientific and Christian, we should be able to discover more intelligent ways of protecting social interests without doing such irreparable damage to so many individuals and to the total social organization to which they belong'.[38] However, the encounter with Hirschfeld, even more than Kinsey's nod towards Christian America, shows up his own need to 'protect' science, making clear that while Kinsey may have been supportive towards his homosexual subjects of study, he was deeply invested in not granting scientific authority to the homosexual to speak for himself.

This kind of policing of authority causes its own kind of damage, as it reshapes expressions of homophobia in a way that allows them to return within new discourse formations. The reception of *Sexual Behaviour in the Human Male* illustrates this point through the ease by which postwar commentators similarly reverted to older assumptions about sexuality when formulating their response to Kinsey's work. Most contemporary American responses to the Kinsey reports tended to hone in on questions about the extent to which Kinsey's findings reflected accurately on the state of the American population, as well as analysing the implications of his findings.[39] Across the Atlantic, some British commentators extended the discussion specifically to allude to older debates about different national sexual characteristics. For instance, the *British Medical Journal* published an early response to *Sexual Behavior of the Human Male* in November 1948. Summarising the critique of the Report by the chairman of the British Social Hygiene Council, Fred Grundy, the article illustrates well how observers wove together complex discursive threads to dissociate their own national context from what is implicitly seen to be the excessive amount of homosexual occurrence found in the American population. Grundy agrees broadly with Kinsey's findings on homosexuality, arguing that 'much the same *pattern* would be found in this country [the UK]'.[40] However, he is quick to continue that 'the incidence of homosexual practices would probably be less'.[41] Ensuring that the point about the lesser frequency of British homosexuality (or the greater occurrence of heterosexuality in Britain) is not lost, Grundy concludes with the observation that while 'Kinsey had brought a fresh breadth of realism to the subject of behaviour', the same was 'perhaps not so much needed over here as it was in the States'.[42] Grundy's rhetoric is resonant of older discourses of national stereotyping by which homosexuality is attributed to a foreign nation, often the direct political rival (such as in the French slang term for homosexuality, *le vice allemand*). It indicates that the 'American turn' of sexology in the postwar period remained subject to pre-existing assumptions about homosexuality as a taboo from which commentators wished to dissociate themselves.

That Hirschfeld's name still had some currency in these debates is indicated by one of the first book length responses to Kinsey's work. In 1949, the London-based Falcon Press published *Sexual Behaviour and the Kinsey Report*, co-written by two Americans, Morris Leopold Ernst and David Loth. The book shifted the tone of debate from Grundy's defensive position of UK heterosexuality towards a more open attack on the 'homosexuality' of German Nazism. Ernst and Loth were influential figures: Loth was a prolific journalist and writer, while Ernst was a well-known American lawyer, most famous, according to the book's jacket, 'for his defence in cases of so-called "obscenity" in books such as Havelock Ellis's *The Psychology of Sex* and James Joyce's *Ulysses*'.[43] Ernst's contribution to the publication of these work (as well for, for example, Radclyffe Hall's *The Well of Loneliness*) in the U.S. is well-documented, as is what appears to be his somewhat paradoxical involvement in both the setting up of the National Civil Liberties Bureau and his support for the FBI as well his strong anti-communist stance.[44] Ernst and Loth celebrate Kinsey's work with patriotic pride, claiming that 'the Kinsey Report sets Americans apart. For today Americans are the only nation who have some sound scientific basis for knowing what the sexual behaviour of their men actually is.'[45] Yet, if Ernst's legal work suggests that he is sympathetic to sexual reform, supportive of the dissociation of sex from moral and other value judgements, the national framing of the discussion makes clear that he and Loth are no neutral observers on sexuality. They contrast progressive America with an old European world where, as they argue, 'the most sensational and widely reported trials for homosexual behaviour have been conducted'.[46] The examples they give are both from a German context including the Eulenburg trials of 1907, in which a journalist accused members of the entourage of Kaiser Wilhelm II of homosexuality, prompting a series of libel trials that dragged both the issue of homosexuality and Hirschfeld, who acted as an expert witness on the subject, into the German public sphere.[47] The second instance Ernst and Loth mention is what they call 'the Munich blood purge of Captain Roehm' in 1934, in which the Nazi founder of the SA was executed in an act excused by Hitler as a necessary protection of national security from Roehm's homosexuality.[48]

While the complex debates about homosexuality and Nazism clearly form part of the distinct national history of Germany, the conceptualisation of the homosexual as a threat to the nation has a transnational scope. It infamously resurfaced in North America during the McCarthy era with a report about the 'Employment of Homosexuals and Other Sex Perverts in the U.S. Government'.[49] This was presented to the U.S. Congress in the winter of 1950 and is considered the motor that drove the persecution of homosexuals in the decade that followed. Ernst and Loth to some extent anticipate these debates. For when they turn to the history of sexology, it becomes clear that their primary aim was not to critique the repressive German state but to identify the particular political danger of homosexuality. Ernst and Loth write:

> One of the great studies in sexual behaviour was that of Hirschfeld, who early in the century persuaded 10,000 men and women to fill out a questionnaire containing 130 questions. They were what he called 'psychobiological' questions, but on the basis of them and of his medical practice, he reached some conclusions about homosexuality in Germany. One of these was that in the Germany of his day, with a population of 62,000,000 there were nearly a million and a half men and women "whose constitutional predisposition is largely or completely homosexual". Just how big a proportion of his estimated million and half German homosexuals found their way into Nazi uniform is not known, of course. But a good many of them were attracted by the Nazi principles and the society of their fellows in a bond which excluded all women.[50]

The chilling change of direction in the argument, which moves from a description of Hirschfeld's 'great' work to the suggestion that 'a good many' of Germany's homosexual men would have been 'attracted by Nazi principles', illustrates the ease by which homosexuality was aligned with the abhorrent without needing further explanation. Dagmar Herzog has scrutinised the complex issues at stake in debates linking homosexuality and Nazism, both during the Nazi reign and in postwar assessments of the origin and rise of German fascism, where, as Carolyn

Dean has argued, male homosexuality was frequently equated with the formation of totalitarian regimes.[51] Morris and Loth show how easily Hirschfeld's name could still be invoked as shorthand for an old, homosexual sexology that was somehow implicated in the rise of Nazism through a discursive slight of hand, which, by foregrounding issues of homosociality, entirely ignored the fact that many sex researchers like Hirschfeld himself were Jewish and victims of the Nazi regime.

Bordering

Kinsey's references to Hirschfeld locate his work in relation to a larger discursive history which sought to disqualify homosexuality, reinforcing that we need to pay close attention to the intersections between textual, experiential and social realities in the scrutiny of the past. It is fair to say that Kinsey himself had a curious relationship with the sexological past. Unlike the founding contributors to the new *scientia sexualis* who found both in the immediate and the distant past inspiration and validation for their theoretical ventures, Kinsey largely mentions past sex research to bury it. 'There are of course', he writes in the 'historical introduction' to *Sexual Behavior in the Human Male*, 'thousands of individual sex histories in the psychiatric and psychologic journals and texts, and in hundreds of other volumes', acknowledging that 'as pioneer studies they contributed materially to the development of a public realization that there were scientific aspects to human sexual behavior, and the present-day student finds it much simpler to undertake an investigation of sex because of the influence which these older studies had'.[52] However, Kinsey overtly focuses on the limits of existing work, arguing that 'none of the authors of the older studies, in spite of their keen insight into the meanings of certain things, ever had any precise or even an approximate knowledge of what people do sexually'.[53] Kinsey's concern with developing a method of sexological research capable of capturing on paper a precise rendering of lived experience curiously evokes older, nineteenth-century models of translation which were underpinned by a similar notion of 'authenticity' through accurate transcription.[54] Translation theorist Naoki Sakai, developing further the work of Canguilhem and Foucault on the establishing of scientific norms, has recently shown what is at stake in this debate.[55] She makes the case that if we want to gain a deeper understanding of the relationship between texts and the social experience they transcribe, we need to add to discussions about the 'problem of boundary, discrimination, and classification' a focus on what she calls 'the problematics of bordering': 'the processes of drawing a border, of instituting the terms of distinction in discrimination, and of inscribing a continuous space of the social'.[56]

By deliberately privileging what appear almost incidental aspects of Kinsey's writing – his (dis)use of Hirschfeld – this chapter has attempted to make visible this complex process in relation to the postwar reshaping of sex research, showing that the 'problematics of bordering' goes beyond debates about sexual identity and identification that lie at the core of the sexological project. Kinsey himself was highly critical of binary modes of thinking, lamenting the fact that for many people, 'sexual behavior is either normal or abnormal, socially acceptable or unacceptable, heterosexual or homosexual; and many persons do not want to believe that there are gradations in these matters from one to the other extreme'.[57] In some ways, Kinsey's work seems to continue Hirschfeld's homosexual emancipation project. His observations on the frequency of homosexual practice normalise difference and in so doing seemingly contribute to a move towards greater tolerance of homosexuality within American society. However, Kinsey's dismissal of Hirschfeld's sexological authority shows up the limitations of Kinsey's own thinking, as it implies that scientific objectivity is contingent on the heterosexuality of the scientist. It makes visible how Kinsey's avowedly apolitical, future-oriented science of sex retains older assumptions about homosexuality and sexology that had first gained currency in the highly politicised debates around the institution of sex research in the earlier twentieth century. Kinsey absorbed these debates into a postwar anti-German rhetoric, paradoxically associating Hirschfeld's homosexuality with Nazism in a way that also allowed him to ignore the fact that many of the early sex researchers were Jewish. If the evidence of the damage caused here is found in brief textual encounters, its reach is much broader. It shows how homophobia was perpetuated in the scientific sphere beyond the debates around homosexual identity as Kinsey's rejection of Hirschfeld marked the 'straight turn' of sex research in the postwar years.

Notes

My thinking on this chapter was partly developed in a paper presented at NeMLA 2010 in Montreal. I am grateful to the British Academy for generously funding my speaking at this conference.

1. See, for instance, Vern L. Bullough, ed., *Before Stonewall: Activists for Gay and Lesbian Rights in Historical Context* (Binghampton: Haworth, 2002); Joseph

Bristow, *Sexuality*, 2nd edition (New York: Routledge, 2011). For an overview of sexology debates, see Chris Waters' excellent 'Sexology', in H.G. Cocks and Matt Houlbrook, eds, *Palgrave Advances in the Modern History of Sexuality* (Basingstoke: Palgrave Macmillan, 2005), 41–63.

2. Key studies of the German and North American sexologies include John D'Emilio and Estelle B. Freedman, *Intimate Matters: A History of Sexuality in America* (New York: Harper & Row, 1988); Lisa Duggan, 'From Instincts to Politics: Writing the History of Sexuality in the U.S.', *The Journal of Sex Research*, 27.1 (1990), 95–109; Janice M. Irvine, *Disorders of Desire: Sexuality and Gender in Modern American Sexology* (Philadelphia: Temple University Press, 2005); Bernd Meyenburg and Volkmar Sigusch, 'Sexology in West Germany', *The Journal of Sex Research*, 13.3 (1977), 197–209; Harry Oosterhuis, *Stepchildren of Nature: Krafft-Ebing, Psychiatry and the Making of Sexual Identity* (Chicago: University of Chicago Press, 2000); James D. Steakley, *The Homosexual Emancipation Movement in Germany* (Salem, New Hampshire: Ayer, 1975); Erwin J. Haeberle, 'Swastika, Pink Triangle, and Yellow Star: The Destruction of Sexology in Nazi Germany', in Martin Duberman, Martha Vicinus and George Chauncey Jr., eds, *Hidden from History: Reclaiming the Gay and Lesbian Past* (London: Penguin, 1991), 365–379.
3. With the exception of the recent study by Elena Mancini, *Magnus Hirschfeld and the Quest for Sexual Freedom: A History of the First Sexual Freedom Movement* (New York: Palgrave Macmillan, 2010), and Charlotte Wolff's *Hirschfeld: A Portrait of a Pioneer in Sexology* (London: Quartet, 1986), most Hirschfeld scholarship is in German, reflecting the fact that this key figure in the institution of modern sexology has become marginalised in Anglo-American histories of sexuality. In contrast, a number of works have been published in German in the last decade, including Ralf Dose, *Magnus Hirschfeld: Deutscher, Jude, Weltbürger* (Teetz: Hentrich und Hentrich, 2005); Manfred Herzer, *Magnus Hirschfeld: Leben und Werk eines jüdischen, schwulen und sozialistischen Sexologen*, 2nd ed. (Hamburg: Männerschwarm, 2001); Elke-Vera Kotowski and Julius H. Schoeps, eds, *Der Sexualreformer Magnus Hirschfeld. Ein Leben im Spannungsfeld von Wissenschaft, Politik und Gesellschaft* (Berlin: Bebra, 2004); and Thomas Mücke, *Magnus Hirschfeld* (Berlin: Bebra, 2004). Scholarly studies of Kinsey vary widely in approach, including James H. Jones, *Alfred C. Kinsey: A Public/Private Life* (New York: W.W. Norton, 1997), which portrays Kinsey as a masochistic homosexual who aims to normalise his own desires, and the recent *Kinsey: A Biography* (London: Pimlico, 2005) by Jonathan Gathorne-Hardy, which is inspired by Bill Condon's film *Kinsey* (2004) and aimed at a general audience. One stand-out study is Miriam G. Reumann's *Sexual Character: Sex, Gender, and National Identity in the Kinsey Reports* (Berkeley: University of California Press, 2005), which offers a detailed account of how sexuality debates underpinned the formation of the postwar ideology of an American national character. Feminist sociologist Liz Stanley in turn has taken the impact of Kinsey's work on British sex research as her prompt for a nuanced re-examination of population surveys throughout the twentieth century, in her *Sex Surveyed, 1949–1994: From Mass Observations 'Little Kinsey' to the National Survey and Hite Reports* (London: Taylor and Francis, 1995).
4. The expression is used by Eve Kosofsky Sedgwick in *Epistemology of the Closet* (Berkeley: University of California Press, 1990), p. 11, in an argument about the difficulties of working through 'the entire cultural network of normative

definitions' attached to the binary opposition of homosexuality and heterosexuality, categories which for Sedgwick are the fundamental 'master terms' around which modernity is structured.

5. Valerie Rohy, 'In the Queer Archive: *Fun Home*', *GLQ*, 16.3 (2010), 343.
6. Lillian Faderman, *Odd Girls and Twilight Lovers: A History of Lesbian Life in Twentieth-Century America* (New York: Penguin, 1992), 140.
7. Regina Markell Morantz, 'The Scientist as Sex Crusader: Alfred C. Kinsey and American Culture', *American Quarterly*, 29.5 (Winter, 1977), 564.
8. Roy Cain, 'Disclosure and Secrecy among Gay Men in the United States and Canada: A Shift in Views', in John C. Fout and Maura Shaw Tantillo, eds., *American Sexual Politics: Sex, Gender, and Race since the Civil War* (Chicago: University of Chicago Press, 1993), 292.
9. Irvine, *Disorders of Desire*, 20.
10. Michel Foucault, *History of Sexuality, Volume 1: an Introduction,* trans.Robert Hurley (London: Penguin Books, 1990), 61.
11. Laura Doyle and Laura Winkiel, 'The Global Horizon of Modernism', in Laura Doyle and Laura Winkiel, eds, *Geomodernisms: Race, Modernism, Modernity* (Bloomington: Indiana University Press, 2005), 3.
12. Heather Love, *Feeling Backward: Loss and the Politics of Queer History* (Cambridge, MA: Harvard University Press, 2007), 5.
13. Love, *Feeling Backward*, 5–6.
14. Love, *Feeling Backward*, 31.
15. The extent of homophobic discursivity has been explored, for instance, by Andrea Friedman who has shown that within the cultural logic of 1950s US politics, homophobia could be used as a political tool 'even against [McCarthy], one of the figures most closely associated with anticommunist and antihomosexual campaigns'. Andrea Friedman, 'The Smearing of Joe McCarthy: The Lavender Scare, Gossip, and Cold War Politics', *American Quarterly*, 57.4 (2005), 1106.
16. The *New York Times*, for instance, wrote that 'Dr Magnus Hirschfeld, the well-known expert on sexual science, died in Munich today of injuries inflicted upon him by an anti-Jewish mob' (12 October 1920).
17. Anon., 'Greatest Expert on Love to Study Romance in US', *New York American* (16 November 1930).
18. Vern Bullough, 'The Development of Sexology in the usa in the Early Twentieth Century', in Roy Porter and Mikuláš Teich, eds, *Sexual Knowledge, Sexual Science: The History of Attitudes to Sexuality* (Cambridge: Cambridge University Press, 1994), 303.
19. Anon., 'Greatest Expert on Love to Study Romance in US', *New York American* (16 November 1930).
20. Alfred C. Kinsey, Wardell B. Pomeroy and Clyde E. Martin, *Sex in the Human Male* (Philadelphia and London: W.B. Saunders, 1948), 620.
21. Magnus Hirschfeld, *Die Homosexualität des Mannes und des Weibes,* Nachdruck der Erstauflage von 1914 mit einer kommentierten Einleitung von E.J. Haeberle (Berlin: de Gruyter, 1984), iv. Translation mine.
22. Freud, Letter to Jung, 2 November 1911, in William McGuire, ed., trans. Ralph Mannheim and R.F.C. Hull, *The Freud-Jung Letters*, (London: Hogarth and Routledge & Kegan Paul, 1974), 453–454. See also Heike Bauer, *English Literary Sexology: Translations of Inversion, 1860–1930* (Basingstoke: Palgrave Macmillan, 2009), viii–xi.

23. James Gilbert, *Men in the Middle: Searching for Masculinity in the 1950s* (Chicago: University of Chicago Press, 2005), 82.
24. Kinsey et al.,–*Sex in the Human Male*, p. 207.
25. Kinsey et al., *Sex in the Human Male*, p. 34.
26. Kinsey et al., *Sex in the Human Male*, p. 620.
27. Kinsey et al., *Sex in the Human Male*, p. 620.
28. Kinsey et al., *Sex in the Human Male*, 4, 34.
29. Kinsey et al., *Sex in the Human Male*, 620.
30. Harriet Mowrer, 'Sex and Marital Adjustment: A Critique of Kinsey's Approach', *Social Problems*, 1.4 (April 1954), 147.
31. Kinsey et al., *Sex in the Human Male*, 623–659.
32. Wardell B. Pomeroy, *Dr Kinsey and the Institute for Sex Research* (London: Thomas Nelson and Sons, 1972), 69.
33. Pomeroy, *Dr Kinsey and the Institute for Sex Research*, 69.
34. Terence Kissack, ed., 'Alfred Kinsey and Homosexuality in the '50s: Recollections of Samuel Morris Steward as told to Len Evans', *Journal of the History of Sexuality*, 9.4 (October 2000), 477.
35. Kissack, ed., 'Recollections of Samuel Morris Steward', 478.
36. Kissack, ed., 'Recollections of Samuel Morris Steward', 476.
37. Love, *Feeling Backward*, 9.
38. Alfred C. Kinsey, Wardell B. Pomeroy, Clyde E. Martin and Paul H. Gebhard, *Sexual Behavior in the Human Female* (Philadelphia and London: W.B. Saunders, 1953), 21.
39. See, for instance, Leo P. Crespi and Edmund A. Stanley Jr., 'Youth Looks at the Kinsey Report', *The Public Opinion*, 12.4 (1948–1949), 687–696; Erdman Palmore, 'Published Reactions to the Kinsey Reports', *Social Forces*, 31.2 (1952), 165–172; W. Allen Wallis, 'Statistics of the Kinsey Report', *Journal of the American Statistical Association*, 44.248 (1949), 463–484. The chapters by Amanda Littauer and Kaye Mitchell in this collection explore in more detail Kinsey's role in the conceptualizations of female teen and adult sexualities and his reception within postwar U.S. lesbian communities.
40. Anon., 'Sex Behavior of the Human Male: Discussion on the Kinsey Report', *British Medical Journal*, 2.4584 (1948), 872. Emphasis mine.
41. Anon., 'Sex Behavior of the Human Male', 872.
42. Anon., 'Sex Behavior of the Human Male', 872.
43. Morris Leopold Ernst and David Loth, *Sexual Behaviour and the Kinsey Report* (London: Falcon Press, 1949).
44. See, for instance, Morris Ernst's own 'Reflections on the *Ulysses* Trial and Censorship', *James Joyce Quarterly* 3.1 (1965), 3–11; Lesley A. Taylor, '"I Made up My Mind to Get It": The American Trial of *The Well of Loneliness*, New York City, 1928–29', *Journal of the History of Sexuality* 10.2 (2001), 250–286.
45. Ernst and Loth, *Sexual Behaviour and the Kinsey Report*, 172.
46. Ernst and Loth, *Sexual Behaviour and the Kinsey Report*, 169.
47. For an account of the Eulenburg affair, see Isabel V. Hull, *The Entourage of Kaiser Wilhelm II, 1888–1918* (Cambridge: Cambridge University Press, 1982), 109–145.
48. For the complex debates about homosexuality and Nazism see Elizabeth D. Heineman, 'Sexuality and Nazism: The Doubly Unspeakable?', in Dagmar Herzog, *Sexuality and German Fascism* (Oxford: Berghahn, 2005), 22–66.

49. *Employment of Homosexuals and Other Sex Perverts in the U.S. Government.* Interim Report submitted to the Committee on Expenditures in the Executive Departments. 81st Congress, no. 241, December 15 (legislative day November 27), 1950. See Mark Blasius, Mark and Shane Phelan, eds, *We Are Everywhere: A Historical Sourcebook of Gay and Lesbian Politics* (New York: Routledge, 1997).
50. Ernst and Loth, *Sexual Behaviour and the Kinsey Report*, 170.
51. Dagmar Herzog, 'Hubris and Hypocrisy, Incitement and Disavowal: Sexuality and German Fascism', in Dagmar Herzog, ed., *Sexuality and German Fascism* (Oxford: Berghahn, 2005), 1–21; and Dagmar Herzog, *Sex after Fascism: Memory and Morality in Twentieth-Century Germany* (Princeton, New Jersey.: Princeton University Press, 2007). Carolyn Dean, *The Fragility of Empathy after the Holocaust* (Ithaca: Cornell University Press, 2004), 109.
52. Kinsey et al., *Sex in the Human Male,* 34.
53. Kinsey et al., *Sex in the Human Male,* 34.
54. See, for instance, Walter Pater's notions of translation as producing an exact copy of the original, described in his 'Introduction' to Dante Alighieri, *The Purgatory,* trans. Charles Lancelot Shadwell (London: Palgrave Macmillan, 1892), xxxvi.
55. Michel Canguilhelm, *On the Normal and the Pathological,* trans. Carolyn R. Fawcett (London: D. Reidel, 1978). Foucault's *History of Sexuality Volume 1*; and his *History of Madness,* trans. Jean Khalfa (Abingdon: Routledge, 2006).
56. Naoki Sakai, 'Translation and the Figure of the Border: Toward the Apprehension of Translation as a Social Action', *Profession* (2010), 25.
57. Kinsey et al., *Sex in the Human Female,* 469.

9

'Who Is She?' Identities, Intertextuality and Authority in Non-Fiction Lesbian Pulp of the 1950s

Kaye Mitchell

For a brief period in the 1950s and early 1960s, the subgenre of lesbian pulp fiction enjoyed enormous success in the US and, to a lesser degree, the UK, with works by the likes of Ann Bannon, Vin Packer and March Hastings selling millions of copies and spawning numerous series and imitations.[1] This chapter turns its attention to a related, but less famous, textual archive: the *non-fiction* lesbian pulp of this period – what we might term 'pulp sexology' – which exists on a continuum with mass market pulp fiction and 'proper' postwar sexology and which seems as significant for the history of lesbianism as the better-known (and arguably more easily recuperable) pulp fictions. In the 1950s, non-fiction pulps allowed current and contentious discourses about sexuality (particularly 'taboo' sexualities such as lesbianism) to be disseminated in a highly marketable, highly accessible format. Reading these texts now offers insights into an era that was less conservative and censorious – or at least more conflicted – than it is usually represented as being, as evidenced by its appetite for the new, the scandalous and the shocking (an appetite that pulp avidly stimulated and supplied). As Michelle Ann Abate argues, the existence of pulps suggests 'that the 1950s was also a decade of dissident desires and alternative value systems'.[2] Reading non-fiction pulps also reveals the significance of sexuality as a major focus of epistemological enquiry, alarmist fantasy and political paranoia in this period, and the significance of the 1950s as a crucial decade in the development of sexual knowledge and forms of sexual regulation. As the brief flowering of pulp so amply demonstrates, the narrative of the development of homosexuality between the late nineteenth and early twenty-first century is by no means one of straightforward emancipation and liberalisation; furthermore, pulp shows us that attempts at the containment and control of supposedly 'perverse' sexualities have frequently involved the most ambiguous of motives and produced the most counter-intuitive of outcomes. Ultimately, it is the very tension between mass-market motive and counter-cultural desires that make an analysis of the pulp genre so productive for examining the complexity of debates about lesbianism in the 1950s.

The non-fiction lesbian pulps of the 1950s and early 1960s presented themselves as more or less serious analyses of lesbian identity and lifestyle, employing case study type scenarios, and engaging in dialogue with the sexological and psychoanalytic writings of the early twentieth century, whilst frequently presenting their 'findings' in a recognisably lurid, salacious, pulp style and boasting covers which rendered them largely indistinguishable from pulp novels. Jennifer Terry has suggested that by the 1950s, homosexuality had become 'a national obsession' in the US, stating that, 'at that moment, the saliency of medical and scientific debates about homosexuality in society, as well as the prominence of lesbian and gay identities and subcultures, reached a critical intensity and visibility.'[3] This peculiarly (although not uniquely) American 'obsession' is marked by the popularisation – even the spectacularisation – of the discourses around sexuality, helped in part by the publicity surrounding the Kinsey reports, in part by the popularity of pulp *novels* with a homosexual theme, and in part by the increasing availability of Freud's work in English and by the consequent dissemination of forms of popular Freudianism. American sexological writings of this period are also distinguished from their European counterparts, Terry claims, by their 'valorization of individualism and identity', as will become evident in my analysis of particular works from this period.[4]

Whilst much of this pulp sexology (like the pulp novels of the period) treated lesbianism as 'A Problem That Must Be Faced',[5] to use the tagline of one work, there also existed the series of non-fiction works on lesbianism by self-identified lesbian author Marijane Meaker (author of *Spring Fire*), under the pseudonym Ann Aldrich. Like pulp novels, these non-fiction pulps are now beginning to receive some critical attention, with Martin Meeker recently claiming that such 'subjective non-fiction accounts of homosexuality' contributed to the emergence of a 'sustained and highly articulated politics of representation'.[6] In fact, I want to suggest that Aldrich's writing, like that of her male heterosexual counterparts, both installs and problematises the very notion of 'lesbian identity', and that what emerges is not anything as coherent as an 'articulated politics of representation'. In describing pulp as a 'queer and contested medium' in 'ways familiar to queer theorists', and linking this idea of queerness to the 'tensions' in Aldrich's writing, Meeker suggests that these works are possessed of an anticipatory queerness and that they can be recuperated as such.[7] Stephanie Foote, who provides the afterwords for the new editions of two of Aldrich's books, also emphasises the 'unexpected, even queer, qualities of Aldrich's work that signal to us that her moment has finally come', and praises her 'productive contradictions'; again, her 'queerness' is located in the books' refusal to cohere, stylistically or politically.[8] Indeed, Foote suggests that 'Aldrich was of her moment in her very capacity for contradiction', in her refusal 'of any unified theory of lesbian behaviour, origins, and desires';[9] in this way, Foote implies that the 1950s, an era viewed as transitional and governed by contradictions in public and private life, was more 'queer' than we might otherwise imagine. Again, I want to counsel caution in our rush to embrace works (and eras, for that matter) as 'queer' primarily on the basis of their incoherence or unintelligibility, whilst also recognising the interestingly dissonant effects of a lesbian-authored account of the 'problem' of lesbianism at this period in history.

Reading Ann Aldrich: authority and intertextuality

Aldrich produced four works in her series, *We Walk Alone* (1955), *We, Too, Must Love* (1958), *We Two Won't Last* (1963) and *Take a Lesbian to Lunch* (1972), in addition to editing a collection of extracts on lesbianism from sexology, psychoanalysis and literature, *Carol in a Thousand Cities* (1960). This last book includes extracts from her own work alongside Freud, de Beauvoir and others, suggesting that she saw her own contributions to the comprehension of lesbian identity and lifestyle as comparable to theirs.[10] I will concentrate on the first two texts, as both have been reprinted recently by the Feminist Press, using the original cover images and adding new prefaces which stress both their significance for twenty-first century lesbian readers and the 'queerness' of the original 1950s context of publication.

My title – 'Who Is She?' – is a chapter heading from *We Walk Alone*, published by pulp press Fawcett Gold Medal in 1955. As well as illustrating the form of rhetorical questioning popular in pulp sexology, this particular question foregrounds the way in which pulp sexological works attempt to establish a definition of 'the lesbian' (implying the singularity and stability of lesbian identity), and yet always fail in this attempt, instead suggesting the multiple possible manifestations and occurrences of lesbianism. So, whilst situating lesbianism as an 'aberration' or anomaly, with a definite morphology and genealogy, such works unwittingly suggest its ubiquity and diversity; whilst attempting to regulate (even 'cure') homosexuality, they arguably produce the effect of a kind of polymorphous perversity. In Aldrich's case, should we then read the suggestions of lesbianism's diversity, ubiquity and invisibility (she writes: 'I have never been able to pick a lesbian out of a crowd') as deliberate and, therefore, subversive?[11]

In pulp sexology, the tacitly masculine tools and language of 'science' are deployed; it is 'scientific' knowledge that facilitates control and social stability, with the books often casting themselves in a preventative role. Lesbianism is defined as a social issue, a matter of public – not merely individual – concern. This language of 'science' and 'knowledge' ostensibly replaces a moralising language, but the latter cannot be utterly displaced or exorcised. For example, sex scientist Frank Caprio writes in *Female Homosexuality* (1954): 'We need less moral condemnation and greater scientific understanding of human frailties.'[12] Yet, 'moral condemnation' lives on in the metaphors and motifs of 'darkness', shadows, versus 'enlightenment' or illumination, in his work. Maurice Chideckel's earlier (1935) account of lesbianism, however, is steeped in a patrician, moralising language almost biblical in its foretelling of doom for all lesbians, suggesting that there *has* been a shift – however small – in the tone and outlook of writings on lesbianism by the 1950s:

> The turbulent life of the sex pervert is doomed to defeat; condemned to eternal night, unless enlightened, analyzed and treated. Enlightenment alone can aid her in the unequal struggle between her impulses and her self....
>
> When lacking the fortitude to repress completely such [abnormal] desires her entire existence becomes a life in death, and death in life – a living sepulchre behind the thick walls of the madhouse.[13]

What does Aldrich do with such language? In this instance, does it matter 'who' is speaking? This question *'who is she?'* therefore serves a wider argumentative function in my essay, as it can be seen as applying to Aldrich herself: who she is, how she speaks, how her authority as a speaker is constituted and whom she might be speaking to and for.

What emerges from pulp sexological works of this period is a kind of hybrid and highly contradictory language; a familiarity of tone and content (even a formula), which yet exhibits a significant degree of generic incoherence and instability. The authority of the author is achieved – but also displaced and even unwittingly undermined – via a process of intertextual citation, which happens through quotation, through argument and counter-argument between and within texts, but also through manipulations (and imitations) of style and genre. Aldrich's first two books exist at the nexus of a series of texts devoted (in whole or in part) to the discussion of female homosexuality, which must be read as being 'in conversation' with each other (some being dedicated to earlier titles, some merely citing earlier titles, all employing forms of imitation and intertextuality in form, structure, style and key questions and objectives). These texts include, most prominently, Maurice Chideckel's *Female Sex Perversion* (1935), George W. Henry's *Sex Variants* (vol. 2) (1941), Donald Webster Cory's *The Homosexual in America* (1951),[14] Kinsey's *Sexual Behavior in the Human Female* (1953), Frank Caprio's *Female Homosexuality* (1954) and Edmund Bergler's *Homosexuality: Disease or Way of Life?* (1956).

We Walk Alone, in particular, is highly indebted to preceding and contemporary sexological, psychoanalytic and literary accounts of lesbianism, and little is done to distinguish between different types of material being cited, or to identify the nuances of quite contradictory arguments and approaches. In the course of the book, Aldrich cites, amongst others, psychoanalysts such as Freud, Helene Deutsch, Marie Bonaparte and Theodor Reik; sexologists including Havelock Ellis, Kinsey, Henry, Krafft-Ebing, John Addington Symonds, Caprio and Otto Weininger; ancient Greek authors and poets including Sophocles, Sappho, Homer and Horace; and twentieth-century writers and poets including Djuna Barnes, Simone de Beauvoir, Anais Nin, Lillian Hellman, Tereska Torres and George Sand. No distinctions are made between literary, avant-garde, popular/pulp, and philosophical writing, and no critical or evaluative judgements are offered. Like Caprio, who devotes a whole chapter to 'the lesbian theme in literature', Aldrich treats literary texts as authoritative sources of information about homosexuality, using fictional characters as case studies. Furthermore, she does not always acknowledge her debts, borrowing a story which is included in Caprio's *Female Homosexuality* and relating it as a hypothetical scenario of her own devising.

If Aldrich treats fictional characters as case studies, she also tends to present case study scenarios as if they are scenes in a novel.[15] She succumbs to some sensationalistic and moralising copy, for example, in her description of certain lesbian stereotypes (the butch is 'the caricature of the "she-man." Tough, trousered, and tart');[16] in her depiction of most lesbians as alcoholics and/or unhappy; in her reiteration of the 'abnormality' of homosexuality (the lesbian is 'grotesque', 'pathetic', 'a freak');[17] in her employment of the tacitly moralising light and dark imagery, and in her ambivalent, even negative endings, which emphasise loneliness and alienation as the lot of the lesbian. The first two Aldrich books end with references to lesbianism as 'the well of loneliness', an obvious allusion to Radclyffe Hall's infamously miserable 1928 novel, which itself sought to engage with sexological discourses on inversion. Aldrich describes the lesbian as 'an immature and abnormal woman' and lesbianism itself as a 'cancer', determining that 'what really makes a woman a lesbian' is 'fear':

> Fear of the "snips and snails and puppy dogs' tails." Fear of pregnancy. Fear of submission, penetration, and the possibility of ensuing rejection. Fear of the unfamiliar as contrasted with the familiar. Fear of inadequacy, and the fear of not being loved because of a seeming physical deficiency. The fear of rivalry and the fear of rejection.... Then the other members of fear's fraternity, resentment, envy, anger, and hatred, follow through in changing a normal girl into a homosexual woman. [18]

Despite her plea for tolerance, Aldrich explains, in the closing pages of *We Walk Alone*, that:

> A permissive attitude towards homosexuality in no way infers that homosexuality is a desirable condition. It simply allows those people who are in the unfortunate position of being homosexual to live without stigma, until such time as science can eradicate or cure homosexuality in the human animal.[19]

More generally, her non-fiction books are full of excitable and exclamatory direct speech, garish scene-setting and description, lurid characterisation, dramatic plot twists and other familiar pulp devices. Such devices encourage and invite a strongly affective, even physical response (shame, fear, arousal, excitement) at the expense of a more reasoned intellectual one, and in doing so they disturb the generic stability of the texts themselves.

What is enacted throughout works such as Caprio's, Bergler's, Sprague's, Cory's and Aldrich's is a battle between the authority of science and the authority of personal experience and/or confession, the case history pitted against – yet often indistinguishable from – the salacious anecdote. All of these books effect a complex negotiation between different kinds of 'evidence' and different narrative standpoints and styles. Yet, as Martin Meeker has claimed, 'with very few exceptions, mostly male, apparently heterosexual "experts" propagated a discourse that tended to pathologize lesbianism', by focusing on the 'troubled' and sensational cases.[20] What different effects are created if the 'expert' in question is female and a self-professed lesbian? Most pulp sexological works suggest that the lesbian lacks even the authority of self-knowledge, much less the authority to make pronouncements on lesbianism itself. So Caprio asserts that, 'lesbians are unable to appreciate the unconscious psychology behind [the] various roles which they assume in an attempt to gratify each other', concluding that, 'as a group [lesbians] do not understand their unconscious. Hence they find it difficult to discipline themselves successfully.'[21] Not only does the lesbian lack self-control, self-awareness and the appropriate scientific knowledge and authority, she is actually *unable to appreciate* the motivations behind her actions, as if lesbianism itself (figured as sickness by psychoanalytically inflected accounts such as this one) disqualifies one from understanding.

This makes Aldrich's narrative standpoint – and her construction of her own authority – particularly interesting.[22] From the outset of *We Walk Alone*, she places an emphasis on knowledge derived from personal experience (that is, on a kind of self-validating knowledge and authority) and on the need for such knowledge, which then becomes more than subjective. In the Foreword to *We Walk Alone*, she writes:

> This book is the result of fifteen years of participation in society as a female homosexual. It is written with the conviction that there is a sincere need and demand for further enlightenment on this subject. I am convinced that the opinions and viewpoints of the lesbian herself are as valuable in arriving at clues about her nature as are those proffered by the psychiatrist, sociologist, anthropologist, jurist, churchman, or psychologist.[23]

She asserts her right to speak for herself, and she adapts and amends the case study format to allow other queer subjects to speak for themselves. The other 'authorities' that Aldrich sets herself up in opposition to represent 'the objective "outsider"', 'the skilled professional', and yet she uses these descriptions to argue that their opinions and evidence are narrow, whilst the information that she offers – as a self-confessed 'subjective "insider"' – may 'disclose facets of the broader and more typical female homosexual life' and, importantly, may 'give voice to much of the opinion from within this group'.[24] In *We, Too, Must Love,* Aldrich reiterates her implication in the discussion, by claiming that 'As a Lesbian, I shall act as a reporter within my own group and those groups with which I am familiar.'[25]

Yet, much of her authority in the first book is, in fact, borrowed from sociologist Donald Webster Cory, who she cites as an inspiration, and who begins *The Homosexual in America* (1951) with the words:

> This book is the result of a quarter of a century of participation in American life as a homosexual. I am convinced that there is a need for dissemination of information and for a free exchange of argument and opinion on this subject. It is my belief that the observations and viewpoints of the homosexual are as essential as those of the psychiatrist, the jurist, or the churchman in arriving at any conclusions on homosexuality.[26]

If the similarities of these two openings are striking, the differences are also worth considering. Aldrich's use of the word 'enlightenment' is telling (invoking both the language of pulp and scientific discourse), and her list of relevant authorities to be consulted suggests the proliferation of material on lesbianism and of sources of viable knowledge on the subject during this period. In seeking to locate 'clues about her nature', Aldrich presents lesbianism as natural, whatever contradictory evidence concerning its inception and inculcation she may provide in the pages that follow. Whilst Cory proceeds to claim that 'I can speak for no others', Aldrich sees herself as 'giving voice' to lesbians as a group, hinting at possibilities of community-formation, despite the fact that much of the time she is a mouthpiece for the pathologising 'expertise' of precisely those authorities that she has set out to supplement or supplant. *We Walk Alone,* nevertheless, proceeds to imitate Cory's work in a number of ways, and the most obvious points of comparison include: the use of medical and psychiatric opinions and the focus on whether homosexuality can be 'cured'; the discussion of homosexuality as a 'problem', whilst asking for 'tolerance' and understanding; the suggestion of the significant scale of homosexuality (Cory asks, 'Is Our Number Legion?'); the consideration of stereotypes; the examination of subculture, bars, and the social scenes of lesbians and gay men (Cory has a chapter titled 'On the Gayest Street in Town'); and the listing of laws against homosexuality/sodomy in different states of the US, which in *We Walk Alone* takes up a full ten pages.

Annamarie Jagose argues that 'lesbian pulp sexology, like lesbian pulp fiction, has played an important part in the self-fashioning of twentieth-century lesbian identities', and she asserts that Aldrich/Meaker's self-identification as lesbian constitutes, 'a disclosure that revitalizes, rather than short-circuits, pulp sexology's generic commitment to an authoritative brokering of sexual ethnography'.[27] Certainly, Aldrich's work raises the question of whether the lesbian can be authoritative, whether sexual identity can be a basis of authority or can constitute a speaking position – or whether her 'sickness' and 'abnormality' (terms that Aldrich herself uses frequently) disqualify her from such a position. Arguably, Aldrich's disclosure and foregrounding of her lesbianism *both* qualify and disqualify her – hence the tenuousness of the authority that she wields, here. What is it to be an 'expert', or 'professional' in this context? How and where do the 'professional' and the 'personal' meet in the examination of sexual lives? Even those whom Aldrich labels as 'objective' – the sexologists and psychoanalysts – find themselves in the position of having to write defensively, to some extent: either defending the popularisation of their discourses or defending themselves against charges of obscenity. It therefore becomes necessary for Aldrich to construct her authority on the very basis of *her implication in the situation* being described: 'I have seen them and I am one of them', she writes, placing herself simultaneously within and without the group of which she writes, as a kind of intermediary.[28] At the same time, she *distances herself* via various narrative means, such as the occasional use of the second person, or the telling of stories from a narrative standpoint that is omniscient but extra-diegetic – the position of the detached observer – often aligning herself with the reader as *both* implicated and at a distance: 'Soon, these members of the circle in the square will arrive at The Dock. We will join them there later. Meanwhile, let's get a cab and head uptown.'[29]

From 'I' to 'we': readers, communities and subcultures

'Authority' in this context is not only a concern for the author; there is also the authority of the readership to take into account. Stephanie Foote has noted the publication in the fifties of 'a range of books that straddled the border between official documents meant to be read only by medical experts and popular books available to anyone'.[30] This suggests that the popularisation of sexual discourse in this period not only empowered and lent authority to the writers and disseminators of that discourse but also at least purported to hand authority (in the form of transferable knowledge and the tools of analysis and self-analysis) into the hands of 'ordinary' readers, thereby aligning them (controversially) with 'medical experts' and professionals. If 'Knowledge is Power' (as Caprio claims), then who is empowered here?[31] In the Aldrich books, I would suggest, knowledge is always tied, simultaneously and troublingly, to both empowerment *and* regulation.

Aldrich develops this idea of reader authority by including reader letters in *We, Too, Must Love* and *We Two Won't Last* and in describing the former book as a direct response to her bulging mailbag. She takes authority from correspondence with readers to validate what she is doing, but also allows her readers to 'speak back'. Lillian Faderman comments that in the 1940s and 1950s, 'lesbianism came to mean, much more than it had earlier, not only a choice of sexual orientation, but a *social* orientation as well, though usually lived covertly', adding that 'suddenly there were large numbers of women who could become part of a lesbian subculture, yet also there were more reasons than ever for the subculture to stay underground.'[32] This development of a social context for lesbianism, and a social understanding of the term 'lesbian', is neatly evidenced by Aldrich's mailbag, but her correspondence illuminates also the continuing emphasis on secrecy and shame. If *We Walk Alone* is in dialogue with recognised authorities and objective insiders, *We, Too, Must Love* speaks to (and of) readers whose responses are definitively subjective – and often dishearteningly downbeat. One writes, 'I hate what I am. ... Is there someway I can see a doctor you could give me the name of who could change me?'; a 16-year-old girl in love with an older woman laments that, 'I do not want to be a Lesbian. I know I would be very unhappy if I could not get married and be normal'; another woman confesses that, 'I am at the point of suicide' and describes herself as 'one of those transvestites that you write about'.[33] Nevertheless, and despite her typical emphasis on 'the lesbian', Aldrich's use of 'we' in her titles implies multiplicity and, more importantly, community, regardless of her emphasis on loneliness and on the near-impossibility of long-term lesbian relationships. The 'we' is here extended to include the (lesbian) reader.

Not all readers, however, were convinced by Aldrich's accounts of lesbian life. In an article entitled 'Aldrich "Walks Alone"', in the June 1957 issue of *The Ladder* – the newsletter of the 1950s US lesbian group, the Daughters of Bilitis – Aldrich's first book is described as 'controversial' and the source of much debate in a recent DoB meeting. She is accused of having 'failed to balance her more bizarre examples of Lesbianism with those who have attained adjustment and are useful, productive citizens in today's society'.[34] *We, Too, Must Love* receives a more favourable review in *The Ladder* – 'Although she includes a number of the objectionable types of Lesbians..., she also treats them with more sympathy and less malice', and the book overall is deemed to be 'more inclusive'[35] – but in Del Martin's 'Open Letter to Ann Aldrich' in April 1958, she still opines that 'you have not reached your objective. You have glossed over that segment of the Lesbian population which we consider to be the "majority" of this minority group...those who have made an adjustment to self and society'.[36] In a subsequent issue, a reader writes to congratulate *The Ladder* on their criticism of Aldrich: 'How can we censure the otherwise-uninformed public for entertaining prejudice when their only acquaintance with the Lesbian is that learned through such writers as Ann Aldrich? Reading these misrepresentations leaves me depressed for days.'[37]

The presence of such dissenting voices works against the idea of the singularity and stability of lesbian identity. If Aldrich's series of books begins with the question 'Who Is She?', then arguably she never answers that question. Jagose has noted in pulp sexology 'a certain historical or ethnographic reach whose almost encyclopedic categorization of lesbianism works against the definitive specification it seems to promise', and she goes on to suggest that 'the prolific and often contradictory information disseminated by pulp sexology never quite congeals as coherent knowledge'.[38] The contradictoriness of Aldrich's arguments and the piecemeal, uncritical nature of her intertextual borrowing bear out this point. In 1948, Kinsey had proclaimed that 'Persons with homosexual histories are to be found in every age group, in every social level, in every conceivable occupation, in cities and on farms, and in the most remote areas of the country.'[39] Caprio, disputing the idea of a 'third sex', argued that 'a homosexual component can be found in every human being. It is either expressed, repressed or sublimated', and in this he is showing the influence of Kinsey, whilst arguably working towards quite different ends.[40] Aldrich develops this point about the potential ubiquity of homosexuality in *We Walk Alone*, as she asks, 'Who is the lesbian?' and responds:

> She is many women.
>
> Look at her, and she cannot be distinguished from her more normal sisters. Test her mental development, and she ranges from feebleminded to superior. Examine her background, and she comes from the smoky slums of Pittsburgh; the exclusive homes of Oak Park, Illinois; the sprawling campuses of Cornell, Radcliffe, Michigan,

> Stephens; the boxed-in Lower East Side of New York City; the sun-baked open plains of Texas and Wyoming. Expose her to psychotherapy, and she is "undersexed" and "oversexed", man-hungry and a man-hater; an overt participant with a "girl friend", a repressed homosexual with a husband and a family; a secretary with a crush on her female boss, a divorcee with nymphomaniac tendencies, a society matron, a widower, a teen-aged high-school girl, a whore.[41]

Later, in *We, Too, Must Love*, she shows, in her gossipy treatment of distinct, but overlapping, lesbian subcultures within New York City, the way that lesbian life within a single city can vary enormously according to class, wealth and precise geographical location. In providing this picture of 'diversity', Aldrich is not subverting but rather is complying with the common formula of pulp sexology; thus, Benjamin Morse similarly focuses his 1961 account of lesbianism around such contrasting case studies as 'the college girl', 'the tomboy', 'the career girl', 'the bored matron', 'the prostitute' and 'the man hater' and in doing so reveals both pulp sexology's dependence upon taxonomic practices, and the moments when the sheer proliferation of 'types' of lesbian and causes for lesbianism renders this particular 'problem' resistant to classification and control.[42] Aldrich, I would suggest, goes a little further than her male heterosexual counterparts in conceding that 'there is no definition, no formula, no pattern that will accurately characterize the female homosexual'.[43]

The preoccupation with lesbian 'lifestyle' is not unique to Aldrich either. Caprio, for example notes that 'lesbians have special meeting places (restaurants, night clubs, taverns, bars, cafes, etc.) in almost all of the large cities in the world. They establish a secret society of their own – a sort of inner group, apart from the outer world.'[44] In a slightly later piece of pulp sexology, *Sexual Deviations of the American Female* (1965), Carlson Wade reveals both the vacuity of such anthropological generalisations about lesbian subcultures and the implicitly admonitory nature of such accounts, in his claim that, 'Lesbians flock together, shunning male company. They often engage in such activities as sun bathing or swimming. They are demonstrative and aggressive towards their partners.'[45] Arguably, the 'secret society' of lesbians takes on a less sinister aspect in Aldrich's work, allowing for a more affirmative suggestion of group identity or shared community, as she moves between bohemian Village bars and snobbish uptown cocktail parties and gallery openings, her own status and affiliations tantalisingly withheld.

Indeed, Aldrich's troubling of (lesbian) identity extends to herself. 'Who is she?' might also be read as: Who is Aldrich? She is a self-identified lesbian (but she never writes of her own affairs here). She is a pioneer historian of lesbian history and lifestyle, yet elicited a decidedly mixed response from lesbian readers in her own time (as her exchanges with the Daughters of Bilitis reveal). She is both elusive and self-mythologising (including references to her own work and publicly documenting her relationship with Highsmith), simultaneously self-aggrandising and self-hating in her pronouncements. Hidden behind a series of pseudonyms, Aldrich worked across different genres and concealed herself further behind a mass of cited and borrowed material, contradictory opinions and discordant styles and influences. There is, then, no stable or singular authorial identity to be unearthed here. Therefore, whilst the Aldrich books seem to be staking a claim for lesbian authority, they actually reveal, even revel in, the dispersal and displacement of authority; whilst they appear to be incipient expressions of a kind of identity politics (and are now being recuperated as such), they also reveal the limitations – even the impossibility – of a politics organised around sexual identity when that identity remains so very difficult to pin down.

Re-reading Aldrich in the twenty-first century

Whether such pulp sexological texts of the 1950s and 1960s are 'queer', in the twenty-first century usage of that term, is another matter and certainly the rediscovery and recuperation of such texts have significant implications for our understanding of queerness in the present. Martin Meeker's reading of Aldrich as 'queer' emerges from the various 'tensions' that he finds in her work: a tension between her 'strategies of demystifying as well as pathologising the lesbian'; her condemnation of sodomy laws yet harsh critique of certain types of lesbianism, particularly those associated with butchness and transvestism; the tension between 'strategies for preventing lesbianism and calls for its tolerance'.[46] The reader letter which Aldrich chooses to excerpt for the opening of *We, Too, Must Love* embodies this rather peculiar ambivalence, as the reader in question writes of Aldrich's first book: 'It doesn't help me, but maybe it'll keep some kid from being like me if she reads it in time, or if her folks do.'[47] Despite the generosity of her reading of *We Walk Alone* (she notes the 'subtle modulations' and 'self-possession' of Aldrich's narrative voice), Foote also points up instances of contradiction or elision, where Aldrich moves 'from a social critique to a psychological diagnosis, not pausing to connect the two'.[48] Having considered such examples, she concludes that 'Aldrich is contradictory, and there is no way to reconcile some of those contradictions' – but for Foote, this makes her an 'agent provocateur', and makes it possible 'to see the value in what she is doing'.[49] Such contradictions can be read as a product of *both* the original context (the postwar era with its numerous competing, contentious public discourses around sexuality, and with the battle for ascendancy still being enacted between morality and science) *and* of distinctly twenty-first century queer reading practices, which can serve to valorise sexual ambiguities; forms of textual and sexual unintelligibility; and feelings of loss, shame and trauma.

Jagose has noted that 'recent considerations' of pulp sexology 'range from dismissals of its scientific authority to camp reclamation', and it seems to me that both responses are misguided to some extent.[50] Such texts *are* important because they demonstrate the widespread, popular dissemination of scientific discourse around sexuality in the 1950s, and the gradual waning of religious and more obviously moralising accounts of homosexuality; they introduce new terminology and new tools of analysis and suggest that these are available to the man – or, indeed, the woman – 'in the street'; they reveal crucial social tensions and anxieties of the Cold War period – when global anxieties could be displaced upon more 'local' concerns about the movement of women into the public sphere and the increased visibility of non-heterosexual relationships; they detail also the emergence of particular subcultures based around sexual preferences and practices, subcultures which would prove vital to the later emergence of a gay liberation movement. As my reading of Aldrich has indicated, however, lesbian pulps – whether fictional or non-fictional – bear the indelible imprint of shame (both literary and sexual) and pathologisation and, as such, dismissal of them might seem by far the best option. Nevertheless, it is possible to argue, as Heather Love does, that:

> Homosexual identity is indelibly marked by the effects of reverse discourse: on the one hand, it continues to be understood as a form of damaged or compromised subjectivity; on the other hand, the characteristic forms of gay freedom are produced in response to this history. Pride and visibility offer antidotes to shame and the legacy of the closet; they are made in the image of specific forms of denigration. Queerness is structured by this central turn; it is both abject and exalted.... This contradiction is lived out on the level of individual subjectivity; homosexuality is experienced as a stigmatizing mark as well as a form of romantic exceptionalism.[51]

Pulps, more forcefully than much 'literary' writing on the subject, express and embody this structuring tension between homosexuality as 'stigmatizing mark' and homosexuality as 'romantic exceptionalism'. Their re-publication can therefore be understood as an articulation of pride (or, more pertinently, of a commercially packaged form of pride), but one made 'in the image of specific forms of denigration'. Intuitions such as Love's (and the affective turn of which they are part) may offer some explanation of pulp's popularity in the present, yet pulp sexological works such as Aldrich's reveal, above all, the availability of homosexuality – as scandal and sensation, even as shame and sickness – for commercial exploitation. Thus the original 'queerness' of these texts may lie less in their contradictions (productive or otherwise) and more in their unwitting prefigurement of a post-political, commercially-driven notion of queerness, which would emerge much later in the twentieth century.

Notes

1. Since 2000, Cleis Press (an independent queer publishing company, based in San Francisco) and the Feminist Press (of City University, New York) have produced new editions of works, including the five novels that comprise Ann Bannon's *Beebo Brinker Chronicles,* as well as the two earliest lesbian pulp novels, Tereska Torres, *Women's Barracks* (New York: Fawcett Gold Medal, 1950), republished by Feminist Press (New York: Feminist Press, 2005). and Vin Packer, *Spring Fire* (New York: Fawcett Gold Medal, 1952), republished by Cleis Press (San Francisco: Cleis Press, 2004). Lesbian pulp fiction has begun to receive critical attention from a growing number of scholars and critics, for example: Michelle Ann Abate, Michele Aina Barale, Susanna Benns, Stephanie Foote, Gabriele Griffin, Diane Hamer, Annamarie Jagose, Yvonne Keller, Lee Lynch, Judith Mayne, Christopher Nealon, Lee Server, Melissa Sky, Susan Stryker, Carol Ann Uszkurat, Amy Villarejo, Suzanna Danuta Walters and Jaye Zimet. This is despite lesbian pulp previously being dismissed as a homophobic and titillating genre by influential cultural historians such as Lillian Faderman. See Faderman's comments in *Odd Girls and Twilight Lovers* (New York: Columbia, 1991), 147. Note also her exclusion of pulp titles from her anthology, *Chloe plus Olivia* (Harmondsworth: Penguin, 1994).
2. Michelle Ann Abate, 'From Cold War Lesbian Pulp to Contemporary Young Adult Novels: Vin Packer's *Spring Fire,* M.E. Kerr's *Deliver Us from Evie,* and Marijane Meaker's Fight against Fifties Homophobia', *Children's Literature Association Quarterly* 32.3 (2007), 231–251 (p. 232).
3. Jennifer Terry, *An American Obsession: Science, Medicine, and Homosexuality in Modern Society* (Chicago: University of Chicago, 1999), 6.
4. Terry, *An American Obsession*, 10.
5. W.D. Sprague, *The Lesbian in Our Society* (New York: Tower Publications, 1962)

6. Martin Meeker, 'A Queer and Contested Medium: The Emergence of Representational Politics in the "Golden Age" of Lesbian Paperbacks, 1955–1963', *Journal of Women's History*, 17.1 (2005), 165.
7. Meeker, 'Queer and Contested', 68.
8. Stephanie Foote, 'Afterword: Ann Aldrich and Lesbian Writing in the Fifties', in Ann Aldrich, *We Walk Alone* [1955] (New York: Feminist Press, 2006), 160; Stephanie Foote, 'Afterword: Productive Contradictions', in Ann Aldrich, *We, Too, Must Love* [1958] (New York: Feminist Press, 2006), 159–185.
9. Foote, 'Afterword: Productive Contradictions', 182.
10. Meaker also produced an (auto)biographical work about her relationship with Patricia Highsmith, *Highsmith: A Romance of the 50s* (San Francisco: Cleis Press, 2003), wrote numerous pulps as 'Vin Packer' (only one of these, *Spring Fire*, is a lesbian pulp, the others are thrillers), and had a successful career as a writer of novels for young adults, using the pseudonym M.E. Kerr.
11. Aldrich, *We Walk Alone*, 6.
12. Frank Caprio, *Female Homosexuality: A Psychodynamic Study of Lesbianism* (New York: Citadel Press, 1954), ix.
13. Maurice Chideckel, *Female Sex Perversion* (New York: Eugenics Publishing Company, 1935), 322.
14. Published in the UK as *The Homosexual Outlook*, 1953.
15. As Annamarie Jagose has commented, in pulp sexology the case history 'closely resembles the novelistic and avowedly unscientific pulp fiction from which it barely distinguishes itself'. Annamarie Jagose, *Inconsequence* (Ithaca: Cornell University Press, 2002), 125. For examples of this, see Sprague, *The Lesbian in Our Society* and Frank Caprio's *Female Homosexuality*.
16. Aldrich, *We Walk Alone*, 34.
17. Aldrich, *We, Too, Must Love*, 157.
18. Aldrich, *We Walk Alone*, 24.
19. Aldrich, *We Walk Alone*, 152.
20. Meeker, 'A Queer and Contested Medium', 166.
21. Caprio, *Female Homosexuality*, 22, 305.
22. Aldrich is not the only lesbian in the postwar period to contribute to the debates around female homosexuality, whilst acknowledging her own homosexuality, nor is she the first to do so. See, for example, Jane MacKinnon, 'The Homosexual Woman', *The American Journal of Psychiatry*, 103.5 (1947), 661–664. MacKinnon announces her own homosexuality in the first paragraph of her article and, despite the generally maudlin tone of the piece ('You are always lonely'), closes with a plea for lesbians to be 'recognized as human beings instead of as material for a chapter in a book on abnormal psychology', 661, 664.
23. Aldrich, *We Walk Alone*, xiii.
24. Aldrich, *We Walk Alone*, xiii–xiv.
25. Aldrich, *We, Too, Must Love*, xiii.
26. Donald Webster Cory, *The Homosexual Outlook* [UK edition of *The Homosexual in America*] (London: Peter Nevill, 1953), xiii.
27. Jagose, *Inconsequence*, 187 n11.
28. Aldrich, *We Walk Alone*, 6.
29. Aldrich, *We, Too, Must Love*, 42.

30. Foote, 'Afterword: Ann Aldrich and Lesbian Writing in the Fifties', 166.
31. Caprio, *Female Homosexuality*, ix.
32. Faderman, *Odd Girls and Twilight Lovers*, 157. My emphasis.
33. Aldrich, *We, Too, Must Love*, 144, 149, 151.
34. Anonymous, 'Aldrich "Walks Alone"', *The Ladder*, 1.9 (1957), 16–17. All *Ladder* quotations taken from reprint (New York: Arno Press, 1975).
35. B.G. [Barbara Grier], 'Ann Aldrich Does a Re-take', *The Ladder*, 2.4 (1958), 12
36. Del Martin, 'Open Letter to Ann Aldrich', *The Ladder*, 2.7 (1958), 4. Aldrich responded by including a scathing chapter on *The Ladder* in her *Carol in A Thousand Cities* (New York: Fawcett, 1960), and more recently has spoken of her dislike for *The Ladder* in an interview with Marcia M. Gallo. See Gallo, *Different Daughters* (New York: Carroll & Graf, 2006), 66–70.
37. Letter signed 'F.L., Peace Dale, R.I.', *The Ladder*, 2.9 (1958), 24.
38. Jagose, *Inconsequence*, 124, 125.
39. Kinsey *et al.*, *Sexual Behavior in the Human Male*, 627, cited in D'Emilio, *Sexual Politics, Sexual Communities*, 36.
40. Caprio, *Female Homosexuality*, 45.
41. Aldrich, *We Walk Alone*, 3.
42. Morse, *The Lesbian*, 9, 34, 45, 55, 68, 90.
43. Aldrich, *We Walk Alone*, 6.
44. Caprio, *Female Homosexuality*, 303.
45. Carlson Wade, *Sexual Deviations of the American Female* (Chicago: Novel Books Inc, 1965), 68.
46. Meeker, 'A Queer and Contested Medium', 168, 170.
47. Aldrich, *We, Too, Must Love*, xiv.
48. Foote, 'Afterword: Ann Aldrich and Lesbian Writing in the Fifties', 176.
49. Foote, 'Afterword: Ann Aldrich and Lesbian Writing in the Fifties', 177.
50. Jagose, *Inconsequence*, 126–127.
51. Love, *Feeling Backward*, 2–3.

10

Queer Profits: Homosexual Scandal and the Origins of Legal Reform in Britain

Justin Bengry

On 25 May 1952, *Sunday Pictorial* readers awoke to dire warnings of 'male degenerates' infesting not only London's West End but even provincial centres throughout the country. So many 'normal people' had already been infected by this menace that it ceased to be simply a medical issue associated with a 'glandular disorder'. It was now a danger so potent that it threatened the very fabric of the British state. Before the war, there had apparently been over one million known homosexuals, readers were alerted, but 'both numbers and percentage have grown steeply since then'. The final instalment in the series asked who was to blame. Parents themselves, it declared, were too often 'responsible for their children growing up to be perverted'.[1]

Queer history scholars have rightfully emphasised the harm caused by press vitriol, like that of the *Pictorial*'s 'Evil Men' series. Looking to such coverage, Jeffrey Weeks has characterised the 1950s and 1960s press in particular as 'magnifiers of deviance' – objectifying and dehumanising homosexuals.[2] Similarly, Patrick Higgins describes the popular press as 'one of the most ruthless antagonists to male homosexuality'.[3] Historian Matt Houlbrook attributes escalating concern with homosexuality in the press to social and cultural instability. The 'queer', he argues, was imagined to be 'a predatory and lustful danger' who 'embodied a wider postwar crisis of Britishness'.[4] Such interpretations tend to characterise the press only as another key partner in the containment and vilification of homosexuality, but I argue here that the press treatment of queer men was more complicated and fraught. Revisiting the most infamous cases of the early 1950s affords the best opportunity to explore what motivated press coverage of queer scandal as well as to identify its political influence. So, whilst it is important to recognise a history of intolerance in the press, and also to understand the social pressures that fuelled it, materialism and capitalist motivations are a key yet under-analysed factor in this sensational press coverage.

Historians, sociologists and business scholars have all considered the intersection of homosexuality and capitalism. As early as 1980, Jeffrey Weeks asked why capitalism and sexuality were 'so inextricably linked'. Rather than the model of capitalist repression promulgated by radical sexual movements, he advocated that capitalism created certain sexual types at particular historical moments.[5] John D'Emilio also looked toward capitalism for the origins of the modern homosexual. Free labour markets, he argued, separated procreation from household economies and created a space for individuals who desired members of their own sex.[6] Later, social and cultural histories of nineteenth- and twentieth-century homosexuality identified pubs and clubs, pornography and prostitution as areas where homosexuality and commerce intersected, demonstrating a continued relationship between queer lives and capitalist forces.[7] More recent work has tended to focus on the 'discovery' of a queer market segment, newly available to advertisers and marketers with the collapse of many legal restrictions on homosexuals.[8] While this phenomenon has opened up marketing and advertising opportunities directed at queer consumers,[9] it has also highlighted the divisive and fragmentary effects of consumer capitalism on sexual minorities.[10] Unlike previous work that seeks to understand capitalism's direct effects on queer communities, I seek to complicate the relationship between homosexuality and consumer forces by identifying how material motivations also have political and social consequences.

Newspapers are consumer goods, their producers seeking methods to increase circulation and revenue. For some, relaying the scandal and titillation at the intersection of sexual aberration and criminal offence promised significant returns. Audiences followed the Sunday papers for this kind of respectable pornography, which provided lurid details of sexual abnormality decontaminated for their consumption through the inclusion of details of legal process and punishment. Press commodification of queer scandal grew so lucrative, in fact, that it contributed to the creation of homosexuality as a public issue attracting government concern and ultimately requiring state intervention. Criminalised in Britain until 1967, male homosexual acts entered public discourse in the early 1950s as never before. But the government was not solely interested in homosexual legal reform. Its initial interest was in commercial exploitation. Paradoxically, then, the profit motivations of the scandal press that both vilified and publicised homosexual desire must be considered part of the history of legal reform in Britain that led to the decriminalisation of homosexuality.

The scandal of homosexuality

In the decade leading up to the *Pictorial*'s 'Evil Men' exposé, both heterosexuality and homosexuality were entering the public consciousness at levels unimagined a generation earlier. During the Second World War, for example, concern over venereal disease made sex a point of public discussion. Particularly after the arrival of US troops in Britain in 1942, both the BBC and newspapers joined government campaigns to educate Britons about syphilis.[11] And with the publication of Alfred Kinsey's *Sexual Behavior in the Human Male* (1948), the public was further exposed to mainstream discussion of (homo)sexuality. Kinsey's report was covered widely in British newspapers, spurring a 'torrent of discussion over the next decade' that would have continuing effects on public opinion.[12] The *Sunday Pictorial* itself in fact spearheaded the public exploration of British sexuality in the press at this time. For five weeks in the summer of 1949, its series 'The Private Life of John Bull' captivated readers with findings from Mass-Observation's so-called 'Little Kinsey' survey of British attitudes toward sex.[13] Sexuality also played a significant role in postwar reconstruction. Sexual delinquency, youth sexuality (particularly female), prostitution and homosexuality were all features of medical, legal and press concerns for reconstructing gender relations, national identity and a modern state following the ravages of war.[14] New protocols were emerging for the public discussion of sexuality, which contributed to the popular press's own move toward more open, but also scandalous, coverage of homosexuality.

Douglas Warth's sensational three-part exposé of the 'homosexual problem' in the *Sunday Pictorial* scandalised readers. But it also accelerated public discussions of homosexuality in the early 1950s that would ultimately promote the movement for legal reform. As the Sunday counterpart to the *Daily Mirror*, the *Pictorial*'s decision to run the controversial series was hardly surprising. The paper had been revamped in the late 1930s by Hugh Cudlipp, then its editor, to be more populist and sensational and to appeal to a broader audience through 'earnest crusading and sense of social purpose'.[15] Cudlipp knew that the striking use of pictures and strong opinions on timely issues would fatten circulation figures. In the 1930s, this included anti-appeasement pieces criticising Prime Minister Chamberlain's foreign policy. In the 1950s, the *Pictorial* turned its attention to what Cudlipp called the last taboo: homosexuality.[16]

According to Higgins, it was Cudlipp, editorial director by 1952, who was responsible for the series.[17] 'Evil Men' ostensibly sought to draw attention to the 'conspiracy of silence' around homosexuality in postwar Britain. Cudlipp described the series as the first attempt to strip away the 'careful euphemistic language in which it had always been concealed'.[18] But this was more than a little disingenuous, and the *Pictorial*'s coverage was not primarily about casting out into the open crimes and criminals that threatened the state. As Cudlipp already knew, sensational stories sold papers. By promising to detail the sins of Britain's homosexuals, these stories could help expand circulation and advertising revenues at a key competitive moment. By 1952, the *Sunday Pictorial* was, according to Cudlipp's own memoirs, in a neck-to-neck race with The *People* for second place in the Sunday newspaper circulation stakes.[19]

The *News of the World* surpassed both by the late 1940s and early 1950s, claiming the world's highest newspaper circulation figure. By the 1950s, under the editorship of Reg Cudlipp (brother of the *Sunday Pictorial*'s Hugh Cudlipp), the paper's circulation exceeded eight million, with an estimated readership of 24 million.[20] By comparison, the *Sunday Pictorial*'s and The *People*'s circulations, though growing, remained under six million, while the respectable *Sunday Times*'s circulation remained below one million.[21] Until the 1950s, the *News of the World* focused coverage exclusively on trials and punishment, using these as an alibi to report vice, name names and ensure that press coverage of homosexuality never completely disappeared. In 1953 alone the paper covered more than one hundred trials for homosexual offences. That was a banner year, but the paper had regularly covered these offences each week for decades, even though words like 'homosexual' and 'homosexuality' rarely appeared in print.[22] Instead, it used a particular lexicon to identify the stories as homosexual. There were, for example, 'grave' or 'serious' offences; 'youths' or 'soldiers' were often implicated.[23]

With a flurry of high-profile queer trials, 1953 saw a growth in column inches as the lucrative potential of the subject became clearer.[24] Homosexual scandals and trials earned front-page headlines and extensive coverage over weeks and even months with promises of ever more lurid details.[25] Trial evidence, character backgrounds and social consequences all appeared in lengthy detail, promoting greater circulation and revenues, and increasing public awareness of the subject of homosexuality and its treatment by the judiciary. Already in January, for example, the *News of the World* latched on to the case of Labour MP William Field, charged with 'persistently importuning men for an immoral purpose'.[26] Police arrested Field following observation over two nights at lavatories in Piccadilly Circus and Leicester Square. Significantly, after its initial coverage, the *News of the World* continued to follow Field's case for the remainder of the year, devoting extensive three-column articles to it for the next two weeks. It remained a feature story throughout January as the paper relayed details of Field's trial, alleged movements and conviction on one of two charges. Ultimately, coverage only ceased with the dismissal of Field's appeal and his resignation from the Commons in October.[27] But by then, the papers had found opportunities to pursue queer stories beyond their wildest expectations.

The conviction of author Rupert Croft-Cooke on 10 October 1953, for gross indecency committed with two sailors was only the first prominent case to appear in the press that month. Found guilty on three charges, Croft-Cooke was sentenced to nine months' imprisonment.[28] Just eleven days later, the arrest of recently knighted Shakespearean actor Sir John Gielgud would throw into further relief the 'problem' of homosexuality in the early 1950s. Pleading guilty and fined £10 for 'persistently importuning male persons for immoral purposes' at a Chelsea public lavatory, Gielgud's case sparked a frenzy in the papers – the case appeared in every national and many local publications.[29] With Gielgud, coverage moved from the Sunday scandal papers to even the respected national and daily papers. The *Daily Mail* gave the case front-page coverage, asking whether Gielgud would still appear at the opening of *A Day by the Sea* the following Monday in Liverpool.[30] The *Daily Express* emphasised his prominence, noting the 267 lines attributed to his career in the 'Who's Who of the Theatre'.[31] Both recognised the import of the case, and how this scandal might be transformed into increased circulation and revenues.

Easily the greatest scandal of the year, indeed of the decade, however, was that of Lord Montagu. It began even before Gielgud's arrest, and continued through two trials across 1953 and 1954. Splashed across virtually every paper in the country, the scandal involved a dizzying cast of characters that expanded to include Lord Montagu of Beaulieu, his cousin, Michael Pitt-Rivers, film director Kenneth Hume, *Daily Mail* diplomatic correspondent Peter Wildeblood, two Royal Air Force men and a pair of boy scouts. Press interference and financial incentives characterised the case from its beginning. After Montagu had decamped to America and then Paris as charges were made, *Sunday Pictorial* correspondent Audrey Whiting found his hideout off the Champs-Élysées. Despite the conflict of interest, she protected Montagu and delayed reports until he could return to England. In exchange, he agreed to return on a Saturday, thereby giving the *Pictorial* a Sunday scoop over competitors.[32] Whiting and her editors clearly recognised the cultural resonance and commercial potential of homosexual scandal as well as the competitive advantage of breaking the story first.

Returning to England via London Airport, Montagu was arrested, charged and delivered to Lymington Magistrates' Court in Hampshire, where he was committed along with Kenneth Hume to trial at Winchester Assizes. At the first trial in December 1953, Montagu and Hume stood accused of the indecent assault of two boy scouts following an incident that August Bank Holiday at a beach hut on Montagu's estate. Montagu was further charged with what the *News Chronicle* only described as 'an unnatural offence' against one of the boys. As the privilege of the peerage to be tried by the House of Lords had only been abolished in 1948, Montagu was reportedly the first peer to stand trial for a felony before judge and jury.[33] Press coverage was extensive and left little to the imagination. On 15 November, the *News of the World* gave the trial front-page prominence, graphically detailing the evidence given by the boy scouts. A second page described medical examinations of one boy, which concluded that while conditions 'were consistent with the nature of the allegation, they were not specifically so'.[34] Naming the offence 'serious' and 'indecent', and appending details of medical examination, the *News of the World* left little doubt as to the exact nature of the alleged crime. Reports of conflicting statements that discredited the boy, and testimony from a 'forensic expert' filled newspapers through mid-December. In the end, conflicting evidence was insufficient to secure Montagu's conviction, and he was found innocent of the primary charge, the second lesser charge being held over till the next assizes.[35] By that time, however, it was not just the Sunday scandal papers that recognised the notoriety and value of the case. Even national dailies like the *Daily Mail* and the *Daily Mirror* followed the trial extensively with sensational cover features to sustain interest and promote circulation.

After Christmas, Lord Montagu recalls in his memoirs being confident of acquittal for the outstanding charge.[36] But he soon came into the public eye even more spectacularly than before. Taken from his bed at eight a.m. on the morning of 9 January 1954, Montagu, along with his cousin Michael Pitt-Rivers and friend Peter Wildeblood, was served with an arrest warrant for offences with two RAF airmen. The charges were for offences alleged to have occurred a full year before those he had been tried for just a few weeks earlier. After another trial alleging a 'decadent' dinner in Wildeblood's London flat, dancing and 'some sort of orgy' at the now infamous Beaulieu estate beach hut and further offences at Pitt-Rivers' estate in Dorset, each man was found guilty on virtually every charge. Wildeblood and Pitt-Rivers, found guilty of felonies, each received 18 months in prison, while Montagu, found guilty of a misdemeanor, was sentenced to 12 months. In one more effort to draw the consuming public to its pages, the *Daily Mail*'s 25 March cover duly announced the guilty verdict in an enormous capitalised headline.[37]

Both Lord Montagu and Peter Wildeblood have written about the press's involvement and interest in their case. Montagu's writings illuminate the lengths and expense to which the *Sunday Pictorial* went to secure its scoop of his initial arrest and trial. Peter Wildeblood, Montagu's co-defendant in the second trial, had been diplomatic correspondent for the *Daily Mail* and was familiar with the priorities on Fleet Street, which were guided by men he termed 'cold-eyed ... businessmen who peddled tragedy, sensation and heartbreak as casually as though they were cartloads of cabbages or bags of cement'.[38] As an insider, as well as both 'hunter' and 'hunted', he had sympathy for reporters. It was the proprietors and editors, Wildeblood contended, who peddled the lucrative combination of sensation and scandal even 'while protesting that they are shocked by what they have to print'.[39]

As Wildeblood recognised, publications also relied on articles that denounced scandal itself to further promote their own coverage while condemning competitors. Even before the cases of Gielgud and Montagu broke in October 1953, press commentators were already decrying the commercial exploitation of sex, queer scandal and press sensationalism. Denunciation of competitors' strategic and calculated exploitation of homosexuality was itself often little more than an excuse to further profit from the titillation of sex. This parallel dialogue explicitly identifies and describes editors' awareness of the lucrative potential of sex and queer scandal. In August 1953, the *Sunday Express*'s John Gordon bemoaned the 'brothel journalism' found in Britain's Sunday press.[40] Described by historian Jeffrey Weeks as one of the paper's 'men of all prejudice' for his hostility to homosexuality, Gordon's rage extended to almost any discussion of sex.[41] Gordon condemned competitors for their 'skillful handling of type, headlines, and layout' to emphasise salacity, even as his own article headline, 'Our Sex-Sodden Newspapers', was itself highlighted in large, capitalised and italicised text. He further railed against competitors who exploited the 'powerful sales stimulant' of sex, which the *Express* – he claimed – avoided.

Gordon did not explicitly reference homosexuality in his diatribe against the 'wallowing' and 'unrestrained glee' that competitors found in their 'cesspool of sex', but the *Daily Mirror* was only too happy to bring homosexuality into the debate in its rejoinder against him.[42] It dismissed accusations of sensationalism and exploitation of sex as 'nonsense' and 'hypocrisy'. And in a cover feature, the paper indicted John Gordon for his own hypocrisy. It charged that after condemning competing papers, he went on just three months later 'with the candour he condemned in others' to rouse the nation against homosexuality. The *Daily Mirror* disputed the financial incentive behind homosexual features as 'rubbish', adding that the *Pictorial*'s 'Evil Men' series had actually threatened circulation figures. This position is hardly surprisingly considering the *Mirror*'s extensive coverage of the ongoing Montagu trial and other articles that kept sex in the public eye. Just five days earlier, in fact, the *Mirror* had defended its coverage of homosexuality for 'serious people' who were 'now waking up to demand action' on the homosexual problem.[43] Proclaiming to act in the public good, the *Mirror* sought further to distance itself from commercial considerations asking whether authorities would now take action.

In November 1953, *The News of the World* also struck back against accusations of sensationalism. It dismissed Gordon's 'pious resolutions', adding that 'Only the searchlight of public opinion will reveal the extent of the evil in our midst'.[44] But perhaps the spate of recent accusations of sensationalism and its economic incentives had come too close to the truth. Vehement protestations from *The News of the World* and others suggest just how important such sensationalist stories were to publications. But they also perpetuated a public dialogue on the volume and detail of press coverage of homosexuality,[45] which continued to present homosexuality as an increasingly urgent public issue, one that was soon taken up by critics of and within the government.

The sensational origins of the Wolfenden Committee

By 1954, interest in homosexuality had grown further, and Winston Churchill's Conservative government was called to act on multiple fronts. Some critics wanted immediate legal reform; others sought stricter enforcement of prohibitions against homosexuality. There were also demands for a royal commission to investigate either the role of the press in publicising homosexuality or the effectiveness of existing homosexual criminal law in addressing it. Churchill responded by convening the Wolfenden Committee (a departmental committee as distinguished from a royal commission) to review the law and practice relating to homosexual offences and prostitution in August.[46] According to the standard narrative, concern with the unequal application of the law, and particularly its attack on prominent men, was the catalyst that finally pushed the government to action. The origins of the committee extended back through the previous year, however, and actually cohered first around concerns with press exploitation of homosexual scandal described above. Even in mid-1953, before the most scandalous stories broke, concerns about extensive and sensationalist press coverage already converged with calls for an official inquiry.

In June 1953, Dr Donald Soper, President of the Methodist Conference, was among the earliest calling for government action to address the exploitation of homosexual scandal by the press. He called for a royal commission into the 'publicity and sensation' that could exaggerate the 'problem' and scope of homosexuality.[47] Sir David Maxwell-Fyfe, Churchill's Home Secretary, felt much the same about dangers of press coverage. In a November speech to the Coningsby Club, a Conservative society for Oxford and Cambridge graduates, Maxwell-Fyfe spoke to the treatment and imprisonment of homosexual offenders. He also elaborated his concerns about press coverage of homosexual vice and crime, arguing that, 'there can be little doubt that their extent depends in some measure on the degree of publicity which is given to them, whether this be by way of condonation or condemnation'.[48] For the Home Secretary, any press attention to homosexuality, whether capitalising on the scandal of high-profile trials and urban vice or advocating reasoned examination of the subject and legal reform, was equally dangerous. His twin concerns of press coverage and incarceration were already apparent.

The question of homosexual legal reform soon entered Parliament, and illustrated how concerns over lucrative press coverage and legal reform comingled. On 3 December 1953, MPs Sir Robert Boothby and Desmond Donnelly called on the government to establish a royal commission to examine laws on sexual offences with particular regard to homosexuality.[49] They wanted the law on homosexuality to be brought into line with prevailing medical opinion. By February 1954, Labor MP George Craddock, however, remained most concerned about the press. He demanded the Home Department call a commission, which would 'inquire into the danger to public morale caused by wide publicity in the Press of gross and unnecessary details in cases of homosexuality ...'[50] For observers like Craddock, the press's interest in homosexuality went far beyond its traditional remit of investigation. It crossed the line to prurient exploitation. Responding to Craddock, Sir David Maxwell-Fyfe did not believe that a committee to examine 'this one aspect of the problem' would be justified. But it would remain, nonetheless, a feature of cabinet-level interest that combined concern with extensive press coverage of homosexual scandal with the issue of legal reform.

The day before Craddock voiced his demands in the House, Maxwell-Fyfe had forwarded a secret memorandum to the Cabinet detailing his concerns on the law and the press. Citing 'serious increases' in offences, Maxwell-Fyfe disputed the position that existing law was 'antiquated and out of harmony with modern knowledge and ideas', concluding there was no case for altering the law.[51] Maxwell-Fyfe instead believed that the focus should be upon improving the 'facilities for the treatment of homosexuals sentenced by the courts', in other words incarceration. Expanding medical or psychological treatment facilities were unnecessary, he believed, because 'only a minority of homosexual offenders are likely to benefit by psychiatric treatment', and that could be adequately provided in prisons.[52] The Home Secretary had never been shy in publicising his opinion that the best place for homosexual offenders was in prison. The previous month, in the Coningsby speech, he also highlighted these views, concluding that, 'to put it at its lowest, even if imprisonment fails to secure any improvement in the homosexual's character and behaviour, it serves to protect the public by the segregation of the offender'.[53] For him, legal reform was undesirable because the important question was not the treatment of homosexual offenders as he implied, but rather the protection society from them. This concern to 'protect' regularly overlapped with the danger posed by press exploitation.

The Home Secretary also introduced the subject of an inquiry into homosexuality in the secret memorandum. Even as public opinion showed growing support for some form of inquiry, Maxwell-Fyfe was nonetheless anxious that a commission might 'expose us to the danger of receiving embarrassing recommendations for altering the law'. But given the fact that the Home Secretary already advocated an inquiry into prostitution, he worried that Churchill's government could be open to criticism if it were to fail to address the question of homosexual offences as well. Significantly, Maxwell-Fyfe's concluding justification for calling an inquiry was its 'value in educating public opinion, which at present is ill-informed and apt to be misled by sensational articles in the press'. Once again, the volume and circulation of press accounts of homosexual scandal were key features in government debate and policy.

When the Cabinet met eight days later to discuss Maxwell-Fyfe's request, it was divided as to how to proceed. Churchill voiced concern that the 'Tory Party won't want to accept responsibility for making [the] law on homosexuality more lenient...'[54] Reaffirming the link between homosexual legal reform and the role of the scandal press, he asked whether the press's publicising of homosexuality could somehow be limited. One possibility was a private member's bill that could allow discussion but still distance the government from the issue of homosexuality. If support were found for prohibiting the press from publishing the details of homosexual prosecutions, the government could then proceed further with the bill. On the related question of an inquiry, R.A. (Rab) Butler, Chancellor of the Exchequer, wanted to avoid one altogether, instead increasing penalties to deal with London's 'public scandal'. Maxwell-Fyfe, however, felt that an inquiry would strengthen his position – if not a royal commission, then a departmental committee. Churchill remained sceptical: 'I wouldn't touch the subject', he declared. The Prime Minister ended the discussion asking his Cabinet to 'Remember that we can't expect to put the whole world right with a majority [in parliament] of 18'.

It was unclear and contested, however, just what 'right' should mean. Most of the Cabinet was still primarily concerned with the exploitation of homosexual scandal by the papers. At the same time, other prominent publications like the *Sunday Times* and *New Statesman* had now parted from the pack by advocating progressive legal reform.[55] The Home Secretary was against changing the law but recognised a growing body of opinion that sought reform, including outright decriminalisation. Cabinet minutes indicate that several ministers remained reluctant when Maxwell-Fyfe appealed again to the Cabinet to form a royal commission to review the laws on prostitution and homosexuality. These included Churchill, fixated instead on the press, still preferring the tactic of a private member's bill.[56] While Maxwell-Fyfe believed that press reports might corrupt the innocent, provoke imitation crimes and even exaggerate their prevalence in the minds of the public, he nonetheless concluded that the danger of such legislation to the liberty of the press and proper functioning of the courts was too great.[57] But the Cabinet remained divided between restricting press coverage of homosexuality and calling an inquiry into the law.

By that time, *The Sunday Times* was again highlighting the issue of homosexuality, publicly calling for an inquiry into legal reform. Just as Churchill was seeking to avoid coverage in the press of the details of homosexual offences and trials, *The Sunday Times* was citing them in support of legal reform in its lead editorial. Foreshadowing language that would later appear in the Wolfenden Report, it found the case very strong 'for a reform of the law as to acts committed in private between adults', concluding that 'the case for authoritative inquiry into it is overwhelming'.[58] Having begun with the lucrative interests of the scandal press in trial details, the issue of homosexual legal reform had now reached the highest levels of press interest and government concern.

When the Cabinet met again two weeks later, Maxwell-Fyfe reiterated objections against legislation to restrict the press. Harold Macmillan, Minister of Housing and Local Government, agreed: press restrictions might make the government appear to be diverting public attention away from scandal. He therefore supported the calling of a departmental committee. Churchill now concurred, and on 15 April 1954, the 'Cabinet agreed that a Departmental Committee should be appointed to enquire into the law relating to prostitution and homosexual offences'.[59] Harold Macmillan could not know that the committee, whose formation he had supported, would in fact propose a complete overhaul of British law on homosexuality or that the 1957 release of its official report would coincide with the first year of his own premiership.

Conclusion

The popular press's invocation of the danger of homosexuality was only ever partially about safeguarding the public and containing or punishing the queer criminal. There were concrete financial incentives as well. At their most basic level, scandalous headlines and open vitriol attracted readers and maintained or increased circulation figures, and therefore potentially advertising revenues as well. Titillating and shocking coverage of homosexuality was an important component of an overall strategy to use scandalous headlines, sensational copy and hyperbole to stir up fear, anger and righteous indignation among consumers – and produce an appetite for more. But to conclude by demonstrating the reliance on queer scandal by many popular titles as calculated marketing and business strategy is only half the story. The effects of this commodification of homosexual scandal by the press extended, I have suggested, to the government.

Home Secretary Sir David Maxwell-Fyfe famously believed 'Homosexuals, in general, are exhibitionists and proselytisers, and a danger to others, especially the young', and assured parliamentarians in 1953, 'I shall give no countenance to the view that they should not be prevented from being such a danger'.[60] For the Home Secretary, preventing this danger required a two-pronged approach that addressed incarceration, but also the damage the press might do by promoting homosexuality through coverage or dialogue on the subject. He was not alone in his concerns. The Cabinet took a keen interest in this coverage by the popular press, leading in part to its decision to convene the Wolfenden Committee.

A fuller understanding of the mid-century press and its treatment of homosexuality offers an opportunity to explore the cultural materialism of queer history. By commodifying homosexual vice and desire as a feature of scandal reportage, the press conjured it as a pressing public issue. Its lucrative potential drove interest for continued and ever more extensive coverage of homosexuality and the social decay it heralded, but also created a space for opposition and greater public dialogue on reform. It was thus, I suggest, more than just mass entertainment, and ultimately pushed Churchill's Cabinet to seek out methods to contain the two problems: homosexual vice on the one hand, and its treatment in the press on the other. Only after exhausting options for limiting press treatment did the Government finally settle on an inquiry into the law. Press vitriol, its lucrative potential and concerns over its containment in the 1950s are thus paradoxically deeply intertwined with the story of homosexual legal reform.

Notes

1. Douglas Warth, 'Evil Men', *Sunday Pictorial*, 25 May 1952, 6 and 15. See also: 1 June 1952, 12; 8 June 1952, 12.
2. Weeks, *Coming Out*, 162–163.
3. Patrick Higgins, *Heterosexual Dictatorship: Male Homosexuality in Postwar Britain* (London: Fourth Estate, 1996), 267.
4. Houlbrook, *Queer London*, 236–239.
5. Jeffrey Weeks, 'Capitalism and the Organization of Sex', in Gay Left Collective, ed., *Homosexuality: Power and Politics* (London: Allison and Busby, 1980), 11–20.
6. John, D'Emilio, 'Capitalism and Gay Identity', in Ann Snitow, Christine Stansell and Sharon Thompson, eds, *The Powers of Desire: The Politics of Sexuality* (New York: Monthly Review Press, 1983), 100–113.
7. For example, see: Chauncey, *Gay New York*; Matt Cook, *London and the Culture of Homosexuality, 1885–1914*, (Cambridge: Cambridge University Press, 2003); D'Emilio, *Sexual Politics, Sexual Communities*; Hugh David, *On Queer Street: A Social History of British Homosexuality* (London: HarperCollins, 1997); Matt Houlbrook, *Queer London*; Marc Stein, *City of Sisterly and Brotherly Loves: Lesbian and Gay Philadelphia, 1945–1972* (Philadelphia: Temple University Press, 2004).

8. See Katherine Sender, *Business, Not Politics: The Making of the Gay Market* (New York: Columbia University Press, 2004); Daniel L. Wardlow, *Gays, Lesbians, and Consumer Behavior: Theory, Practice, and Research Issues in Marketing* (New York: Haworth, 1996).
9. See M.V. Lee Badgett, *Money, Myths, and Change: The Economic Lives of Lesbians and Gay Men* (Chicago: University of Chicago Press, 2001); Steven Kates, *Twenty Million New Customers! Understanding Gay Men's Consumer Behavior* (New York: Haworth Press, 1998); Grant Lukenbill, *Untold Millions: Secret Truths About Marketing to Gay and Lesbian Consumers* (New York: Harrington Park Press, 1999).
10. See Alexandra Chasin, *Selling Out: The Gay and Lesbian Movement Goes to Market* (Basingstoke: Palgrave Macmillan, 2000); Rosemary Hennessey, *Profit and Pleasure: Sexual Identities in Late Capitalism* (New York: Routledge, 2000).
11. On the history of syphilis in Britain since the 1920s, see Richard Davenport-Hines, *Sex, Death and Punishment: Attitudes to Sex and Sexuality in Britain since the Renaissance* (London: Fontana Press, 1991), 245–285.
12. Weeks, *Coming Out*, 152–153. Kinsey's *Sexual Behaviour in the Human Female* (1953) would be no less shocking.
13. *Sunday Pictorial*, 1–31 July 1949. Adrian Bingham, 'The "K-Bomb": Social Surveys, the Popular Press, and British Sexual Culture in the 1940s and 1950s', *Journal of British Studies*, 50.1 (January 2011), 156–179.
14. Gillian Swanson, *Drunk with the Glitter: Space, Consumption and Sexual Instability in Modern Urban Culture* (London: Routledge, 2007).
15. Hugh Cudlipp, *At Your Peril* (London: Weidenfeld and Nicolson, 1962), 56.
16. Anthony Howard, 'Cudlipp, Hubert Kinsman [Hugh], Baron Cudlipp (1913–1998)', *Oxford Dictionary of National Biography*, Oxford University Press, Sept 2004, online edn., <http://www.oxforddnb.com/view/article/69790>, accessed 30 January 2009.
17. The series was part of the *Sunday Pictorial*'s regular treatment of inflammatory issues. See Higgins, *Heterosexual Dictatorship*, 288–293.
18. Cudlipp, *At Your Peril*, 317.
19. From unpaginated graph of Sunday newspaper circulations 1947–1961. Cudlipp, *At Your Peril*.
20. Higgins, *Heterosexual Dictatorship*, 278.
21. Unpaginated graph in Hugh Cudlipp, *At Your Peril*.
22. Higgins, *Heterosexual Dictatorship*, 275 and 281.
23. On the history of the *News of the World*, see Higgins, *Heterosexual Dictatorship*, 278–279.
24. On homosexual trials that appeared primarily in 1953 and 1954 see Higgins, *Heterosexual Dictatorship*, 179–230.
25. According to Jeffrey Weeks, it was this 'shockability' that interested the papers more than any real engagement with the issue of homosexuality. Weeks, *Coming Out*, 162.
26. 'M.P. Changes Plea to "Not Guilty"', *News of the World*, 11 January 1953. On this and the Montagu case, see H. Montgomery Hyde, *The Other Love: An Historical and Contemporary Survey of Homosexuality in Britain* (London: Heinemann, 1970), 216–226.
27. See 'M.P.'s Appeal is Dismissed', *News of the World*, 11 October 1953; 'Labour M.P. to Resign', *News Chronicle*, 14 October, 1953.

28. 'Author Sentenced to Nine Months', *News of the World*, 11 October 1953.
29. For extensive discussion, see Higgins, *Heterosexual Dictatorship*, 268–270.
30. 'Gielgud sees agent after £10 fine', *Daily Mail*, 22 October 1953.
31. 'Sir John Gielgud stays on the stage', *Daily Express*, 22 October 1953.
32. Edward Montagu, Lord Montagu of Beaulieu, *Wheels Within Wheels: An Unconventional Life* (London: Weidenfeld and Nicolson, 2000), 100–102.
33. George Glenton, 'Judge questions boy in Montagu trial', *News Chronicle*, 15 December 1953.
34. 'Lord Montagu: Court Cleared While Scouts Give Evidence', *News of the World*, 15 November 1953.
35. According to Jeffrey Weeks, subsequent charges against Montagu, Michael Pitt-Rivers and Peter Wildeblood, including conspiracy, were 'carefully designed to jeopardize Montagu's retrial'. Weeks, *Coming Out*, 161. But when the remaining charge came to trial, the prosecution offered no evidence against Montagu, and on the judge's direction the jury returned a verdict of not guilty. 'Montagu Charge Dropped', *News Chronicle*, 7 April 1954.
36. Montagu, *Wheels Within Wheels*, 105.
37. Peter Woods, 'Guilty: Montagu—12 Months', *Daily Mirror*, 25 March 1954.
38. Peter Wildeblood, *Against the Law* (London: Weidenfeld and Nicolson, 1955), 31.
39. Wildeblood, *Against the Law*, 31.
40. Though he focused on the press 'orgy' following the release of Kinsey's *Sexual Behavior in the Human Female* (1953), Gordon was well known for his thoughts on homosexuality. John Gordon, 'Our Sex-Sodden Newspapers', *Sunday Express*, 23 August 1953.
41. He shared this distinction with fellow *Sunday Express* writer James Douglas. Weeks, *Coming Out*, 160.
42. 'Sex, Crime and The Press', *Daily Mirror*, 11 November 1953.
43. 'Now Will They Act?', *Daily Mirror*, 6 November 1953.
44. 'An Evil in Our Midst', *News of the World*, 1 November 1953.
45. The Archbishop of Canterbury also called on 'responsible' consumers to stop buying publications exploiting sex for profit. 'Primate Hits Sex Press', *Daily Mail*, 25 November 1953.
46. See especially Weeks, *Coming Out*, 156–167; Grey, *Quest for Justice*, 19–33. Higgins, *Heterosexual Dictatorship*, 3–7 and 267ff., however, suggests the influence of the press in the government's decision to pursue a commission.
47. 'Royal Commission Urged', *Guardian*, 11 June 1953.
48. Notes for the Secretary of State's Speech at the Coningsby Club [hereafter Coningsby], 19 November 1953. The National Archives, London [hereafter TNA], HO 45/24955.
49. *Hansard Parliamentary Debates*, 5th ser., vol. 521 (1953), cols. 1295–1299. For coverage of this early call for a royal commission, see Ronald Camp, 'Fyfe: My Duty To Guard Youth', *Daily Mail*, 4 December 1953; 'Amazing Figures Show Growth of an Evil', *Daily Mirror*, 4 December 1953.
50. *Hansard Parliamentary Debates*, 5th ser., vol. 523 (1954), cols. 228–229.
51. 'Sexual Offences: Memorandum by the Secretary of State for the Home Department and Minister of Welsh Affairs', C. (54) 60, 17 February 1954 [The memorandum was signed 16 February]. TNA, CAB 129/66.
52. 'Sexual Offences', C. (54) 60, 17 February 1954. TNA, CAB 129/66.

53. Coningsby, 19 November 1953. TNA, HO 45/24955.
54. Cabinet Secretary's Notebooks, C.C. 11 (54), 24 February 1954. TNA, CAB 195/11. Cabinet Minutes, C.C. (54) 11th Conclusions, 24 February 1954. TNA, CAB 128/27. All subsequent quotes from members of the Cabinet in this paragraph are taken from CAB 195/11, while further discussion and contextualisation of the meeting by the Cabinet Secretary is offered in the minutes in CAB 128/27.
55. 'A Social Problem', *The Sunday Times,* 1 November 1953. E.M. Forster, 'A Magistrate's Figures', *New Statesman,* 31 October 1953. See also 'Law and Hypocrisy', *The Sunday Times,* 28 March 1954.
56. Cabinet Minutes, C.C. (54) 20th Conclusions, 17 March 1954. TNA, CAB 128/27.
57. 'Restrictions on Reporting of Proceedings for Homosexual Offences: Memorandum by the Secretary of State for the Home Department and Minister for Welsh Affairs', C. (54) 121, 1 April 1954 [signed 31 March 1954]. TNA, CAB 129/67.
58. 'Law and Hypocrisy', *The Sunday Times,* 28 March 1954.
59. Cabinet Secretary's Notebooks, C. 29 (54), 15 April 1954. TNA, CAB 195/12; Cabinet Minutes, C.C. (54) 29th Conclusions, 15 April 1954. TNA, CAB 128/27.
60. *Hansard Parliamentary Debates,* 5th ser., vol. 251 (1953), c. 1298.

11

Geeks and Gaffs: The Queer Legacy of the 1950s American Freak Show

Elizabeth Stephens

The 1950s were the decade in which the traditional freak show, which had enjoyed such popularity during the heyday of nineteenth-century amusement parks and funfairs, finally came to an end. By the 1950s, the reputation of the freak show was as it remains today: widely held to be an unpleasant anachronism, degrading people with unusual anatomies for putting them on display before a curious staring public. In the middle of the century, however, this perception of the freak show was still a very new one, representative of a recent and steep decline in its cultural standing after the Second World War. Thus, the 1950s are the final chapter in a much longer history of the modern freak show, which is usually dated to the first part of the nineteenth century. More particularly, the freak show itself – as distinguished from earlier traditions of publicly exhibiting people with unusual anatomies – is often identified as beginning with P.T. Barnum's first exhibition in 1832: that of an African-American woman, Joice Heth, whom he promoted as the 161-year-old former nursemaid of George Washington.[1]

Although, as Mark Chemers recognises, Barnum himself never used the word 'freak' to advertise his exhibits, his shows are widely recognised as the site of emergence of the new concept of the 'freak'. It was Barnum who devised the methods of display that would become synonymous with the freak show, and it was Barnum who established such exhibitions as an important and culturally central spectacular space.[2] In a nineteenth-century cultural context in which public displays of natural curiosities, mechanical novelties and technical inventions were celebrated as educational and improving, cultivating an appreciation of civilisation and progress, the freak show occupied a respectable position. Even at the end of the nineteenth century, as James Cook argues, freak shows were 'still considered solid family entertainment, an exhibition worthy of visits by the upper crust as well as respectable workers, women and children as well as men, serious naturalists as well as fun-seekers'.[3] During the first half of the twentieth century, however, and especially after the Depression, freak shows experienced a dramatic fall in popularity and cultural status. By the mid-twentieth century, freak shows were widely seen as an affront to decency, a byword for sleaze and disrepute, running on the abuse of the poor and often unwell. Despite the much-obituarised death of the freak show in the 1950s, however, in recent years large numbers of performers – many of them people with some form of unusual embodiment themselves – have returned to this historical moment, exploring the traditional acts and aesthetics of the freak show as it was coming to an end in the 1950s as a means by which to both reflect upon and intervene in its legacy for people with visible forms of physical difference. The aim of this chapter is therefore to demonstrate that the freak show represents an important episode in the history of the queer 1950s and that its legacy lives on in its reimagining by contemporary performers, which constitutes a queer rereading of this history.

Queer freak histories

Freak shows are rarely considered within the context of queer history or culture. However, Judith Halberstam has recently reminded us that the term 'queer' should be understood to refer not only to same-sex relationships and practices but also to the lifestyles and experiences of those who 'live outside of reproductive and familial time as well as on the edge of the logics of labour and production'.[4] Halberstam gives examples of other practices and experiences – such as homelessness, drug taking, middle-aged punks and rave parties – that might also be recognised as queer. This focus on non-normative bodies and practices, rather than stable sexual identities, is widely understood as the defining difference-between a 'gay, lesbian and bisexual' concept of sexuality, on the one hand, and the more fluid and contingent queer conceptualisation, on the other. Yet, it is also true that, in practice, queer scholarship and activism have remained strongly focused on same-sex practices and desires.[5] As such, the history of freak performers, and the institution of the freak show, have potentially important contributions to make to queer history by expanding the sites in which it is recognised to take place and the variety of bodily and subjective experiences of which it is composed.

Freak shows do include a number of acts that feature what would now be considered gender queer bodies, such as 'bearded ladies' or 'half-men/half-women'. Additionally, however, and perhaps less obviously, traditional freak performances centre on acts of bodily penetration: blockheads hammer nails up their noses, performers lay on beds of nails or contort themselves into tiny spaces, geeks and sword swallowers swallow strange objects. Freak shows and performers also share with other queer institutions a tendency towards itinerancy, and like other transient populations, travelling performers often report being greeted by local populations with suspicion or hostility. This distrust was especially evident during the 1950s, when the freak show reached its nadir of popularity and prestige and was often met with active public resistance and distaste. The 1950s were hence representative of the sleaziest, most marginal era in the history of the freak show, in which the display of vulnerable and marginalised people was itself becoming marginalised and imperilled. By the 1950s, freak shows could only be found on cultural margins: at a geographical remove, like New York City's Coney Island, situated on the fringes of the city; ghettoised in seedy inner-city entertainment districts like the Bowery; or attached to travelling circuses or fairs as side shows. Freak shows, then, were often 'nomadic' not just in the literal sense but also in the Deleuzian one described by Rosi Braidotti, in which it refers to 'the kind of critical consciousness that resists settling into socially coded modes of thought and behaviour'.[6]

If freak shows aroused much negative public feeling in the 1950s, during which decade the number of professional troupes rapidly declined, it was largely because of this fact: freak shows are spaces that upset or disturb prevalent 'modes of thought and behaviour' towards the differently embodied. Prior to the twentieth century, public exhibition of unusual bodies was widely accepted and presumed to be both instructive for the audience and profitable for the exhibited. By the middle of the twentieth century, however, public standards had changed, transforming the cultural significance of putting those bodies on display. As Robert Bogdan argues, 'the meaning of being different had changed in American society. Scientific medicine had undermined the mystery of certain forms of human variation.... People who were different had diseases and were now in the province of physicians, not the general public.'[7] Rather than being subjected to a public gaze, people performing freakery were increasingly understood as suffering from medical conditions requiring professional treatment. Rachel Adams also attributes the demise of the freak show during the 1950s to an increasing medicalisation of anatomical difference at this time: 'Diagnosed in terms of recognisable pathologies, freaks lost the aura of mystery and wonder that once made them objects of visual fascination.'[8] As a result, argues Rosemarie Garland Thomson, 'By 1940, the prodigious body had been completely absorbed into the discourse of medicine, and the freak shows were all but gone.'[9] Although 'scientific and sideshow discourses had been entangled during the freak show era, they diverged towards opposite ends of a spectrum of prestige and authority as time went on', Garland Thomson continues, so that 'scientists had transformed the freak into the medical specimen.'[10]

While changing cultural standards about the treatment of people with unusual anatomies were undoubtedly an important factor in the decline of the freak show during the 1950s, changing tastes in popular entertainment also played a significant role. As Joe Nickell recognises, in the 1950s the travelling carnivals and circuses to which freak shows were usually attached were undergoing a rapid shift in their economics that had a very negative impact on their viability: 'the decline of sideshows began in the mid-1950s with the advent of the big rides,' writes Nickell. Citing the showman Ward Hall, he adds, 'They were like a vacuum cleaner. They'd just suck money up off the midway.'[11] As the proprietor of Coney Island's Side Shows by the Seas Shore, Dick D. Zigun, noted in an interview with the *New York Times*, the state-subsidised re-opening of that sideshow was largely motivated by a desire to preserve Coney Island itself from a similar fate to that of the freak show as an institution: 'Coney Island was at the crossroads', Zigun explained. 'It was getting dangerously small and could have been rezoned for residential housing.'[12]

Reclaiming the freak

Despite this critical consensus that the freak show came to a definitive end in the 1950s, however, over the past decade the freak show has been experiencing a cultural resurgence, marked by a sharp return of popularity. Many of these troupes evidence a pronounced enthusiasm for a distinctively 1950s aesthetic. Part of a wider international network of neo-vaudeville and neo-burlesque performance cultures, these performers often embrace a lowbrow, kitschy aesthetic that strongly recalls that of B-grade circus and sideshow movies of this era. The widespread contemporary use of orange and yellow banner art is a visible legacy of a style, which, as Bosker and Hammer note, only developed in the mid-twentieth century.[13] Coney Island's Side Shows by the Seashore was the first of this new generation of freak shows, reopening on the site of the old Dreamland side show in 1982.[14] Coney

Island makes extensive use of banner art, which features highly-stylised portraits of acts such as Madame Twisto, Serpentina, Eak the Geek and Insectavora. Over the last decade, in the wake of Coney Island's success, the number of professional freak shows has proliferated rapidly. Popular troupes such as the Jim Rose Circus Side Show (US), the Happy Sideshow (Australia) and the performer Mat Fraser (UK) have rediscovered traditional sideshow acts, including sword swallowing, snake handling, magic and contortionism. Often, these troupes include very explicit references not simply to the history of the freak show generally but to its 1950s incarnation in particular. Mat Fraser, a British actor and writer with phocomelia (or foreshortened arms), wrote and starred in 'Sealboy: Freak', a performance piece which recreated the life and sideshow act of the 1950s performer Sealo, or Stanley Berent. Fraser's most recent show is 'The Freak and the Showgirl', with the neo-burlesque performer Julie Atlas Muz, which draws on the aesthetics of mid-century burlesque and vaudeville performance. Similarly, the cover art of Jim Rose's memoir, *Snake Oil: Life's Calculations, Misdirections, And Manipulations,* also reflects a 1950s-influenced aesthetic, reproducing the cover art style of mid-century pulp fiction, while its title references the quack medical shows that travelled so extensively during that era.

Both in its aesthetics and in what these signify for queer subjects, the 1950s freak show finds a close correspondence in the contemporaneous world of queer pulp fiction. As Susan Stryker demonstrates in *Queer Pulp: Perverted Passions from the Golden Age of the Paperback,* despite their negative, pathologising representations of the characters and narratives they treated, these texts played an important role in the formation of early queer and gay/lesbian cultures. They provided people who felt themselves marginalised and isolated with a place to read about experiences and lives similar to their own. And they did so while inventing a distinctive aesthetics through their sensationalised cover design that is still instantly recognisable, and is still the object of widespread fond nostalgia (as evidenced in the continual reproduction of pulp cover art as postcards and fridge magnets). Queer pulp texts were mass produced, cheap and circulated widely in sites like train stations that catered to mobile and transient populations, and they offered a site for potential queer self-representation and self-identification that remains an important to many queer cultures today.[15] Despite the fact that queer pulp texts feature largely negative representations of queer life, then, they remain important to queer history in their negativity, which can nonetheless be harnessed as a productive political force. This is Heather Love's argument in *Feeling Backward: Loss and the Politics of Queer History*, in which she argues that queer itself is often marked by a turn away from the 'positive affirmations' that characterised so much important work in gay and lesbian studies and towards a reconsideration of negativity, 'attempting to counter stigma by incorporating it. The word "queer," like "fag" or "dyke" but unlike the more positive "gay" or "lesbian," is a slur. When queer was adopted in the late 1980s it was chosen because it evoked a long history of insult and abuse – you could hear the hurt in it.'[16] Noting the importance of negative histories and experience to queer culture, Love argues that: 'Turning away from past degradation to a present or future affirmation means ignoring that past as past; it also makes it harder to see the persistence of the past in the present.'[17] In consequence, Love suggests, investigations of this history of negativity are imperative to a queer critical practice: 'Rather than disavowing this history of marginality and abjection, I suggest that we embrace it, explaining the ways it continues to structure queer experiences in the present.'[18]

It is precisely this strategy one finds in contemporary queer and disabled performers' appropriations of the traditional freak show. Many of these performers are viscerally aware of the negativity of this history, and explicitly frame their engagement with this history as an act of critical intervention and historical recovery. We can see this in the work of Mat Fraser. Once performing at Coney Island with the word 'freak' inscribed on his chest, Fraser's work confronts the history of the freak show in a defiant, even belligerent, way. His reclamation of the word 'freak', and his recognition of the way it is culturally inscribed upon his body, recalls Robert McRuer's attempt to reclaim the word 'crip' within the context of critical disability studies. Like McRuer, Fraser's use of the term 'freak' can be seen as a politically-motivated appropriation of an historically negative term.[19] Fraser's work provides one of the most sustained interrogations of the legacy of the freak show for people with unusual forms of embodiment, and over the past fifteen years he has produced a significant body of work that reflects critically on this history. In addition to 'Sealboy: Freak', Fraser's works include *Thalidomide: The Musical!*, the documentary *Born Freak* (which included historical accounts of the freak show).

Despite Fraser's critical engagement with the form of the freak show and his very evident familiarity with its history, his decision to work within this space has been critically contentious. For the disability studies scholars David Mitchell and Sharon Snyder, Fraser's performance at Coney Island (filmed as part of *Born Freak*) represents less a critical intervention in the history of the freak show than an exposure to an institutional and discursive system of spectacularisation that he cannot control, and which ultimately defines his body in negative ways that he does not have the power to reinscribe. On the Coney Island stage, Mitchell and Snyder claim, what Fraser experiences is:

> his own inevitable degradation. His stage performance, which literally recreates an exhibition of one of his nineteenth-century freak show ancestors, Seal-o, fails to achieve the desired level of political satire. In the process of duplicating the comments and actions of his predecessor, we watch as the act increasingly mires the performer in degrading spectacle. Fraser finds no effective politicized venue within the carnival tent and, as if to emphasize this fact, the camera performs various pans across the faces of Fraser's audiences; they stare at the performance with a collective discomfort and the show seems almost too humiliating to witness from an 'enlightened' freak show audiences' perspective. The act of simply occupying an objectifying gaze is no longer possible – if it ever was to begin with – and the performer's audiences are caught either looking away in embarrassment or staring with some difficulty.[20]

For Mitchell and Snyder, Fraser's work pits the reinscriptive capacities of the individual performer against the weight of a long and very negative history in a way that is doomed to failure.

That Fraser's experience of and at Coney Island differ markedly from that attributed to him by Mitchell and Snyder is, however, indicated by the fact that Fraser has continued to perform in this space – most recently at the 2011 'Congress of Curious Peoples'. In an opinion piece for the *Guardian* newspaper he wrote in 2008, Fraser expresses his frustration at the critical response to disabled performers investigating the legacy of the freak show. This article was written in protest at the exclusion of Richard Butchins' documentary, *The Last American Freak Show*, from the London International Disability Film Festival. Fraser argued that the refusal to screen this documentary silenced a potentially important discussion about the reasons 'some disabled film-makers are returning to the freak show.' He was especially critical of the fact that the reason given for the exclusion of this documentary was that it made BAFTA's head of events 'feel uncomfortable'.[21] As Fraser remarks: 'Heaven forbid that anyone should be made to feel uncomfortable by a film about disability made by a disabled person'.[22] Making audiences feel uneasy by confronting them with the recent histories in which polite society was quite happy to pay promoters to star at the bodies of people with unusual anatomies is very much the point and purpose of Fraser's work. His performances are explicitly grounded in the history of such public exhibitions, and his uncomfortable mobilisation of this history is both queer itself and a reminder of an important moment in queer history. Considered from this perspective, the discomfort Mitchell and Snyder identify in the audience at Fraser's Coney Island show might be understood not as evidence of his degradation or humiliation but of the audience's own uncomfortable confrontation with the spectre of that history.

A similar productive appropriation of the negative history of the freak show can be seen in the work of Jennifer Miller, founder of New York's queer performance group Circus Amok and occasional 'bearded lady' at Coney Island. As Miller noted during an interview about her experiences performing as a 'bearded lady', she saw such an engagement with the freak show tradition not as choice but as a cultural imperative, because the freak show is still the lens through which people with noticeable forms of physical difference are still seen. Miller, like Fraser, explicitly frames her performance practice as a critical commentary on the history of the freak show, explaining that she had 'always had this image of the bearded lady as kind of this little icon sitting on my shoulder, you know, battling with me and how I was seen in the world. So when the opportunity came to work in the sideshow, I wanted to give it a try. I wanted to meet this person, this image, this history that I had been in dialogue with, sort of face to face.'[23] As Miller's comment makes clear, whether or not she chose to perform the role of the bearded lady on the sideshow stage, this figure would remain the one through which her own bodily difference is popularly interpreted and understood. Moreover, while it is generally understood that what occurs on the space of the stage is, precisely, a performance, on the street Miller is still likely to be seen by passing strangers as a 'bearded lady' without any awareness of the extent to which this is a constructed, theatrical category. The sideshow stage thus affords a valuable opportunity to talk back to and critique this figure – one that does not readily exist outside it.

In choosing to step into the role of the 'bearded lady', then, Miller, like Fraser is, on the one hand, making the same compromise made by generations of people with unusual anatomies before her, profiting from a public curiosity whose effects no individual can control; on the other hand, however, her actual performance attests to the institutional changes the freak show has undergone since the 1950s and during its recent revival, which makes that space more available for resistant queer performances. Whereas earlier incarnations of Coney Island's sideshow, such as Dreamland and Wonderland, used inside and outside talkers to provide tantalising accounts of their acts, Miller speaks for herself during her performance in a way that allows her to talk back, critically, to the tradition that had constructed public perceptions about her corporeal difference. This change – the move from using talkers to allowing performers to speak for themselves – represents an important and epochal shift in the nature of the freak show. Miller's performance as a bearded lady is in this regard exemplary of the way performers in twenty-first century freak shows critically reflect on the tradition they also continue, interrogating the cultural assumptions about unusual forms of embodiment that circulate in and through the public sphere.

Performers like Fraser and Miller, who are confronted with the legacy of the freak show on a daily basis, thus embody and confirm the point made above by Heather Love: it is through an engagement with the negativity of this history that its full impact can be both measured and resisted – often precisely by stirring up the sort of discomfort that Mitchell and Snyder experienced while watching Fraser's performance at Coney Island. While Mitchell and Snyder are right to note that no performer can single-handedly dismantle a history or a cultural framework within which physical difference is seen, performances like Fraser's and Millers are able to exert a recognisable influence over time on the way anatomically unusual bodies are represented in the public sphere. Changes in dominant cultural mores and the public sense of what is acceptable occur slowly: audience members may have one response during a live performance and different memories of that performance later on, while audiences' expectations about what it is acceptable to see on a public stage also reflect substantive changes when measured over longer periods of time.

Conclusion: freak fifties

The capacity of contemporary freak shows to bring about changes in dominant ways of seeing even as they appear to reproduce them is what makes them so queer and their engagement with their late, 1950s period so potentially productive for contemporary performers. However, it is instructive to recognise that the reinscriptive and resignificatory potential within the freak show so successfully exploited by recent troupes is one that can be identified within the tradition of the freak show itself, from its very inception in the nineteenth century, and this is undoubtedly another reason the form has remained popular with contemporary performers. One of the distinguishing features of the freak show, differentiating it from other, earlier forms of public display of non-normative anatomies, has always been its explicit construction of the freak show stage as a space of uncertainty, in which the status and meaning of the bodies on display are framed as objects for discussion and debate, rather than simply explained to the audience. This is evident even in P.T. Barnum's very exhibition of Joice Heth. On his first tour of Heth to Boston, Barnum discovered he had rented an exhibition room next door to one of the most popular and celebrated curiosities of the day – Johann Maelzel's automaton chess-player. Shortly afterwards, 'anonymous' notices began to appear in the local press, questioning whether Heth really was the prodigiously old woman she was advertised to be, or whether she was actually an automaton herself. Audiences thronged to the exhibition, many arguing that Heth was quite obviously a mechanical figure. 'What made Barnum's new (and seemingly counterproductive) marketing scheme innovative', argues James Cook, was his recognition that

> artful deception was never a hard and fast choice between complete detection and total bewilderment, honest promotion and shifty misrepresentation, innocent amusement and social transgression. Rather, Barnum suggests, it was precisely the blurring of these aesthetic and moral categories that defined his brand of cultural fraud and generated much of its remarkable power to excite curiosity.[24]

This aspect of Barnum's exhibitory practice, in which he mischievously advertised his exhibits as fraudulent and constantly drew attention to his enthusiasm for 'humbug', is recognised as one of his most influential contributions to American popular culture. In framing the freak show in this way, Barnum established it as a well-known site of trickery and hoaxing, in which audiences always ran the risk of being gulled by promoters of performers.

This, in turn, constituted the freak show as a space in which the usual power relations between the (dominant) spectators and (marginal) freaks were open to sudden reversals. Thus, while the freak show has certainly earned its reputation as a space in which the poor and vulnerable with unusual anatomies were exploited for profit and the amusement of a leering crowd, it was also a site of the reciprocal exploitation of the audience by the performers, particularly through fake exhibits, or gaffs, that served to destabilise the category of the 'freak' even as they constructed it. Half-men/half-women performers, for example, were almost always fakes, while the eleventh exhibit in a traditional ten-in-one sideshow is called the 'blow-off', an obviously gaffed exhibit designed to remove one audience from its seats and to make way for new paying customers.[25] It is this capacity of the freak show to conspicuously trick or wrong-foot its audiences, to explicitly announce that it is gulling its audiences even as it successfully does so, that makes it such a productive space for contemporary performers, and that transforms it from simply a site of repression or control into a space of public exhibition that allows for a variety of readings and possibilities. If contemporary performers like Fraser and Miller have found in the freak show a productive space within which to reflect on the historical and cultural conditions in and through which perceptions about their own physical difference have been constructed, it is primarily because the freak show itself, even in its most traditional forms, contains the potential for different kinds of signification and different dynamics of power.

This potential has only been intensified by the 'death' of the traditional freak show in the 1950s. Rather than bringing about an end to the freak show as a popular spectacle, it is precisely the death of its traditional form that has enabled it to be appropriated so productively by contemporary queer and disabled performers. That is, the resurgence in popularity of the freak show is not despite its death but because of it, making it available for subsequent appropriation and resignification. When contemporary performers draw on the aesthetics and acts of the 1950s freak show, then, they reference not simply a tradition that has constructed non-normative bodies in negative ways, but its sleazy and degraded end. The ambivalence of this gesture, which both recovers the freak show as a site of queer history and critically interrogates its negative construction of those performing in it, is itself an exemplary queer one.

Notes

1. The public exhibition of anatomically unusual bodies has, of course, a much longer history than that of the freak show. Histories of the freak show that contextualise its emergence within longer histories can be found in Robert Bogdan's *Freak Show: Presenting Human Oddities for Amusement and Profit* (Chicago and London: University of Chicago Press, 1988); Rosemarie Garland Thomson's edited collection *Freakery: Cultural Spectacles of the Extraordinary Body* (New York: University of New York Press, 1996) Margrit Shildrick's *Embodying the Monster: Encounters With the Vulnerable Self* (London; Thousand Oaks, California: Sage, 2002); and Marlene Tromp's *Victorian Freaks: The Social Context of Freakery in Nineteenth-Century Britain* (Columbus: Ohio State University Press, 2008).

2. Mark Chemers, *Staging Stigma: A Critical Examination of the American Freak Show* (New York: Palgrave Macmillan, 2008), 1–9.
3. The cultural prestige enjoyed by freak shows during this period is reflected in popular representations of their performers: acts such as General Tom Thumb (a dwarf), Millie-Christine (African conjoined twins) and Julia Pastrana (a hirsute woman billed as 'the missing link') were the objects of frequent and favourable press coverage, touring internationally before audiences comprised of medical professionals, and members of government and the aristocracy as well as the general public. James Cook, *The Arts of Deception: Playing with Fraud in the Age of Barnum* (Cambridge, MA: Harvard University Press, 2001), p.140.
4. Judith Halberstam, *In a Queer Time and Place*, 10. Robert McRuer's *Crip Theory: Cultural Signs of Queerness and Disability* (New York and London: New York University Press, 2006) has taken account of the intersection between critical disability studies and queer theory, and critical disability theorists such as Margrit Shildrick and Rosemarie Garland Thomson have written extensively and insightfully on the freak show (in *Embodying the Monster* and *Extraordinary Bodies: Figuring Physical Disability in American Culture and Literature* (New York: University of Columbia Press, 1997), respectively. However, Marie-Hélène Bourcier's *Sexpolitiques: Queer Zones 2* (Paris: La fabrique, 2005) is one of the few texts to take account of the history of freak performance and its legacy within contemporary queer cultures.
5. Halberstam's own work has examined non-normative forms of embodiment such as monsters and post-human subjects, in *Skin Shows: Gothic Horror and the Technology of Monsters* (Durham and London: Duke University Press, 1995) and the collected co-edited with Ira Livingston, *Posthuman Bodies* (Bloomington, Illinois: University of Indiana Press, 1995).
6. Rosi Braidotti. *Nomadic Subjects: Embodiment and Sexual Difference in Contemporary Feminist Theory* (New York: Columbia University Press, 1994), 5. This idea of movement is also central to definitions of queer: as many queer theorists, such as Eve Kosofsky Sedgwick, have noted, the etymology of the word 'queer' derives from 'the Indo-European root *twerkw*, which also yields the German *queer* (traverse) [and] Latin *torquere* (to twist)'. Eve Kosovsky Sedgwick, *Tendencies* (Durham: Duke University Press, 1993), xii. Queer is thus associated with passage or traversing, with movement rather than identity, or, in David Halperin's often-cited formulation, with positionality rather than positivity. David Halperin, *Saint Foucault: Towards a Gay Hagiography* (Oxford and New York: Oxford University Press, 1995), 62.
7. Bogdan, *Freak Show*, 274.
8. Rachel Adams, *Sideshow USA: Freaks and the American Cultural Imagination* (Chicago: University of Chicago Press, 2001), 118.
9. Garland Thomson. *Extraordinary Bodies*, 70.
10. Garland Thomson, *Extraordinary Bodies*, 75. It should be noted, however, that evidence of the ongoing popular appeal of the freak show can be found even during the period of its widespread decline. A promotional film made the very year Garland Thomson identifies as the end of the freak show, *Coney Island 1940*, shows the Dreamland side show thronged with people, and an outside talker touting for business by placing the show's resident 'pinhead' (or microcephalic) on the bally platform, with little evident concern about

the public suitability of putting such a body on display for the amusement of a funfair crowd.

11. Joe Nickell, *Secrets of the Sideshow* (Lexington: University of Kentucky Press, 2005), 346. See also Fred Siegel, 'Theatre of Guts: An Exploration of the Sideshow Aesthetic', in *The Drama Review* 35.4 (1991), 107.
12. Denny Lee, 'The Nickel Empire Longs To Recapture Its Seedy Glory', *New York Times* (16 June 2002), 6.
13. Gideon Bosker and Carl Hammer, *Freak Show: Sideshow Banner Art* (San Francisco, California: Chronicle Books, 1996), 9.
14. While Coney Island's show is called a 'side show', it is also, and very emphatically, publicised as a freak show. The word 'freak' features prominently on the theatrical space: it is painted on the awning between the banner panels for each act, appears in the large sign advertising the 'Freak Bar' and is repeated in the neon 'freaks' sign hung in the theatre entrance way. Side Shows by the Seashore also hosts regular series of special events such as the Girlie Freak Shows and the Super Freak Weekends.
15. Susan Stryker. *Queer Pulp: Perverted Passions from the Golden Age of the Paperback* (San Francisco: Chronicle Books, 2001).
16. Love, *Feeling Backward* 2.
17. McRuer, *Crip Theory,* 19.
18. McRuer, *Crip Theory,* 29.
19. McRuer explains his own use of the term 'crip' by arguing: 'Stigmatised in and by a culture that will not or cannot accommodate their presence, crip performers ... have proudly and collectively shaped stigmaphilic alternatives in, and through, and around that abjection'. McRuer, *Crip Theory,* 35–36.
20. David Mitchell and Sharon Snyder, 'Exploitations of Embodiment: Born Freak and the Academic Bally Plank', *Disability Studies Quarterly*, 25.3 (2005) http://www.dsq-sds.org/article/view/575/752. Accessed 7 January 2010.
21. Mat Fraser, 'Go Ahead: Take a Good Look', *The Guardian* (15 February 2008), 6.
22. Fraser, 'Go Ahead', 6.
23. *Freaks: The Sideshow Cinema* (Warner Brothers, 2004). DVD.
24. James W. Cook, *The Arts of Deception: Playing With Fraud in the Age of Barnum.* (Cambridge, Mass.: Harvard University Press, 2001), 16.
25. Barnum's crowded American Museum, for instance, had a sign that read, 'This way to the Egress', which led his surprised visitors, who were expecting an additional exhibit, back out onto the street.

Bibliography

Adams, Kate, 'Making the World Safe for the Missionary Position: Images of the Lesbian in Post-World War II America', in Karla Jay and Joanne Glasgow, eds, *Lesbian Texts and Contexts: Radical Revisions* (New York: New York University Press, 1990), 255–274.

Adams, Rachel, *Sideshow USA: Freaks and the American Cultural Imagination* (Chicago: University of Chicago Press, 2001).

Adelman, Marcy, ed., *Lesbian Passages: True Stories Told by Women over 40* (Los Angeles: Alyson Publications, 1986).

Aldrich, Ann, *We Walk Alone* [1955] (New York: Feminist Press, 2006).

Aldrich, Ann, *We Too, Must Love* [1958] (New York: Feminist Press, 2006).

Badgett, M.V. Lee, Money, *Myths, and Change: The Economic Lives of Lesbians and Gay Men* (Chicago: University of Chicago Press, 2001).

Batten, Rex, *Rid England of This Plague* (London: Paradise, 2006)

Bauer, Heike, *English Literary Sexology: Translations of Inversion, 1860–1930* (Basingstoke: Palgrave Macmillan, 2009).

Bauer, Heike, '"Race", Normativity and the History of Sexuality: The Case of Magnus Hirschfeld and Early Twentieth-Century Sexology', *Psychology and Sexuality*, 1.3 (2010), 239–249.

Beehre, Mark, *Men Alone – Men Together* (Wellington: Steele Roberts, 2010).

Bell, Melanie, *Femininity in the Frame: Women and 1950s British Popular Cinema* (London: IB Tauris, 2010)..

Bennett, James, 'Medicine, Sexuality and High Anxiety in Peter Jackson's Heavenly Creatures (1994)', *Health and History*, 8 (2006), 147–174.

Bergler, Edmund, *Homosexuality: Disease or Way of Life?* (New York: Hill & Wang, 1956).

Bingham, Adrian, 'The "K-Bomb": Social Surveys, the Popular Press, and British Sexual Culture in the 1940s and 1950s', *Journal of British Studies*, 50.1 (January 2011), 156–179.

Blackwood, Evelyn, ed., *Anthropology and Homosexual Behavior* (New York: The Haworth Press, 1986).

Bogdan, Robert, *Freak Show: Presenting Human Oddities for Amusement and Profit* (Chicago and London: University of Chicago Press, 1988)..

Bourcier, Marie-Hélène, *Sexpolitiques: Queer Zones 2* (Paris: La fabrique, 2005).

Boyarin, Daniel, *Unheroic Conduct: The Rise of Heterosexuality and the Invention of the Jewish Man* (Berkeley: University of California Press, 1997).

Boyd, Nan, *Wide Open Town: A History of Queer San Francisco to 1965* (Berkeley: University of California Press, 2003). Braidotti, Rosi, *Nomadic Subjects: Embodiment and Sexual Difference in Contemporary Feminist Theory* (New York: Columbia University Press, 1994).

Brickell, Chris, *Mates & Lovers: A History of Gay New Zealand* (Auckland: Random House, 2008)..

Brickell, Chris, 'Sexuality, Morality and Society', in Giselle Byrnes, ed., *The New Oxford History of New Zealand* (Melbourne: Oxford University Press, 2009).

Brickell, Chris, 'Visualizing Homoeroticism: The Photographs of Robert Gant, 1887–1892', *Visual Anthropology*, 23.2 (2010), 136–157.
Britain, Sloane, *First Person, Third Sex* (Chicago: Newsstand Library Books, 1959).
Bristow, Joseph, *Sexuality*, 2nd edition (New York: Routledge, 2011).
Brooke, Stephen, 'Gender and working class identity in Britain during the 1950s', *Journal of Social History*, 34.4 (2001), 773–796.
Bullough, Vern L., ed., *Before Stonewall: Activists for Gay and Lesbian Rights in Historical Context* (Binghampton: Haworth: 2002)..
Cahn, Susan, *Coming On Strong: Gender and Sexuality in Twentieth-Century Women's Sports* (Harvard University Press, 1998).
Cain, Roy, 'Disclosure and Secrecy among Gay Men in the United States and Canada: A Shift in Views', in John C. Fout and Maura Shaw Tantillo, eds, *American Sexual Politics: Sex, Gender, and Race since the Civil War* (Chicago: University of Chicago Press, 1993), 25–45.
Cairns, Lucille, *Sapphism on Screen: Lesbian Desire in French and Francophone Cinema* (Edinburgh: Edinburgh University Press, 2006).
Caprio, Frank, *Female Homosexuality: A Psychodynamic Study of Lesbianism* (New York: Citadel Press, 1954).
Caprio, Frank, *Variations in Sexual Behavior* (New York: Grove Press, 1955).
Chasin, Alexander, *Selling Out: The Gay and Lesbian Movement Goes to Market* (Basingstoke: Palgrave, 2000).
Chauncey, George, *Gay New York: Gender, Urban Culture, and the Making of the Gay Male World, 1890–1940* (New York: Basic Books, 1994).
Chemers, Mark, *Staging Stigma: A Critical Examination of the American Freak Show* (New York: Palgrave Macmillan, 2008).
Chideckel, Maurice, *Female Sex Perversion* (New York: Eugenics Publishing Company, 1935).
Clarke, Eric O., *Virtuous Vice: Homoeroticism and the Public Sphere* (Durham: Duke University Press, 2000).
Cocks, H.G. and Houlbrook, Matt, eds, *Palgrave Advances in the Modern History of Sexuality* (Basingstoke: Palgrave Macmillan, 2005).
Cohen, Stanley, *Folk Devils and Moral Panics: The Creation of the Mods and Rockers* (Oxford: Martin Robertson, 1980).
Conekin, Becky, Frank Mort and Chris Waters, eds., *Moments of Modernity: Reconstructing Britain 1945–64* (London: Rivers Oram, 1999).
Coney, Sandra, ed., *Standing in the Sunshine: A History of New Zealand Women Since They Won the Vote* (Auckland: Viking, 1993).
Cook, Hera, *The Long Sexual Revolution: English Women, Sex, and Contraception 1800–1975* (Oxford: Oxford University Press, 2004).
Cook, James W., *The Arts of Deception: Playing With Fraud in the Age of Barnum* (Cambridge, MA.: Harvard University Press, 2001).
Cook, Matt, *A Gay History of Britain: Love and Sex Between Men Since the Middle Ages* (Oxford: Greenwood World Publishing, 2007).
Cory, Donald Webster, *The Homosexual Outlook* (London: Peter Nevill, 1953).
Cory, Donald Webster, 'Lesbianism', in Albert Ellis, ed., *Sex Life of the American Woman and the Kinsey Report* (Greenberg, 1954).
Cory, Donald Webster, *The Lesbian in America* (New York: Citadel Press, 1964).
Cox, Pamela, *Gender, Justice and Welfare: Bad Girls in Britain, 1900–1950* (London: Palgrave Macmillan, 2003).

Crespi, Leo P., and Stanley, Edmund A. Jr., 'Youth Looks at the Kinsey Report', *The Public Opinion*, 12.4 (1948–1949), 687–696.
David, Hugh, *On Queer Street: A Social History of British Homosexuality* (London: Harper Collins, 1997).
Davenport-Hines, Richard, *Sex, Death and Punishment: Attitudes to Sex and Sexuality in Britain since the Renaissance* (London: Fontana Press, 1991).
Davies, Alistair and Alan Sinfield, *British Culture of the Postwar: An Introduction to Literature and Society 1945–1999* (London: Routledge, 2000).
Dean, Carolyn, *The Fragility of Empathy after the Holocaust* (Ithaca: Cornell University Press, 2004).
D'Emilio, John and Estelle B. Freedman, *Intimate Matters: A History of Sexuality in America* (New York: Harper & Row, 1988).
D'Emilio John, 'Capitalism and Gay Identity', in Ann Snitow, Christine Stansell and Sharon Thompson, eds, *The Powers of Desire: The Politics of Sexuality* (New York: Monthly Review Press, 1983), 100–113.
D'Emilio John, *Sexual Politics, Sexual Communities* (Chicago: University of Chicago Press, 1983).
D'Emilio, John, *Making Trouble: Essays on Gay History, Politics, and the University* (New York: Routledge, 1995).
Dose, Ralf, *Magnus Hirschfeld: Deutscher, Jude, Weltbürger* (Teetz: Hentrich und Hentrich, 2005).
Doyle, Laura and Laura Winkiel, eds, *Geomodernisms: Race, Modernism, Modernity* (Bloomington: Indiana University Press, 2005).
Duberman, Martin, Martha Vicinis, and George Chauncey, *Hidden from History: Reclaiming the Gay and Lesbian Past* (New York: Plume, 1990).
Duggan, Lisa, 'From Instincts to Politics: Writing the History of Sexuality in the U.S.', *The Journal of Sex Research*, 27.1 (1990), 95–109.
Dyer, Richard, 'No place for homosexuality: Marcel Carné's *L'Air de Paris* (1954)', in Susan Hayward and Ginette Vincendeau, eds, *French Film: Texts and Contexts* (London and New York: Routledge, 2000), 127–141.
Dyer, Richard, *Heavenly Bodies: Film Stars and Society* (New York: Routledge, 2003).
Echlin, Shirley, *At Home in the 1950s* (Harlow: Longman, 1983).
Ellenzweig, Allen, *The Homoerotic Photograph: Male Images from Dureiu/Delacroix to Mapplethorpe* (New York: Columbia University Press, 1992).
Ernst, Morris Leopold and David Loth, *Sexual Behaviour and the Kinsey Report* (London: Falcon Press, 1949).
Faderman, Lillian, *Odd Girls and Twilight Lovers* (New York: Columbia University Press, 1991).
Faderman, Lillian, *Surpassing the Love of Men* (New York: Harper, 1998).
Fass, Paula, *The Damned and the Beautiful* (Oxford: Oxford University Press, 1979).
Forrest, Katherine V., ed., *Lesbian Pulp Fiction: The Sexually Intrepid World of Lesbian Paperback Novels, 1950–1965* (San Francisco: Cleis Press, 2005).
Freeman, Elizabeth, *Time Binds: Queer Temporalities, Queer Histories* (Durham and London: Duke University Press, 2010).
Friedman, Andrea, 'The Smearing of Joe McCarthy: The Lavender Scare, Gossip, and Cold War Politics', *American Quarterly*, 57.4 (2005), 1105–1129.

Gallo, Marcia M., *Different Daughters: A History of the Daughters of Bilitis and the Rise of the Lesbian Rights Movement* (Emeryville: Seal Press, 2007).
Galus, Henry S., *Unwed Mothers: A Penetrating Study of the Alarming Rise of Illegitimacy in America* (Derby: Monarch Books, 1962).
Gardiner, Jill, *From the Closet to the Screen: Women at the Gateways Club, 1945–85* (London: Pandora Press, 2003).
Garfield, Simon, *Our Hidden Lives, The Everyday Diaries of a Forgotten Britain, 1945–1948* (London: Ebury, 2004).
Giddens, Anthony, *Modernity and Self-Identity: Self and Society in the Late Modern Age* (Cambridge: Polity, 1991).
Giffney, Noreen, Michelle Sauer and Diane Watt (eds), *The Lesbian Premodern* (Basingstoke: Palgrave Macmillan, 2011).
Gilbert, James, *Men in the Middle: Searching for Masculinity in the 1950s* (Chicago: University of Chicago Press, 2005).
Giles, Jane, *The Cinema of Jean Genet: Un Chant d'Amour* (London: BFI, 1991).
Glamuzina, Julie and Alison Laurie, *Parker & Hulme: A Lesbian View* (Auckland: New Women's Press, 1991).
Goldman, Jason, 'Nostalgia and the Photography of Wilhelm von Gloeden', *GLQ: A Journal of Lesbian and Gay Studies*, 12.2 (2006), 237–258.
Haeberle, Erwin J., 'Swastika, Pink Triangle, and Yellow Star: The Destruction of Sexology in Nazi Germany', in Martin Duberman, Martha Vicinus and George Chauncey Jr., eds, *Hidden from History: Reclaiming the Gay and Lesbian*
Past (London: Penguin, 1991).
Halberstam, Judith, *In a Queer Time and Place: Transgender Bodies, Subcultural Lives* (New York and London: New York University Press, 2005).
Halberstam, Judith, *Female Masculinity* (Durham: Duke University Press, 1998).
Hall, Lesley, *Sex, Gender and Social Change in Britain since 1880* (Basingstoke: Palgrave Macmillan, 2000).
Halperin, David, *Saint Foucault: Towards a Gay Hagiography* (Oxford and New York: Oxford University Press, 1995).. Haworth, Dianne and Diane Miller, *Freda Stark: Her Extraordinary Life* (Auckland: HarperCollins, 2000).
Hayward, Susan, *Les Diaboliques* (London and New York: I.B. Tauris, 2005).
Heineman, Elizabeth D., 'Sexuality and Nazism: The Doubly Unspeakable?', in *Dagmar Herzog, Sexuality and German Fascism* (Oxford: Berghahn, 2005).
Heineman, Elizabeth D., 'The Economic Miracle in the Bedroom: Big Business and Sexual Consumption in Reconstruction West Germany', *Journal of Modern History*, (December 2006), 846–877.
Hennessey, Rosemary, *Profit and Pleasure: Sexual Identities in Late Capitalism* (New York: Routledge, 2000).
Herdt, Gilbert, ed., *Moral Panics, Sex Panics. Fear and the Fight over Sexual Rights* (New York and London: New York University Press, 2009).
Herzer, Manfred, *Magnus Hirschfeld: Leben und Werk eines jüdischen, schwulen und sozialistischen Sexologen*, 2nd ed. (Hamburg: Männerschwarm, 2001).
Herzog, Dagmar, *Sexuality and German Fascism* (Berghahn, 2005).
Herzog, Dagmar, *Sex After Fascism: Memory and Morality in Twentieth-Century Germany* (Princeton: Princeton University Press, 2007).
Higgins, Patrick, *Heterosexual Dictatorship: Male Homosexuality in Postwar Britain* (London: Fourth Estate, 1996).

Hornsey, Richard, *The Spiv and the Architect: Unruly Life in Postwar London* (Minneapolis: University of Minnesota Press, 2010).
Houlbrook, Matt and Chris Waters, 'The Heart in Exile: Detachment and Desire in 1950s London', *History Workshop Journal*, 6 (2006), 142–163.
Houlbrook, Matt, *Queer London: Perils and Pleasures in the Sexual Metropolis, 1918–1957* (Chicago: University of Chicago Press, 2005).
Howard, John, ed., *Carryin' On in the Lesbian and Gay South* (New York: New York University Press, 1997).
Howard, John, *Men Like That: A Southern Queer History* (Chicago: University of Chicago Press, 1999).
Hull, Isabel V., *The Entourage of Kaiser Wilhelm II, 1888–1918* (Cambridge: Cambridge University Press, 1982).
Hyde, H. Montgomery, *The Other Love: An Historical and Contemporary Survey of Homosexuality in Britain* (London: Heinemann, 1970).
Inness, Sherrie A., ed., *Delinquents and Debutantes: Twentieth-Century American Girls' Cultures* (New York: New York University Press, 1998).
Irvine, Janice M., *Disorders of Desire: Sexuality and Gender in Modern American Sexology* (Philadelphia: Temple University Press, 2005).
Jagose, Annamarie, *Queer Theory: An Introduction* (New York: New York University Press, 1996).
Jackson, Julian, *Living in Arcadia: Homosexuality, Politics and Morality in France from the Liberation to AIDS* (Chicago: University of Chicago Press, 2009).
Jagose, Annamarie, *Inconsequence: Lesbian Representation and the Logic of Sexual Sequence* (Ithaca: Cornell University Press, 2002).
Jennings, Rebecca, *Tomboys and Bachelor Girls: A Lesbian History of post-war Britain 1945–71* (Manchester: Manchester University Press, 2007).
Jones, James H., *Alfred C. Kinsey: A Public/Private Life* (New York: W.W. Norton, 1997).
Juvonen, Tuula, 'Shadow Lives and Public Secrets: Queering Gendered Spaces in 1950s and 60s Tampere', *SQS: Journal of Queer Studies in Finland*, 1.1 (2006), 49–70.
Kates, Steven, *Twenty Million New Customers! Understanding Gay Men's Consumer Behavior* (New York: Haworth Press, 1998).
Keller, Yvonne, 'Pulp Politics: Strategies of Vision in Pro-Lesbian Pulp Novels, 1955–1965', in Patricia Juliana Smith, ed., *The Queer Sixties* (New York: Routledge, 1999), 1–26.
Kennedy, Hubert, *The Ideal Gay Man: The Story of Der Kreis* (New York: Routledge, 1999).
Kennedy, Elizabeth Lapovsky and Madeline D. Davis, *Boots of Leather, Slippers of Gold: The History of a Lesbian Community* (New York: Penguin Books, 1993).
King, Michael, *After the War: New Zealand Since 1945* (Auckland: Hodder and Stoughton, 1988).
Kinsey, Alfred C., Wardell B. Pomeroy and Clyde E. Martin, *Sexual Behavior in the Human Male* (Philadelphia and London: W.B. Saunders, 1948).
Kinsey, Alfred C., Wardell B. Pomeroy, Clyde E. Martin and Paul H. Gebhard, *Sexual Behavior in the Human Female* (Philadelphia: W.B. Saunders, 1953).
Kissack, Terence, ed., 'Alfred Kinsey and Homosexuality in the '50s: Recollections of Samuel Morris Steward as told to Len Evans', *Journal of the History of Sexuality*, 9. 4 (2000), 474–491.

Kotowski, Elke-Vera and Schoeps, Julius H., eds, *Der Sexualreformer Magnus Hirschfeld. Ein Leben im Spannungsfeld von Wissenschaft, Politik und Gesellschaft* (Berlin: Bebra, 2004).
Kunzel, Regina, 'Pulp Fictions and Problem Girls: Reading and Rewriting Single Pregnancy in the Postwar United States', *American Historical Review*, 100 (1995), 1465–87.
Kunzel, Regina, 'Queer Studies in Queer Times: Conference Review of "Rethinking Sex," University of Pennsylvania, 4–6 March 2009', *GLQ: A Journal of Lesbian and Gay Studies*, 17.1 (2011), 155–165.
Kynaston, David, *Family Britain, 1951–1957* (New York: Walker & Co, 2009).
Langhamer, Claire, 'Adultery in Post-war England', *History Workshop Journal*, 62 (2002), 87–115.
Langhamer, Claire, 'Love and Courtship in Mid-Twentieth-Century England', *The Historical Journal*, 50.1 (2007), 173–196.
Laurie, Alison, *'Lady-husbands and Kamp Ladies: Pre-1970 Lesbian Life in Aotearoa/ New Zealand'*, PhD thesis, Victoria University of Wellington, 2003.
Leighton, Sophie, *The 1950s Home* (Oxford: Shire, 2009).
Levine, Judith, *Harmful to Minors: The Perils of Protecting Children from Sex* (Minneapolis, London: University of Minneapolis Press, 2002).
Lewin, Ellen, ed., *Inventing Lesbian Cultures in America* (Boston: Beacon, 1996).
Lewis, Jane, *Women in Britain since 1945* (Oxford: Blackwell, 1992).
Lloyd, Christopher, *Henri-Georges Clouzot* (Manchester and New York: Manchester University Press, 2007).
Löfström, Jan, *The Social Construction of Homosexuality in Finnish Society, from the Late 19th Century to 1950s*, Unpublished PhD thesis, Department of Sociology, University of Essex, 1994.
Love, Heather, *Feeling Backward: Loss and the Politics of Queer History* (Cambridge, MA: Harvard University Press, 2007).
Lukenbill, Grant, *Untold Millions: Secret Truths About Marketing to Gay and Lesbian Consumers* (New York: Harrington Park Press, 1999).
Lyons, Andrew P. and Harriet D. Lyons, *Irregular Connections: A History of Anthropology and Sexuality* (Lincoln and London: University of Nebraska Press, 2004).
Mancini, Elena, *Magnus Hirschfeld and the Quest for Sexual Freedom: A History of the First Sexual Freedom Movement* (New York: Palgrave Macmillan, 2010).
Manning, A.E., *The Bodgie: A Study in Psychological Abnormality* (Wellington: Reed, 1958).
Martin Meeker, 'A Queer and Contested Medium: The Emergence of Representational Politics in the "Golden Age" of Lesbian Paperbacks, 1955–1963', *Journal of Women's History*, 17.1 (2005), 165–188.
Meeker, Martin, *Contacts Desired: Gay and Lesbian Communications and Community, 1940s–1970s* (Chicago: University of Chicago Press, 2006).
Meyenburg, Bernd and Sigusch, Volkmar, 'Sexology in West Germany', *The Journal of Sex Research*, 13.3 (1977), 197–209.
Micheler, Stefan, 'Homophobic Propaganda and the Denunciation of Same-Sex-Desiring Men under National Socialism', *Journal of the History of Sexuality*, 11 (2002), 95–130.
Millar, Paul, *No Fretful Sleeper: A Life of Bill Pearson* (Auckland: Auckland University Press, 2010).

Moeller, Robert, 'Private Acts, Public Anxieties, and the Fight to Decriminalize Male Homesexuality in the Federal Republic of Germany', *Feminist Studies*, 36.3 (October 2010), 528–552.

Montgomerie, Deborah, *The Women's War: New Zealand Women 1939–45* (Auckland: Auckland University Press, 2001).

Montagu, Edward, Lord Montagu of Beaulieu, *Wheels Within Wheels: An Unconventional Life* (London: Weidenfeld & Nicolson, 2000).

Montgomery, Heather, *An Introduction to Childhood: Anthropological Perspectives on Children's Lives* (Oxford: Wiley-Blackwell, 2009).

Morantz, Regina Markell, 'The Scientist as Sex Crusader: Alfred C. Kinsey and American Culture', *American Quarterly*, 29.5 (Winter, 1977), 563–589.

Morse, Benjamin, *The Lesbian* (Derby, Connecticut: Monarch Books, 1961).

Morse, Benjamin, *Adolescent Sexual Behavior* (New York: Monarch Books, 1964).

Mort, Frank, 'Scandalous Events: Metropolitan Culture and Moral Change in Post-Second World War London', *Representations*, 93 (2006), 106–137.

Mort, Frank, *Capital Affairs: London and the Making of the Permissive Society* (New Haven: Yale University Press, 2010).

Mowrer, Harriet, 'Sex and Marital Adjustment: A Critique of Kinsey's Approach', *Social Problems*, 1.4 (April 1954), 147–152.

Mücke, Thomas, *Magnus Hirschfeld* (Berlin: Bebra, 2004).

Munoz, Jose, *Disidentifications: Queers of Color and the Performance of Politics* (Minneapolis: University of Minneapolis Press, 1999).

Murray, Heather, *Not in this Family: Gays and the Meaning of Kinship in Postwar North America* (Philadelphia: University of Pennsylvania Press, 2010).

Mustola, Kati and Jens Ryström, eds., *Criminally Queer. Homosexuality and Criminal Law in Scandinavia 1842–1999* (Amsterdam: Aksant, 2007).

Neild, Suzanne and Pearson, Rosalind, eds, *Women Like Us* (London: The Women's Press, 1992).

Nero, Charles I., 'Why Are Gay Ghettoes White?' and other essays in E. Patrick Johnson and Mae G. Henderson, eds, *Black Queer Studies* (Durham: Duke University Press, 2005).

Newton, Esther, *Cherry Grove Fire Island: Sixty Years in America's First Gay and Lesbian Town* (Boston: Beacon Press, 1995).

Nickell, Joe, *Secrets of the Sideshow* (Lexington: University of Kentucky Press, 2005).

Odette, Catherine 'New York, 1959', in Julia Penelope and Sarah Valentine, eds, *Finding the Lesbians* (University of Michigan: The Crossing Press, 1990), 239–249.

Oram, Alison and Turnbull, Annmarie, *The Lesbian History Sourcebook: Love and Sex between Women in Britain from 1780–1970* (London: Routledge, 2001).

Oram, Alison, '"A Sudden Orgy of Decadence": Writing about Sex between Women in the Interwar Popular Press' in Laura Doan and Jane Garrity, eds, *Sapphic Modernities: Sexuality, Women and National Culture* (New York: Palgrave Macmillan, 2006), 165–182.

Oram, Alison, *Her Husband Was a Woman!: Women's Gender-Crossing in Modern British Popular Culture* (London: Routledge, 2007).

Palmore, Erdman, 'Published Reactions to the Kinsey Reports', *Social Forces*, 31.2 (1952), 165–172.

Pomeroy, Wardell B., *Dr Kinsey and the Institute for Sex Research* (London: Thomas Nelson and Sons, 1972).

Pretzel, Andreas and Volker Weiss, *Ohnmacht und Aufbegehren: Homosexuelle Männer in der frühen Bundesrepublik* (Hamburg: Männerschwarm, 2010).

Pulkinnen, Tuija and Antu Sorainen, eds, *Siveellisyydestä seksuaalisuuteen – poliittisen käsitteen historia* [From Decency to Sexuality – History of a Political Concept] (Helsinki: Finnish Literature Society, 2011).

Rees, John Tudor, *They Stand Apart. A Critical Survey of the Problems of Homosexuality* (London: Heinemann, 1955).

Reumann, Miriam G., *American Sexual Character: Sex, Gender, and National Identity in the Kinsey Reports* (Berkeley: University of California Press, 2005).

Roseneil, Sasha and Stephen Frosh, *Social Research After the Cultural Turn* (London: Palgrave Macmillan, 2011).

Ross, Kristin, Fast Cars, *Clean Bodies: Decolonization and the Reordering of French Culture* (Cambridge,: MIT Press, 1996).

Rydström, Jens, *Sinners and Citizens: Bestiality and Homosexuality in Sweden 1880–1950* (Stockholm: Akademitryck, 2001). Sankar A., 'Sisters and Brothers, Lovers and Enemies: Marriage Resistance in Southern Kwantung', in E. Blackwood, ed., *Anthropology and Homosexual Behavior* (New York: The Haworth Press, 1986), 69–81.

Savage, Gail 'Erotic Stories and Public Decency: Newspaper Reporting of divorce Proceedings in England', *The Historical Journal*, 41.2 (1998), 511–528.

Schickedanz, Hans-Joachim, ed., *Wilhelm von Gloeden: Akte in Arkadien* (Dortmund: Harenberg, 1987).

Schofield, Michael, *A Minority: A Report on the Life of the Male Homosexual in Great Britain* (London: Longmans, 1960). Scott, Joan W., 'The Evidence of Experience', *Critical Inquiry* 17.4 (1 July 1991), 773–797.

Sedgwick, Eve Kosovsky, *Tendencies* (Durham: Duke University Press, 1993).

Sedgwick, Eve Kosofsky, *Epistemology of the Closet* (Berkeley: University of California Press, 1990).

Sender, Katherine, *Business, Not Politics: The Making of the Gay Market* (New York: Columbia University Press, 2004). Shildrick, Margrit, *Embodying the Monster: Encounters With the Vulnerable Self* (London; Thousand Oaks: Sage, 2002).

Siegel, Fred, 'Theatre of Guts: An Exploration of the Sideshow Aesthetic', in *The Drama Review* 35.4 (1991), 107–124.

Sinfield, Alan, *Literature and Culture in Postwar Britain* (Berkley: University of California Press, 1997).

Smith, Patricia Juliana, ed., *The Queer Sixties* (New York: Routledge, 1999).

Sorainen, Antu, 'Foreign Theories and Our Histories: The Emergence of the Modern Homosexual and Local Research on Same-Sex Sexualities', *Suomen Antropologi: Journal of the Finnish Anthropological Society*, 24.3 (1999), 61–74.

Spain, Nancy, *Why I'm Not a Millionaire: An Autobiography* (London: Hutchinson, 1956)..

Sprague, W.D., *The Lesbian in Our Society* (New York: Tower Publications, 1962).

Steakley, James D., *The Homosexual Emancipation Movement in Germany* (Salem, New Hampshire: Ayer, 1975).

Steedman, Carolyn, *Landscape for a Good Woman: A Story of Two Lives* (London: Virago, 1986).

Stein, Marc, *City of Sisterly and Brotherly Loves: Lesbian and Gay Philadelphia, 1945–1972* (Philadelphia: Temple University Press, 2004).
Strecker, Edward A., and Vincent T. Lathbury, *Their Mothers' Daughters* (Philadelphia: J.B. Lippincott, 1956).
Stryker, Susan, *Queer Pulp: Perverted Passions from the Golden Age of the Paperback* (San Francisco: Chronicle Books, 2001).
Swanson, Gillian, *Drunk with the Glitter: Space, Consumption and Sexual Instability in Modern Urban Culture* (London: Routledge, 2007).
Terry, Jennifer, *An American Obsession: Science, Medicine, and Homosexuality in Modern Society* (Chicago: University of Chicago, 1999).
Thane, Pat, 'Family Life and "Normality" in Postwar British Culture', in Richard Bessel and Dirk Schumann, eds, *Life after Death: Approaches to a Cultural and Social History of Europe during the 1940s and 1950s* (Cambridge: Cambridge University Press, 2003), 193–210.
Thomas, Nick, 'Will the Real 1950s Please Stand Up? Views of a Contradictory Decade', *Cultural and Social History*, 5.2 (2008), 227–236.
Thomson, Rosemarie Garland, ed., *Freakery: Cultural Spectacles of the Extraordinary Body* (New York: University of New York Press, 1996).
Thomson, Rosemarie Garland, *Extraordinary Bodies: Figuring Physical Disability in American Culture and Literature* (New York: University of Columbia Press, 1997).
Thorpe, Roe, 'The Changing Face of Lesbian Bars in Detroit, 1938–1965', in Brett Beemyn, ed., *Creating a Place for Ourselves* (New York: Routledge, 1997), 165–182.
Turner, William B., *A Genealogy of Queer Theory* (Philadelphia: Temple University Press, 2000).
Vicinus, Martha, *Intimate Friends: Women Who Loved Women, 1778–1928* (Chicago and London: The University of Chicago Press, 2004).
Wade, Carlson, *Sexual Deviations of the American Female* (Chicago: Novel Books Inc., 1965).
Wallis, Allen W., 'Statistics of the Kinsey Report', *Journal of the American Statistical Association*, 44.248 (1949), 463–484. Wardlow, Daniel L., *Gays, Lesbians, and Consumer Behavior: Theory, Practice, and Research Issues in Marketing* (New York: Haworth, 1996).
Warner, Michael, *Publics and Counterpublics* (New York: Zone Books, 2005).
Waters, Chris, 'Havelock Ellis, Sigmund Freud and the State: Discourses of Homosexual Identity in Interwar Britain', in Lucy Bland and Laura Doan, eds, *Sexology in Culture: Labelling Bodies and Desires* (Cambridge: Polity Press, 1998).
Waters, Chris, 'Disorders of the Mind, Disorders of the Body Social: Peter Wildeblood and the Making of the Modern Homosexual', in Becky Conekin, Frank Mort and Chris Waters, eds, *Moments of Modernity: Reconstructing Britain 1945–1964* (London: Rivers Oram, 1999).
Weeks, Jeffrey, 'Capitalism and the Organization of Sex', in Gay Left Collective, eds, *Homosexuality: Power and Politics* (London: Allison and Busby, 1980), 11–12.
Weeks, Jeffrey, *Sexuality and Its Discontents. Meanings, Myths, and Modern Sexualities* (London: Routledge, 1990).

Weeks, Jeffrey, *Coming Out: Homosexual Politics in Britain, from the Nineteenth Century to the Present* (London: Quarter, 1977).
Weeks, Jeffrey, *The World We Have Won* (Abingdon: Routledge, 2007).
Weeks, Jeffrey and Porter, Kevin, eds., *Between the Acts: Lives of Homosexual Men, 1885–1967* (London: Rivers Oram, 1998).
Wekker, Gloria, *The Politics of Passion: Women's Sexual Culture in the Afro-Surinamese Diaspora* (New York: Columbia University Press, 2006).
Williams, H.E., 'Homosexuality: Aspects of This Problem Aboard Ships', *Preventive Medicine Dissertation* (Dunedin: University of Otago, 1962).
Williams, James S., *Jean Cocteau* (Manchester and New York: Manchester University Press, 2006).
Wolff, Charlotte, *Hirschfeld: A Portrait of a Pioneer in Sexology* (London: Quartet, 1986).
Wotherspoon, Garry, *City of the Plain: History of a Gay Subculture* (Sydney: Hale & Iremonger, 1991).
Yska, Redmer, *All Shook Up: The Flash Bodgie and the Rise of the New Zealand Teenager in the Fifties* (Auckland: Penguin, 1993).

Index